PUBLIC OPINION
Micro and macro

THE DORSEY SERIES IN POLITICAL SCIENCE

AKE   *A Theory of Political Integration*

BEST   *Public Opinion: Micro and Macro*

BIRNBACH   *American Political Life: An Introduction to United States Government*

BROWN & WAHLKE (eds.)   *The American Political System: Notes and Readings*
rev. ed.

DRAGNICH   *Major European Governments*   3d ed.

EDELMANN   *Latin American Government and Politics: The Dynamics of a Revolutionary Society*   rev. ed.

EVERSON & PAINE   *An Introduction to Systematic Political Science*

FROHOCK   *The Nature of Political Inquiry*

GOLDMAN   *Behavioral Perspectives on American Politics*

GRIPP   *Patterns of Soviet Politics*   rev. ed.

ISAAK   *Scope and Methods of Political Science: An Introduction to the Methodology of Political Inquiry*

ISMAEL   *Governments and Politics of the Contemporary Middle East*

JACOB, ATHERTON, & WALLENSTEIN   *The Dynamics of International Organization*   rev. ed.

JACOBINI   *International Law: A Text*   rev. ed.

LUTTBEG (ed.)   *Public Opinion and Public Policy: Models of Political Linkage*

MACRIDIS & BROWN   *The De Gaulle Republic*

MACRIDIS & BROWN (eds.)   *Comparative Politics: Notes and Readings*   4th ed.

MANGONE   *The Elements of International Law*   rev. ed.

MEEHAN   *Contemporary Political Thought: A Critical Study*

MEEHAN   *Explanation in Social Science: A System Paradigm*

MEEHAN   *The Foundation of Political Analysis: Empirical and Normative*

MEEHAN   *The Theory and Method of Political Analysis*

MEEHAN   *Value Judgment and Social Science: Structures and Processes*

MINAR   *Ideas and Politics: The American Experience*

MURPHY   *Political Theory: A Conceptual Analysis*

NAGEL   *The Legal Process from a Behavioral Perspective*

NASH   *American Foreign Policy: Response to a Sense of Threat*

OSBORN   *Soviet Social Policies: Welfare, Equality, and Community*

ROBINSON   *Congress and Foreign Policy-Making: A Study in Legislative Influence and Initiative*   rev. ed.

ROELOFS   *The Language of Modern Politics: An Introduction to the Study of Government*

ROSENBLUM & CASTBERG   *Cases on Constitutional Law: Political Roles of the Supreme Court*

SARGENT   *Contemporary Political Ideologies: A Comparative Analysis*   rev. ed.

SARGENT   *New Left Thought: An Introduction*

SIGLER   *Courts and Public Policy: Cases and Essays*

SIGLER   *An Introduction to the Legal System*

SPIRO   *World Politics: The Global System*

WASBY   *The Impact of the United States Supreme Court: Some Perspectives*

WESSON   *Soviet Foreign Policy in Perspective*

Public opinion
MICRO AND MACRO

JAMES J. BEST, Ph.D.
University of Washington

1973
THE DORSEY PRESS *Homewood, Illinois 60430*
IRWIN-DORSEY LIMITED *Georgetown, Ontario*

ISBN 0-256-01412-4
Library of Congress Catalog Card No. 72–93548
Printed in the United States of America

Preface

This book stems from my experience teaching graduate and undergraduate public opinion courses and the growing recognition that, although there is extensive public opinion research, there is little theory which serves to integrate that research.

A book on public opinion can be many things. This is not a book to use in order to learn public opinion polling. Nor does this book seek to explore previously unreported data. Rather, in it I have attempted to define public opinion in a way which seems to make sense of the diverse kinds of research that deal with the subject. In the process, the book makes a natural progression from the examination of public opinion at the individual level to the distribution of public opinion regarding several enduring topics and then concludes by examining the process by which public opinion is fed into the policy-making process.

To make sense of a rich diversity of research findings I have developed models—one for the process by which children develop political orientations and the other for looking at the role of public opinion in the policy process. Through these models I have run much of the relevant social science research to see if *it* yields the insights anticipated. In a number of cases there is no research, and I can only suggest what the research might find if it were to be done.

This book is not a total review of the research on public

opinion; there is too much of it, scattered throughout a multitude of disciplines, for any one person to keep up with, let alone master. Instead I have relied on those pieces which struck me as being particularly useful or insightful and would readily be available for others to use if they wanted to explore the subjects in more depth or challenge my interpretations.

In summary, this book is not written to explore uncharted ground but to integrate what we do know so that it makes sense in a larger context and yields even greater understanding of why we respond to our political environment the way we do and what is the impact it has on public policy.

Acknowledgments

To those students in my public opinion classes and the searching questions they asked, I owe a profound debt. To my professional colleagues in the social sciences, whose research and theories provided me with much to think about and to synthesize, I also acknowledge my debt, which is repaid in some small way by including their works in the footnotes.

Some authors acknowledge the assistance their wife gave in editing or typing the manuscript, or making substantive changes in the content of the book. My wife did none of those things. Instead she maintained our household as a warm and friendly place and shouldered more than her share of raising our children, enabling me to devote my time more fully to writing this book. Only she can know the debt I owe her.

February 1973   JAMES J. BEST

Contents

Introduction

Although a great many social scientists have dealt with the concept of public opinion, there has been remarkably little consensus as to definition. Public opinion has been alternatively defined as "an aggregate of individual views, attitudes, or beliefs shared by a significant portion of the community,"[1] "a multi-individual situation in which individuals are expressing themselves as favoring or disfavoring some definite condition, person, or proposal of widespread importance in such a proportion of number, intensity, and constancy as to give rise to the probability of affecting action, directly or indirectly, toward the subject concerned,"[2] or "those opinions held by private persons which governments find it prudent to *heed*."[3] Public opinion can be individual or aggregate, held by a majority or concerned minority, and having some or no influence on public policy. Given this disparity in definition, it is no wonder that V. O. Key has noted, "To speak with precision of public opinion is a task not unlike coming to grips with the Holy Ghost."[4]

---

[1]Jack C. Plano and Milton Greenberg, *The American Political Dictionary*, 2d ed. (New York: Holt, Rinehart and Co., 1967), p. 116.

[2]Gordon Allport, "Toward a Science of Public Opinion," *Public Opinion Quarterly* 1 (1937), p. 23.

[3]V. O. Key, Jr., *Public Opinion and American Democracy* (New York: Alfred A. Knopf, 1961), p. 14.

[4]Ibid., p. 8.

One way to understand the definitional conflict is to recognize that definitions are often the result of differing preoccupations in psychology, sociology, and political science. The psychologist views opinions as performing an important basic function for the individual—they enable him to cope with his external environment and are projections of his psyche onto his external environment.[5] Sociologists focus on the agents instrumental in the creation of public opinion; opinions are seen as the end product of a social interaction process between and within "publics."[6] Political scientists are most often concerned with the role of public opinion in the policy-making process, assuming that the existence of democratic government requires that the public's opinions play an important role in determining public policy.[7] Thus the psychologists view opinions as individual phenomena, sociologists view them as a group phenomena, and political scientists see them as mass phenomena.

Each definition provides a useful focus for looking at some aspect of what is commonly called public opinion. At the same time these differing definitions make it difficult to develop a holistic perspective on the concept. One solution to this dilemma would be to recognize that public opinion has conceptual significance at both the macro and micro level, i.e., public opinion is both an individual and mass phenomenon and any discussion of the concept must recognize that fact. By focusing on public opinion as the product of the individual interacting with his social and political environment (the micro level) and as the aggregation and articulation of individual opinions within a given functional unit (the macro level) we can begin to

---

[5]See Daniel Katz, "The Functional Approach to the Study of Attitudes," *Public Opinion Quarterly* 24 (Summer, 1960), pp. 163-76, and M. Brewster Smith, Jerome Bruner, and Robert W. White, *Opinions and Personality* (New York: John Wiley and Sons, 1956).

[6]See William Albig, *Modern Public Opinion* (New York: McGraw-Hill, 1956); and George A. Lundberg, Clarence C. Schrage, and Otto N. Larsen, *Sociology* (New York: Harper and Co., 1954).

[7]James A. Rosenau, *Public Opinion and Foreign Policy* (New York: Random House, 1961); Gabriel Almond, *The American People and Foreign Policy* (New York: Harcourt, Brace, and Co., 1956); and Walter Lippman, *Public Opinion* (New York: Harcourt, Brace, and World, 1922) share this perspective although the authors disagree on the role public opinion should play in the policy-making process.

make sense of the sometimes discrepant emphases of the various disciplines. In conceptualizing public opinion in this way definitional differences are merely differences in analytic level; public opinion is what a respondent tells a Lou Harris interviewer and also what Lou Harris reports the nation as saying.

Moreover, we must realize that two definitions of public opinion are needed to handle the concept at both analytic levels. For the purposes of this book public opinion at the micro level will be defined as *the individual expression of beliefs, values, and attitudes about political objects*, while macro level public opinion will be defined as *the aggregation and articulation of individual opinions, as perceived by political decision makers*.

The micro level definition has several components. (1) Public opinion is an individual phenomenon. At this level we are concerned with how an individual forms and maintains his opinions. (2) We are interested in only those opinions which are expressed. The use of the adjective "public" implies that opinions, if they are to be heard and understood, must be expressed in some form. The expression need not be verbal or written; some forms of non-verbal communication can express opinions as well as verbal expressions. (3) Opinions are the surface manifestations of more basic attitudes, values, and beliefs. For this reason it will be necessary to construct a schema which ties together and interrelates the concepts of attitudes, values, and beliefs, and their verbal expression in the form of public opinion. (4) We are concerned only with opinions relating to political objects. In this sense we are studying a subset of the totality of public opinion which we could call political opinions. Delineating of the concept to political opinions allows us to make important decisions. In choosing whether to explain an individual's opinion about a movie star or a leading presidential contender there is no difficulty.

Analysis of micro level public opinion focuses our attention on the individual and forces us to ask how his values, beliefs, and attitudes are interrelated, how they are formed and how and under what circumstances they change. These questions form the framework for the first part of this book. Chapters One and Two will explore the conceptual interrelationship between attitudes, values, beliefs, and public opinion, and develop a theory to explain the process by which attitudes, values, and beliefs are formed. Chapters Three and Four will examine the agents which play important roles in the formation of opinions, particularly in the pre-adult period.

The macro level definition has several important dimensions. (1) It is concerned only with those opinions which are aggregated and articulated. Public opinion, according to this definition, is "public" in two senses—if it represents the collection of more than one opinion and if it is expressed. Two men, standing quietly together on a subway platform, do not have a public opinion, while those same two men, cheering for a candidate at a political rally, do. (2) Aggregated and articulated opinions must be perceived by governmental decision makers. This is a restatement of the classical philosophical question, "If a tree falls in a forest where no one hears it does it make a sound?" For public opinion to play a positive role in the policy-making process, governmental leaders must be aware of it.

The macro level definition of public opinion takes off from where the micro definition ends. The micro definition is concerned with looking at what opinions an individual has and how he uses them to deal with his environment. The macro definition asks what is the distribution of public opinion toward a given set of political objects in the environment and how and under what circumstances does public opinion play a role in the policy-making process. In Chapter Five we will examine the end product of the socialization process—the attitudes and opinions which people hold about their government and the processes by which it operates. Chapter Six assumes that if public opinion is to have an impact in the policy-making process it must be communicated to governmental officials, and the chapter examines the institutions, channels and styles of opinion aggregation and articulation. Chapter Seven develops a model for examining the policy-making process and through which we can look at the role played by public opinion.

CHAPTER ONE

The bases of micro public opinion

Although it is unanimously held that opinions are manifestations of deeper psychological states—beliefs, attitudes, and values—there is less agreement on how these states differ from one another and how they interrelate to enable an individual to hold and express opinions. Frequently we have investigated these concepts separately, thereby escaping the necessity to define them or deal with their organization and operation. After reviewing much of this literature Steiner and Berelson were forced to conclude, "Usually the term 'opinion' refers to more superficial and transitory issues, the term 'attitude' to somewhat deeper and longer-lasting convictions, and the term 'value' or 'belief' to the deepest of all."[1] After differentiating between them on the basis of the "endurance" of each, Berelson and Steiner then proceed to use the concepts interchangeably. Are there any differences between attitudes, values, and beliefs and, if so, does it make any difference? The remainder of this chapter will be devoted to answering those two questions.

Attitudes

Since Steiner and Berelson feel that attitudes are the level "below" that of opinions perhaps we should start with them. Of

---

[1] Gary Steiner and Bernard Berelson, *Human Behavior* (New York: Harcourt, Brace, and World, 1967 ed.), p. 102.

the three concepts attitudes provide the greatest point of agreement; they are most frequently defined as more or less enduring orientations toward an object or situation and predispositions to respond positively or negatively toward that object or situation.[2]

From this definition there are several inescapable conclusions. First, as Steiner and Berelson suggest, attitudes must be conceptualized as being more or less enduring. Without enduring attitudes toward objects and situations opinions would be subject to daily or even hourly change. But research on voting behavior indicates that attitudes toward political candidates, parties, and issues are remarkably stable within an election period, and attitudes toward political parties remain stable between elections, providing an enduring base for opinions toward party candidates.[3] Second, attitudes are orientations toward both objects and situations. Rokeach correctly criticizes much of our research for not recognizing that attitude-toward-situation is as important as attitude-toward-object in determining an individual's opinion.[4] Our opinions toward an object are the result of our attitudes toward the object itself and the situation in which we find the object. We may have an attitude toward blacks and another toward work but what would our opinion be about working with blacks? At the same time, what would our opinion be toward working with Italians, or Poles, or eating in a restaurant with blacks? The determinant of our opinion is not our attitude toward either blacks (object) or work (situation) but the combination of the object in a specific situation.

Third, attitudes involve a predisposition to respond positively or negatively toward the relevant object or situation. For a person to have an attitude he must be aware of the object or situation and it must evoke some sort of evaluative response. In

---

[2]For a good discussion of the concept see Marie Jahoda and Neil Warren, eds., *Attitudes* (Baltimore: Penguin Books, 1966).

[3]Particularly Angus Campbell et al., *The American Voter* (New York: Wiley, 1960); and Bernard Berelson, Paul Lazarsfeld, and William McPhee, *Voting* (Chicago: University of Chicago Press, 1954).

[4]Milton Rokeach, *Beliefs, Attitudes, and Values* (San Francisco: Jossey-Bass, 1970), pp. 118-19.

addition the evaluation may be differential; we don't merely like or dislike, we like or dislike in "degrees." In order to determine an attitude toward an object we must know whether the person being studied is aware of the object and, if so, the degree of his evaluation of the object. "Have you ever heard of Medicare?" and "How do you evaluate its operation?" enable us to measure attitudes toward Medicare.

Beliefs and values

There have been comparatively few attempts to deal conceptually with beliefs and values. Rokeach defines a belief as "any simple proposition, conscious or unconscious, inferred from what a person says or does, capable of being preceded by the phrase "I believe that. . . ."[5] The important part of this definition (which is operational rather than conceptual) is that a belief is a "proposition"—a hypothesis, and expectation about how the world will or should behave. Bem sheds further light on the problem by defining a belief as a perceived relationship between two things or between some thing and a characteristic of it.[6] When a person says "I believe . . .," he is stating that he sees a relationship existing, regardless of whether that relationship exists or not. "The Republican Party favors labor unions" is a belief, regardless of the truth of the proposition, for the individual who states it.

Beliefs also represent basic elements of a more or less complex framework, a belief system, which the individual uses for understanding and dealing with himself and his environment. "A belief system may be defined as having represented within it, in some organized psychological but not necessarily logical form, each and every one of a person's countless beliefs about physical and social reality."[7]

Not all beliefs are equally important. My belief that a two-party system is a prerequisite for a democratic political system

[5]Ibid., p. 113, and Milton Rokeach, *The Open and Closed Mind* (New York: Basic Books, 1960), pp. 31-32.
[6]Daryl J. Bem, *Beliefs, Attitudes, and Human Affairs* (Belmont, Calif.: Brooks/Cole Publishing Co., 1970), pp. 4ff.
[7]Rokeach, *Beliefs*, p. 2.

is more important to me than my belief that there are nine planets in the solar system. The former is more important because I am a social scientist and not an astronomer. Beliefs can be classified on a "central-peripheral" dimension; "the more a given belief is functionally connected or in communication with other beliefs, the more implications and consequences it has for other beliefs and, therefore, the more central the belief."[8] The most central beliefs, which Bem and Rokeach call "primitive beliefs," are those which the individual accepts unquestioningly about himself and his environment and about which the individual feels everyone agrees, i.e., "Death is inevitable" or "Democracy is the best form of government."[9] Less central are those beliefs which are idiosyncratic to the individual and for which he does not seek validation; i.e., "The Democratic Party represents my interests the best." Even less central are those beliefs which are based on some external authority source, a source which is accepted as a legitimate information source for the belief, i.e., "The Democrats don't care for the little man, according to President Nixon." For those areas of our lives where we don't have the capacity to determine our beliefs experientially we look to the guidance of outside experts. We have specific authorities who are used as the basis for establishing specific kinds of beliefs; the college and basketball polls help fashion our beliefs about the best basketball and football teams in the nation, just as Julia Child is recognized as an authority on French cooking. Not only do we use authority sources but we also differentiate between authority sources. Women who are fashion leaders are not likely to be sources of political information[10] just as legislators who are perceived as influential in one policy area are unlikely to be influential in other policy areas.[11] The furthest end of the continuum—the most "peripheral" beliefs—is composed of those beliefs which are derived from more central beliefs. "For ex-

---

[8]Ibid., p. 5.

[9]Ibid., p. 15; and Bem, op. cit., pp. 4ff.

[10]Elihu Katz and Paul F. Lazarsfeld, *Personal Influence* (New York: Free Press, 1955).

[11]Wayne L. Francis, "Influence and Interaction in a State Legislative Body," *American Political Science Review* 56 (December, 1962): pp. 953-60.

ample, favorable or unfavorable beliefs about such things as birth control, the New Deal, and the theory of repression would be considered peripheral beliefs because they are derivable from the formal content of one's beliefs about the Catholic Church, Roosevelt, and Freud."[12] And beliefs about the Catholic Church, Roosevelt, and Freud, in turn, may be derived from more central beliefs about religion, politics, and sex.

There are also variations in the organization of individual belief systems. People will vary in the *range* of their belief systems. Some systems may be quite broad and serve to explain substantial portions of one's political world while others may serve to interpret only those parts of the political world in which the person is interested. Why bother to construct and maintain a set of beliefs which will never be used? People actively involved in politics are thus more likely to have wide-ranging belief systems than those less involved.[13]

In addition we can also examine the *integration* of beliefs within a belief system—the degree to which the individual's beliefs are related to one another—and the extent to which subsystems of beliefs are related to one another. A person can have a wide range of beliefs which are isolated and unrelated to one another so he can take contradictory positions on separate issues because those positions reflect separate beliefs.[14]It is not difficult to find Americans who label themselves Conservatives while believing that government should play no role in the economy and approving of medical care for the aged and binding arbitration for labor disputes. Free and Cantril have found, as we shall see in a later chapter, that some Americans have liberal and conservative beliefs at the same time.[15] Converse determined that, within the mass public, there is relatively little correlation between specific issue beliefs on domestic as well as foreign issues.[16]

---

[12]Rokeach, *Open and Closed Mind*, p. 47.

[13]See Phillip E. Converse, "The Nature of Belief Systems in Mass Publics," in *Ideology and Discontent*, David Apter, ed. (New York: Free Press, 1964).

[14]Ibid., pp. 228-30.

[15]Lloyd A. Free and Hadley Cantril, *The Political Beliefs of Americans* (New York, Simon and Schuster, 1968).

[16]Converse, op. cit.

"Beliefs, then, differ from one another in the degree to which they are differentiated (vertical structure), in the extent to which they are broadly based (horizontal structure), and in their underlying importance to other beliefs (centrality). These are some of the major factors that contribute to the complexity of our cognitive belief systems."[17] Several consequences flow from the organization of belief systems on these three dimensions. First, we can now classify people on the basis of the organization of their beliefs as well as their content. An "ideologue" would not be someone with whom we disagree ideologically nor would he necessarily be a person who did "rely in some active way on a relatively abstract and far-reaching conceptual dimension as a yardstick against which political objects and their shifting policy significance over time were evaluated."[18] Instead, an ideologue is a person whose beliefs are highly integrated and serve to explain a wide range of political objects and events which are important to him. He could be a liberal or a conservative and his beliefs could be abstract or concrete—the label is dependent on the organization of the beliefs, not their content or conceptual level. The antithesis of the ideologue would be that person who holds isolated beliefs on a narrow range of political objects which are unimportant to him. Second, the differentiation, range and centrality of beliefs determine the extent to which they can be changed. Beliefs which are psychologically interrelated and form the basis for other beliefs, all of which are critical to a person's understanding of his world, will be very difficult to change. For an ideologue to change one belief would require his changing related beliefs; to alter one belief calls for redefining one's self and one's way of looking at the world. In an insightful study Festinger showed how a group of people who believed in the end of the world adjusted to its continuance past the predicted date; rather than change their belief they merely redefined their perception of when the world was ending.[19]

---

[17]Bem, op. cit., p. 12.
[18]Converse, op. cit., pp. 215-16.
[19]Leon Festinger, *When Prophecy Fails* (Minneapolis: University of Minnesota Press, 1956).

If a person can have a great many beliefs about his political world it is also true that he can have relatively few values. Bem and Rokeach argue that values are a special subset of beliefs, "centrally located within one's total belief system, about how one ought or ought not to behave, or about some end-state of existence worth or not worth attaining."[20] There is a difference between the belief that Communism is spreading across the globe and having as a value that Communism is bad. Notice that the normative content of the value colors the meaning of the belief; the belief that Communism is spreading across the globe has entirely different opinion consequences, depending on your evaluation of Communism as good or bad. And your evaluation of Communism as good or bad can color a wider range of beliefs about actors and events in the domestic and international environment.

It is not surprising that social scientists who have attempted to deal with human values have suggested that a limited number of values universally guide men's actions. Allport,[21] in an early work, and Lasswell begin by assuming that men as political actors have the pursuit of power as their overwhelming value.[22] In a subsequent work Lasswell added respect, rectitude, affection, well-being, wealth, skill, and enlightment to the pursuit of power.[23] Knowing values which people hold does not tell you much about the opinions they will express. Like beliefs, values can probably be arrayed on a continuum of importance for the person; those values which are important for someone, which provide him with normative guidelines for action and interpretation, are more likely to be directly tied to a person's opinions. Values which are more peripheral are less likely to be important components of someone's opinions. Thus, the opinion which springs from the belief that Communism is spreading across the globe and the value that Communism is bad will depend on the relative strength of each belief and value.

---

[20]Rokeach, *Beliefs*, p. 124.
[21]Gordon Allport, *Personality* (New York: Holt, 1937).
[22]Harold Lasswell, *Power and Personality* (New York: Viking, 1962 ed.)
[23]Harold Lasswell and Abraham Kaplan, *Power and Society* (New Haven, Conn.: Yale University Press, 1950).

The structure and function of attitudes, values, and beliefs

Although it is conceptually difficult to differentiate between values, beliefs, and attitudes it appears that these three concepts "do not stand in isolation to one another. They are related in a number of interesting ways."[24] From the preceding discussion it is clear that I share with Bem and Rokeach the idea that it is conceptually useful to view values, beliefs, and attitudes as being organized hierarchically, with attitudes being reflections of one or more basic values and beliefs. Values and beliefs, at the same time, are interconnected and form a more or less well organized belief system, offering the person a more or less stable and comprehensive framework for interpreting and responding to his environment. In specific situations attitudes which are derived from the belief system become articulated as opinion. For this reason it is imperative that we look at how beliefs enable a person to deal with his environment.

The more structured the belief system—the greater its range and the more integrated—the easier it is to interpret events and objects in the environment. The belief system provides a ready-made set of cues for interpretation and criteria for evaluation.[25] At the same time the fact that beliefs are structured forces perceptions of the external world into preexisting and preformed categories. Without beliefs and values we would have to spend a large part of each day classifying and evaluating anew events and objects with which we regularly deal. Without the belief that people will obey traffic laws every street corner would become a novel and potentially dangerous challenge. Without the belief that "my political party represents everything I believe in" every election would be a totally new event; with party labels and a belief in the "goodness" of one party, choosing between candidates on election day is a comparatively easy task. A belief system serves for most people as a labor-saving device, saving the time and energy of con-

---

[24]Lewis A. Froman, *People and Politics* (Englewood Cliffs, N.J.: Prentice-Hall, 1962), p. 21.

[25]For a discussion of categorization see Jerome Bruner, Jaqueline Goodnow, and George A. Austin, *A Study of Thinking* (New York: Science Editions, 1966).

tinually relearning criteria for judging their political environment.

An overly rigid belief system, however, can limit a person's ability to adapt to new situations. Most people, when faced with a new situation, strive to classify it as analogous to a situation which they have encountered in the past. The more unchanging the person's belief system the more he is forced to respond to new situations as merely variations of old experiences, thereby stifling innovation and limiting adaptation. Such a person runs the risk of becoming a captive of the time and place during which his belief system was formed. The ideologue, whose beliefs are highly integrated and important to him, is frequently a victim of his time in history; the liberals of one generation are often the conservatives of the next. The belief system remains the same but the environment changes.

The ideologue's ability to interpret a changing environment is seen in Holsti's research on the belief system of John Foster Dulles, U.S. Secretary of State during the Eisenhower administration.[26] The key to Dulles' foreign policy beliefs can be found in his view of "moral power" as the basic factor determining success in the international political arena.

> His theory began with the premise that man is basically self-seeking—selfishness being the primary motive of human activity. Man has, however, a duty to exhibit spiritual attributes in the quest for his own ends; in so doing he will fulfill his moral obligation, and society will automatically benefit. Since Christianity directs the actor toward proper goals, the Christian who seeks his own ends simultaneously fulfills his social and spiritual duties.[27]

The United States, both its leaders and its people, represent the epitomy of those moral virtues which guarantee success. Conversely, the Soviet Union was seen by Dulles as the moral enemy of the U.S.: "Soviet Communism starts with an atheistic godless premise. Everything else flows from that premise."[28]

---

[26]In David J. Finlay, Ole R. Holsti, and Richard R. Fagen, *Enemies in Politics* (Chicago: Rand-McNally, 1967), Chapter II.

[27]Ibid., p. 38.

[28]Ibid., p. 49.

This basic belief colored Dulles' opinions about the Soviet Union and his interpretation of changes in Soviet actions and intentions. Decreased Soviet hostility, for example, was not seen as an attempt to reach a detente with the U.S. but a sign of weakness and failure of Soviet foreign policy. The end of the Korean War, on the other hand, was seen as a Communist failure militarily to defeat the United States and an example of the efficacy of Dulles' policy of nuclear brinksmanship. Thus we find that Dulles' beliefs about the Soviet Union colored his interpretation of their actions and were immutable to change. Shifts in Soviet action or intention were interpreted and further substantiated with that central belief, making it difficult, if not impossible, for him to change that belief or cease using it as the basis for evaluating changes in Soviet foreign policy.

If the ideologue were in a stable environment, where his world was the same from day to day, a stable and unchanging belief system would be an asset. But our current historical period, as Toffler so cogently points out, is not characterized by its stability but by its accelerating rate of change.[29] Starting from Toffler's premise we can argue that the future will require that a person have a belief system which is not so open that it offers no criteria for evaluating and judging the environment nor so closed that it precludes adaptation to new situations.

In addition to changes in the environment, a person's need to know and understand his political world, or some segment of it, will influence the structure and flexibility of his belief system. For those continually exposed to political stimuli, such as candidates and political activists, a political belief system must be highly developed in order economically to process the vast number of political stimuli to which it is constantly exposed.

For most citizens politics does not create a very great need for a complex belief system to aid in their understanding the political world. The voting studies have consistently shown that the American electorate does not respond to election campaigns in highly ideological terms. The Survey Research Center at the University of Michigan has found that the vast

---

[29]Alvin Toffler, *Future Shock* (New York: Random House, 1970).

majority of the electorate responded to the political campaigns of the 1950s in terms of what the party or candidate promised to do for a group with which the voter identified or displayed an amorphous mood response to a political environment in which the voter was disinterested or about which he had little information.[30] Only one out of every nine Americans responded to a major political event—a presidential election—in ideological terms, and even these people were not necessarily "ideologues" in the sense used here. When asked what she liked and disliked about the Democratic and Republican parties, an Ohio woman answered:

(Like about Democrats?) Well, that depends on what you are thinking of—historically or here lately. I think they are supposed to be more interested in the small businessman and low tariffs. (Is there anything in particular that you like about the Democratic party?) Nothing except it is being a more liberal party, and I think of the Republicans as being more conservative and interested in big business.

(Dislike about Democrats?) I think extravagance, primarily. (Is there anything else?) Nothing that occurs to me offhand.

(Like about Republicans?) Well, I never thought so. I have been a Republican the last several years because of personalities involved, I guess.

(Dislike about Republicans?) This again is tradition—just that they give too much support to big business and monopoly concerns. (Any other things you don't like about the Republican party?) No.[31]

The voting studies of the 1952 and 1956 elections substantiate the claim that Americans tend to respond to political campaigns in simplistic terms.[32] A very small proportion of the American electorate have a sense of the differences in ideology between "liberal" and "conservative" and those who do tend to respond to politics with a reasonably sophisticated belief system. Those who are aware of ideological differences and have ideologies of their own are also the best educated and most politically active segment of the electorate. For the bulk of the

---

[30]Campbell et al., op. cit.
[31]Ibid., p. 229.
[32]Ibid.

population, however, beliefs about domestic and foreign policy issues are not tightly integrated.[33] For most people politics is a marginal portion of their environment and so they have little need for a political ideology.

More intensive studies of small populations by Lane;[34] Smith, Bruner, and White;[35] and Keniston confirms the lack of ideology among some segments of the American electorate.[36] Smith, Bruner, and White found that Russia was a salient political object for only four of their ten men; the men were unable to differentiate the various dimensions of Russians and tended to respond to Russians on the basis of "an immediate and self-evident goodness or badness, desirability or fearsomeness."[37] While they all had opinions about Russia very few of those opinions were the result of a complex belief system.

Lane has found that working class men in New Haven, Connecticut, do not have belief systems which are broad ranged or well articulated while college students do. College students are able to differentiate between liberals and conservatives on the following dimensions:[38]

Liberal	*Conservative*
Opportunity for all, especially underdogs	Opportunity for the able
Inclusive personal and social orientation toward ethnic and other groups	Exclusive personal and social orientation toward ethnic and other groups
Greater equality for other nations in world affairs	Focus on priority of American interests and rights
Belief in positive government	Suspicion of government, restrictive view of government
Capitalism as a neutral symbol	Capitalism as a positive symbol

[33]Converse, op. cit.

[34]Robert Lane, *Political Ideology* (New York: Free Press, 1962), and *Political Thinking and Consciousness* (Chicago: Markham, 1969).

[35]M. Brewster Smith, Jerome Bruner, and Robert White, *Opinions and Personality* (New York: Wiley & Sons, Inc., 1956).

[36]Kenneth Keniston, *Young Radicals* (New York: Harcourt, Brace, & World, 1968).

[37]Smith, Bruner, and White, op. cit., p. 245.

[38]Lane, *Political Thinking and Consciousness*, pp. 51-53.

| Greater acceptance of social change | Greater faith in the status quo |
| No identification with business and businessmen | Identification with business and businessmen |

Although these liberal-conservative concepts can be drawn from the writing of Lane's college subjects a caveat is necessary. These beliefs are often unconscious and unarticulated and the college men did not readily articulate them as "their" ideologies. At the same time the philosophical premises which underlie these beliefs are unquestioned or unarticulated. These college students may call themselves liberals or conservatives but they are not easily able to define what those ideological terms mean and one has the impression that their definitions, while they do overlap, are not congruent.

Even people as politically involved as the college students active in the 1967 Vietnam summer were not ideologically committed.

> Formal statements of rationalized philosophy, articulated interpretations of history and political life, and concrete visions of political objectives were almost completely absent in the interviews. . . . But what did emerge was a strong, if often largely implicit, belief in a set of basic moral principles: justice, decency, equality, responsibility, nonviolence, and fairness.[39]

The motive force behind their political activities, according to Keniston, was not their ideological commitment but their involvement with others and the use of that involvement as a means of self-discovery and self-fulfillment. The "commitment" of these college-age radicals is not to the ideology of the New Left but to the "idea" of the New Left, to its movement and activities.

For those who do have ideologies, the more highly organized the belief system the greater the need for internal consistency and logic if it is to have functional utility as a "world view." If the person has a wide range of beliefs which are integrated and if he operates in a highly politicized world the individual beliefs must be consistent if the individual is to receive consistent evaluations of his environment. Using three elements, the indi-

---

[39]Keniston, op. cit., p. 28.

vidual P, and other person O, and the object X, there are four classical cases where P's attitudes, values, and beliefs are congruent:[40]

FIGURE 1–1

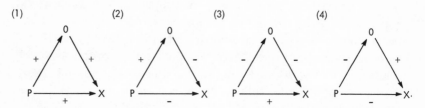

(1) P likes O and X and perceives that O likes X, (2) P dislikes X and likes O whom he perceives dislikes X, (3) P likes X and dislikes O whom he perceives as disliking X, and (4) P dislikes X and O whom he perceives as liking X. In cases (1) and (2) we have two friends who like or dislike the same political candidate. In cases (3) and (4) we have two enemies who, to remain enemies, cannot like the same object; if the Soviet Union favors Egypt we must oppose Egypt and if we favor Israel the Russians must oppose. When the two friends disagree or the two enemies agree (as in Figure 1-2) cognitive dissonance or imbalance occurs.[41] The lack of agreement within the belief system produces conflict and discomfort. Since dissonance is psychologically uncomfortable and the individual seeks to reduce the dissonance and to avoid the dissonance-producing situation.

Conflict between elements in the belief system or between attitudes does not automatically lead to change in beliefs or attitudes or withdrawal from the dissonance-producing situation.

---

[40]The literature in this field is too large for easy summary but the major works include Leon Festinger, *A Theory of Cognitive Dissonance* (New York: Harper, 1957), and *Conflict, Decision, and Dissonance* (Stanford, Calif.: Stanford University Press, 1964); and Morris J. Rosenberg et. al., *Attitude Organization and Change* (New Haven, Conn.: Yale University Press, 1960).

[41]For an excellent analysis of cognitive dissonance theories see Harold P. Taylor, *Balance in Small Groups* (New York: Van Nostrand Reinhold, 1970).

FIGURE 1–2

(5)   (6)

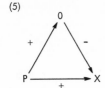

Three factors are necessary. First, the amount of dissonance created must be above a threshold tolerance level in order to move the person to seek to reduce the dissonance. Most people live with a certain level of dissonance; like the background noise of a radio when you are studying it may be necessary for efficient functioning. It is only when the dissonance becomes too annoying or psychologically crippling that people seek to eliminate it. In order to know whether a person will reorder or change his beliefs or attitudes we must know his tolerance for dissonance. Second, the importance of the cognition to the individual and the centrality of the belief are significant conditions. The more central the belief the more likely it is that dissonance will be high and the individual will move to reduce it. A friend's negative beliefs about the chief justice of the Supreme Court will not create much dissonance, even if I personally like the chief justice, unless I like my friend a great deal or care equally greatly about the chief justice. A third factor is the cost of removing the source of the dissonance. My wife and I may have differing attitudes toward my mother-in-law but shooting my mother-in-law is a personally expensive way of eliminating a dissonance-creating object. This is one reason why the electorate will often tolerate the development of a political problem until it reaches crisis proportions. As long as air and water pollution were not widespread and did not affect many people personally the costs of acting against them were high. Once the problem had reached crucial dimensions and affected many people intimately—they were no longer able to swim or fish in unpolluted waters or breath on hot summer days—even though the costs of action had increased they were now "worthwhile" for many people.

Consider for a moment the case of a Catholic woman, a member of her church sodality, who is also a local and state officer of the League of Women Voters. Suppose that within a space of one or two days the League comes out with a strong statement in favor of legalizing abortion while the Pope issues a papal encyclical emphasizing the primacy of human life and condemning abortion. The woman's opposition to the League's policy may well signal the end of an effective and worthwhile public service career, while opposition to the Pope's encyclical may mean excommunication from the Church. This is clearly a dissonance-producing situation.

The Catholic woman has three alternatives: She can change her belief, she can misperceive the situation, or she can withdraw from the dissonance-producing situation, by withdrawing from the League, the Catholic Church, or both. If the belief is to be changed, which one will change? Festinger predicts that the change will be in the direction of the most salient attitude or the more central belief and the change will be of sufficient magnitude or direction to reduce the dissonance to a tolerable level. The woman in our example will change her attitudes toward abortion in the direction of either the Catholic Church or the League of Women Voters, depending on which is the more important to her.

Another way of reducing the dissonance is through the processes of *selection exposure, perception* and *retention.* People tend to expose themselves only to information which reinforces already held predispositions rather than information which produces dissonance.[42] Once you make a decision to buy a car you begin to expose yourself selectively to only the advertisements of that car manufacturer.[43] If possible the Catholic League of Women Voters officer will selectively expose herself to information regarding abortion. In the case we have described she cannot, however, since both organizations have

[42]Lance Canon, "Self-confidence and Selective Exposure to Information," in Festinger, *Conflict, Decision, and Dissonance,* pp. 83-95, argues that a certain amount of dissonance-producing information is useful for a person since it provides him with a rationale for making the decision he made.

[43]For a classic description of this process see D. Ehrlich et al., "Post-decision Exposure to Relevant Information," *Journal of Abnormal and Social Psychology,* 54 (1957), pp. 98-112.

taken public positions on the issue. Being unable to avoid the information the next process, selective perception, becomes operative. She will misperceive, distort, the information which is least sympathetic to her position; she will argue that the League's interest in abortion is only symbolic or that the papal encyclical doesn't conflict with the aims of the League's activity. Having selectively exposed and perceived contradictory information the individual will now forget that information which it could not avoid or distort. Our forgetfulness is another way of stating our lack of desire to remember something distasteful. Having been told what was wrong with our newly purchased car by a well-meaning friend we then proceed to forget his information as we take off for a ride in the car.

In addition to these three primary processes Rosenberg and Abelson have identified a number of *microprocesses* to assist in dissonance reduction.[44] One such process is *denial*. If a friend says something with which you disagree you can deny that he means what he said. Or a person can *differentiate* and *segregate*. If your friend says something disagreeable you can argue that it is merely one of his quirks and that this line is not very important to the maintenance of your friendship. And in a friendship in which politics is not a very salient item for the friends, opinions about candidates, parties, and issues will do little to create dissonance which cannot be handled by one or both the friends. A third process is called *bolstering*. Instead of listening to your friend talking about a candidate you dislike you will seek out friends who support your position, even while you maintain the original friendship. McGuire[45] and Tannenbaum[46] point out three more microprocesses which operate in dissonance situations. One alternative is to *decrease the importance* of the object which is the source of controversy between

---

[44]Morris Rosenberg and Robert Abelson, "An Analysis of Cognitive Balancing," in Rosenberg, et al., op. cit., pp. 112-63.

[45]William McGuire, "The Current Status of Cognitive Consistency Theories," in *Cognitive Consistency*, S. Feldman, ed. (New York: Academic Press, 1966).

[46]P.H. Tannenbaum, "The Congruity Principle Revisited: Studies in the Reduction, Induction, and Generalization in Persuasion," in *Advances in Experimental Social Psychology*, Leon Berkowitz, ed., vol. 3 (New York: Academic Press, 1967).

the two friends; by decreasing the salience of the object the amount of dissonance created also diminishes, perhaps to acceptable levels. Another alternative is to *change one's cognitions of the object*. Having objected to a candidate because he is a politician one of the friends can now become aware of his more statesmanlike qualities, which become the new criteria for evaluating him. A last alternative is merely to *tolerate* the dissonance because it is below the threshold level or to *change the threshold level* so that the existing amount of dissonance is not enough to move the person to reduce it.

The more central a belief (or value) the more it will resist change. Since central beliefs and values deal with those things which are most important to the person and are a reflection of his self-image, they are highly interrelated and tightly held. To change them means changing some dimension of a person's self-image—an act of far-reaching consequence. Changes in more central beliefs produce greater changes than do alterations in peripheral beliefs, where the lower level of interrelatedness means changes in one belief have limited impact on other beliefs. Peripheral beliefs, as a result, can be more contradictory than central beliefs; they are less salient and less important in interpreting one's political world and, as a result, they can tolerate some contradiction.

The central-peripheral dimension is important for our understanding of how people evaluate political phenomena. According to Sherif, Sherif, and Nebergall[47] the more central the belief—the more ego involved—the more likely the person is to make a judgment about the political object, the smaller his range of indifference, and the more clearly delineated his acceptance or rejection of the object. The more peripheral the relevant belief the less likely the person is to make a judgment, the larger his range of indifference in evaluation, and the wider the range of acceptance and rejection of the object. A person who is unconcerned about the war in Vietnam will find that he is largely indifferent to many of the proposals to end the conflict; a person moderately concerned will find that he can

---

[47]Carolyn Sherif, Muzafer Sherif, and Roger Nebergall, *Attitude and Attitude Change* (Philadelphia: W. B. Saunders Co., 1965).

accept any policy alternative between unilateral withdrawal and attacking North Vietnam; and the deeply concerned person will find himself committed to one, and only one.

FIGURE 1–3

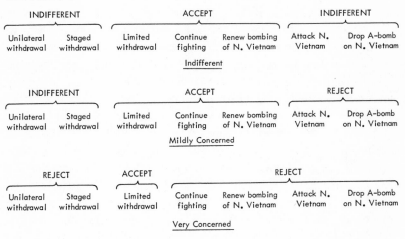

It is easy to see under what conditions attitudes can be formed and how. The less central the belief the more likely it can be changed, either by linking it to another belief or value, or by making the belief more central and forcing the person to form an opinion. Increasing the salience of an issue does not change the attitude; it makes it imperative that the person have an attitude toward the object. What appears to be attitude change, then, is nothing more than the crystallization of values and beliefs which had previously been unimportant. The process of crystallization, Gabriel Almond argues, is particularly important in the area of attitudes toward foreign political objects, where the public tends to have undifferentiated beliefs which crystallize in response to specific foreign policy crises.[48] The movement from an amorphous "mood" to a climate of "opinion" occurs as the foreign policy crisis deepens and

[48]Gabriel Almond, *The American People and Foreign Policy* (New York: Praeger, 1960).

foreign policy questions become more salient for a larger segment of the American population. Almond's discussion of a foreign policy mood implicitly assumes that foreign policy questions are of very low salience for most of the electorate most of the time; when foreign policy becomes salient the citizen begins to crystallize his opinions.

The less salient a belief the less important a role it plays in interpreting the environment. Salience appears to be a function of two factors. First, the more immediate and concrete the stimulus from the environment, the more salient the belief, so that beliefs about abstract concepts such as patriotism are less salient than beliefs about how to raise children or earn a living. Because of the marginal role of politics in our lives political beliefs are often far less salient than other kinds of beliefs. Grodzins argues that we are loyal, not to the flag or the national anthem, but to the immediate social life which these symbols represent.[49] Second, the more personal the belief the more salient it is—the more central the belief, the more important it is to someone, the more salient it is. Symbolic of this are white attitudes toward blacks.

> It can now be said that in 1966 America simply was not ready for open housing. Under the pressure of the law, the Negro protest, and his conscience, the American white has begun to yield—however grudingly—*in the areas that touch his private life the least*—voting rights, or public accommodations, or jobs. Even education is in a sense peripheral, for the white child need spend only a few hours with Negroes in an integrated school; after that the Negroes vanish somewhere into a private world of their own. But the white man is not quite ready to see the Negro move in next door, and the battle there has scarcely been joined.[50]

As blacks became more active in civil rights demonstrations they also became more visible and threatening to members of the white community. In 1964 only 34 percent of the white population felt that the pace of civil-rights progress was too fast; by 1965 49 percent agreed; and by 1966 85 percent of the white

---

[49]William Brink and Louis Harris, *Black and White* (New York: Simon and Schuster, 1966), p. 41.

[50]Ibid., p. 41.

population agreed. As a result of the increased visibility of blacks and the occurrence of urban riots whites in the mid-1960s also felt increasingly unsafe on city streets.[51]

From the foregoing discussion it is clear that a person has many belief systems to deal with a multifaceted and complex environment. He has one belief system to deal with his political environment, another to deal with his immediate social environment, and still a third to deal with some other segment of his life. There are probably as many belief systems as there are roles for an individual to play. What is less clear is the relationship between belief systems. Converse's research indicates relatively little interconnection between beliefs about domestic and foreign policy questions, except for the political elite.[52] Those people who have well-developed political belief systems probably have belief systems equally well developed for dealing with other aspects of their life. Lane found that the working man's ideology in New Haven was partly related to his ideas about the economic system.[53]

Belief systems perform a variety of important functions for the individual.[54] By providing a viable framework for interpreting the environment the belief system serves as a filter, a perceptual screen,[55] between the individual and his environment, screening out those stimuli which are potentially threatening and admitting those which are rewarding or nonthreatening. This filtering process means that a person is most aware of those aspects of his world which are compatible with his belief system and least aware of those which are antagonistic. The screening function preserves the balance and integrity of the individual's belief system, safeguarding its utility for him. If we are Democrats we don't read Republican campaign materials; if we do read them (by accident) we distort them to fit our

[51]Ibid., pp. 120-39.

[52]Converse, op. cit., pp. 228-30.

[53]Lane, *Political Ideology*, pp. 228-67.

[54]The following discussion owes much to Daniel Katz, "The Functional Approach to the Study of Attitudes, *Public Opinion Quarterly*, 24 (Summer, 1960), pp. 163-76.

[55]The Term has been used by Campbell et al., op. cit., and Lester Milbrath, *Political Participation* (Chicago: Rand McNally, 1966).

perceptions of what Republicans say; and then we forget what' we have read.[56] In that way we are able to maintain our basic beliefs about the nature of the Democratic and Republican parties.

Besides serving as a filter the belief system also acts as a buffer between the individual and his environment. The belief system represents a projection of one's self-image and a protection against threats to that self-image; with it "the individual avoids facing either the inner reality of the kinds of person he is, or the outer reality of the dangers the world holds for him."[57] For Lane, liberal and conservative belief systems are the result of basic motives and needs: the need to be liked, the need to express or inhibit aggression, the need for status, the need for moral self-imagery, and the need for identity through the family and separate from the family. The need to be liked finds its political expression in the following way: "A need to be liked which is somehow complicated and constrained by a fear of intimacy tends to work itself out in social thought in the form of bidding for the affection of distant groups."[58] Smith, Bruner, and White found the same complex interplay between environment and personality. Opinions regarding Russia were found to be the result of the need to relate Russia with their own interests and goals, related to a person's group membership and serving to define one's social identity, and reflections of a person's inner fears.[59]

Lane and Smith, Bruner, and White see the belief system as a mediator between the individual, his personality, his needs and his fears, and the larger environment—a protection of the one and a buffer against the other. A person's opinion can thus be viewed as the consequence of how he views himself and his environment. If he views the environment as threatening and feels personally inadequate to cope with it, his attitudes will

---

[56]For an analysis of these processes in a presidential election, see Paul F. Lazarsfeld, Bernard Berelson, and Hazel Gaudet, *The People's Choice* (New York: Columbia University Press, 1948); and Berelson, Lazarsfeld, and McPhee, op. cit.

[57]Katz, op. cit., p. 171.

[58]Lane, *Political Thinking and Consciousness*, p. 123.

[59]Smith, Bruner, and White, op. cit., pp. 241-79.

reflect that fact; he will be hostile to others and seek to dominate them for fear of being dominated by them. If he sees the world as a hospitable place and perceives an active and positive role in it for himself his opinions will reflect that fact; trusting himself and his capabilities he will have faith in his fellow men and in the basic goodness of nature itself.

Micro public opinion can be conceptualized as an individual's verbal expression of the interaction between his personality and the environment, mediated by his attitudes, values, and beliefs. Acting as his perceptual screen these attitudes, values, and beliefs serve to define "reality" for a person, giving him cues as to how he should react to the environment in ways which are most meaningful for him as a person and as a part of a social setting.

The personality base of micro public opinion

Most political scientists who deal with public opinion accept the idea that opinions are, in some way or another, reflective of personality. There is less agreement as to what constitutes "personality." Smith, Bruner, and White define personality as "an inferred construct to which we ascribe certain dynamic properties—striving, adaptation, defense, etc."[60] Since we cannot "see" personality, or lay it on a table to measure and feel, we must define it in terms of its manifestations—attitudes, values, beliefs, and opinions—which then must be examined in terms of the function they play for the personality. Following up on a later work by Smith[61] Greenstein suggests that

> Attitudes, then, can be thought of as the "face" of personality closest to the situational antecedents of political behavior: indeed, it is the situation, *as perceived by the actor,* an attitudinal datum, that is of central importance for predicting and explaining behavior.[62]

---

[60]Smith, Bruner and White, op. cit., p. 29.

[61]M. Brewster Smith, "A Map for the Analysis of Personality and Politics," *Journal of Social Issues* 24 (1968), 15-28.

[62]Fred Greenstein, *Personality and Politics* (Chicago: Markham, 1969), p. 24.

But this definition merely begs the question; it doesn't define personality, doesn't delineate the linkage between personality and attitudes, and doesn't suggest how one infers personality from attitudes.

Lane argues

> The properties of the personality are more or less enduring qualities that permit men to cope with the world: their internal conflicts and the way they solve them, their dominant drives and needs, the habitual ways in which they relate to people, their consciences and regulatory mechanisms, their moods and affective states, their concepts of self and ideal self.[63]

Lane's definition has merit for several reasons. First, it recognizes what most psychologists recognize—that there are a number of ways of defining and analyzing "personality"—and any definition is wise to view personality as a complex of different dimensions. Second, Lane's definition suggests that personality must take into account two basic themes in defining personality; it is possible to define personality in terms of the *needs* which motivate human action and it is necessary to talk of personality in terms of *ego strength*, the ability to perceive and master one's internal and external environment. Personality, defined on these two dimensions, leads Lane to conclude, "Opinions are the products of personalities and minds as these respond to situations, but the way the situation is defined affects the opinion given."[64] And it is a person's attitudes, values, and beliefs which determine how we define a situation.

Recognizing the importance of personality has led investigators to study the relationship between personality and opinion and political behavior. Most of these studies can be described as typological studies, which focus on a single personality trait in a number of people, and single case studies, which focus on the personalities of one or a small number of political actors.[65] From these studies we may be able to establish the relationship between personality and micro level public opinion.

---

[63]Lane, *Political Thinking and Consciousness*, p. 95.
[64]Ibid., p. 95.
[65]This distinction is taken from Greenstein, op. cit., pp. 14-17.

Typological studies

One of the first large-scale studies of personality traits was *The Authoritarian Personality*, by Adorno and his associates.[66] The research was initially designed to determine the basic personality types which could be classified as anti-Semitic, by means of questionnaires and in-depth interviews. The hope was to find anti-Semites by means of questionnaires and then use the in-depth interviews to find the historical and familial roots of the anti-Semitism. Having identified the anti-Semites on the basis of their questionnaire answers they were then classified as more or less "authoritarian" on the basis of their answers to another questionnaire. Studying nonrandom groups of subjects —college students, members of service clubs, psychiatric clinic patients, veterans, members of the merchant marine, working-class women, and prison inmates—they found an authoritarian personality syndrome composed of the following traits:

1. Conventionalism: rigid adherence to conventional, middle-class values.
2. Authoritarian submission: submissive, uncritical attitude toward idealized moral authorities of the "in" group.
3. Authoritarian aggression: tendency to be on the lookout for, and to condemn, reject, and punish people who violate conventional values.
4. Anti-intraception: opposition to the subjective, the imaginative, the tender-minded.
5. Superstition and stereotype: the belief in mystical determinants of the individual's fate; the disposition to think in rigid categories.
6. Power and toughness: preoccupation with the dominance-submission, strong-weak, leader-follower dimension; identification with power figures; overemphasis upon the conventionalized attributes of the ego; exaggerated assertion of strength and toughness.

---

[66]T.W. Adorno et al., *The Authoritarian Personality* (New York: Harper and Bros., 1950). For an extensive critique of the Adorno study see Richard Christie and Marie Jahoda, eds., *Studies in the Scope and Method of "The Authoritarian Personality,"* (Glencoe: Free Press, 1954), and Greenstein, op. cit., pp. 96-119.

7. Destructiveness and cynicism: generalized hostility, vilification of the human.
8. Projectivity: the disposition to believe that wild and dangerous things go on in the world; the projection outwards of unconscious emotional impulses.
9. Sex: exaggerated concern with sexual "goings on."

The authoritarian personality syndrome[67] is not a pretty one. Authoritarians are straight-laced, moral, and overly concerned with controlling their external world and their internal self. Ambivalence toward authority, for example, manifests itself in submission to those who are perceived to have more "power" or to be like oneself and aggression toward those perceived as "weaker." The ingroup is idealized and the authoritarians' hostilities are projected outward toward people who are different from himself. Fearing himself, the person fears others, and seeks to protect himself from his own inner drives and from the threats, real and fancied, of hostile others.

The authoritarian personality syndrome (measured by the F-Scale) was then found to relate to political beliefs concerning anti-Semitism, ethnocentrism in general, and political-economic conservatism. People scoring high on the authoritarianism scale were also likely to have

> ... stereotyped negative opinions describing the Jews as threatening, immoral and categorically different from non-Jews, and of hostile attitudes urging various forms of restriction, exclusion, and suppression as a means of solving "the Jewish problem."[68]

and

> ... stereotyped negative imagery and hostile attitudes regarding outgroups, stereotyped positive imagery and submissive attitudes regarding ingroups, and a hierarchical, authoritarian view of group interaction in which ingroups are rightly dominant, outgroups subordinate.[69]

and

> support of the *status quo* and particularly of business; support of conservative values; desire to maintain a balance of

---

[67]Adorno et al., op. cit., pp. 222-79.
[68]Ibid., p. 71.
[69]Ibid., p. 150.

power in which business is dominant, labor subordinate, and the economic functions of government minimized; and resistance to social change.[70]

Given these definitions of anti-Semitism, ethnocentrism, and political-economic conservatism, respectively, it is not surprising to find that the three measures correlated quite highly, particularly the first two, with authoritarianism. Anti-Semitic and ethnocentric beliefs are little more than restatements of the characteristics attributed to the authoritarian personality syndrome and in measuring various dimensions of the same phenomenon—authoritarianism—it is not surprising that the various measures have high levels of statistical correlation. The high correlations also raise another question: if authoritarian personality traits are highly correlated with anti-Semitic and ethnocentric beliefs, can authoritarianism be a measure of a belief system or are anti-Semitism and ethnocentrism measures of personality?

In addition, the F-Scale, the name for the authoritarianism measure, is historically and culturally bound. Some of the original questions, such as, "After we finish off the Germans and Japs, we ought to concentrate on other enemies of the human race such as rats, snakes, and germs," and "Homosexuals are nothing but degenerates and ought to be severely punished," seem curiously dated, both in time and in social customs. The construction of the questions, particularly the use of simple-sounding "truths" created a response set problem[71] among the lower educated.

In addition Lipset,[72] Shils,[73] and Rokeach[74] have been critical of *The Authoritarian Personality* for its emphasis on the basic conservatism of the authoritarian. All three suggest that the authoritarian personality is characteristic of all ideologues, of both the right and left. Rokeach responded by developing a measure of general intolerance, focusing on the structure of the

---

[70]Ibid., p. 157.

[71]A response set is a general tendency to agree or disagree with interview questions, regardless of their content.

[72]Seymour M. Lipset, *Political Man* (Garden City, N.Y.: Doubleday, 1963), pp. 87-186.

[73]Edward A. Shils, "Authoritarianism: 'Right' and 'Left'," in Christie and Jahoda, op. cit., pp. 24-49.

[74]Rokeach, *The Open and Closed Mind*, pp. 11-19.

person's belief system rather than its content. He is then able to deal with authoritarianism as a special form of dogmatism, where a person has a set of beliefs which are basic to him and which are immune to change, regardless of whether the beliefs are liberal or conservative, democratic or fascist. At the same time he eliminated the problem of whether "dogmatism"[75] or authoritarianism is a personality syndrome or a belief system by stating, "During the course of our investigation we have come more and more to view a given personality as an organization of beliefs or expectancies having a definable and measurable structure."[76] Beliefs are not a reflection of personality, they *are* personality.

Even with different populations Rokeach found his Dogmatism Scale correlated quite highly with the Adorno Authoritarianism and Ethnocentrism Scales. At the same time there was very little correlation between the Dogmatism Scale and liberal-conservative ideology—both liberals and conservatives apparently could be dogmatic about the beliefs which they held.

Subsequent research has validated many of the Adorno et al. findings. H. J. Eysenck has explored in some depth the relationship between anti-intraception, or "tough" versus "tender"-mindedness and radicalism and conservatism among party members in Great Britain, defining the "tough-minded" syndrome as composed of such personality traits as extroversion, aggression, dominance, rigidity, intolerance of ambiguity, narrow-mindedness, and mental concreteness.[77] Relating these personality traits to party identification and conservatism-radicalism he found that Fascists were tough-minded conservatives, Communists were tough-minded radicals, Conservatives and Socialists were conservative and radical, respectively, while being intermediate on the tough-tender-mindedness scale, and Liberals were tender-minded and intermediate on the conservative-radical scale. With these data in hand Eysenck

---

[75]Dogmatism is used as a measure of openness of one's belief system. People who score high on the Dogmatism Scale are assumed to have relatively closed belief systems.

[76]Ibid., p. 7.

[77]H. J. Eysenck, *The Psychology of Politics* (London: Routledge and Kegan Paul, 1954).

then argues that party identification is nothing more than a projection of personality traits onto the relevant political parties. In other words not only political beliefs but political party identification as well as a reflection of the way one looks at the world and one's need to master or be mastered by it.

Lane's study of 15 men in New Haven, Connecticut, suggests that this lack of self-control, characterized by a loss of identity, alienation from self, high levels of anxiety, irrationality, and anti-intraception are part of the core personality of the "undemocratic" man. A loss of personal identity, of connection to and control over one's personal environment is reflected in feelings of alienation from the political environment.[78] But Lane does not find many "impoverished" men in New Haven, just as Adorno and Rokeach found few authoritarians or dogmatics. Lane found that most of his men in New Haven had more or less healthy egos, were interested in and participated in politics and were "happy democratic citizens."

Rosenberg feels that how a person views his world and others in his world around him is related to how he views his political world. Rosenberg's thesis is that one of the most important determinants of political attitudes is the individual's well being; consequently much of his research has focused on the relationship between self-esteem and misanthropy and various political attitudes[79] He finds that people with high self-esteem are more interested in national and international affairs than those with low self-esteem, who are uninterested in politics generally. One reason for their lack of interest is that they feel threatened by political discussions which will expose their political ignorance or their lack of interest and understanding.[80]

Self-esteem, however, is only one aspect of a general personality syndrome which has certain attitudinal consequences. Rosenberg is concerned about how an individual's sense of identity—his ability to relate meaningfully to himself and others—is correlated with his view of the political world.

---

[78]Lane, *Political Ideology*, pp. 400-412.

[79]Morris Rosenberg, "Self-Esteem and Concern with Public Affairs," *Public Opinion Quarterly* 26 (Summer, 1962): 201-11 and "Misanthropy and Political Ideology," *American Sociological Review* 21 (1956), pp. 690-95.

[80]Rosenberg, "Self Esteem," pp. 201-11.

In sum, these data suggest that the way a man looks at people has a bearing upon the way he looks at certain political matters. There are many political matters, of course, which are unrelated to the individual's view of humanity. For example, faith in people has little to do with being a Democrat or a Republican, a liberal or a conservative (in the formal sense). But low faith in people is related to a distrust of the public, the conviction of public officials' unresponsiveness to the people, a belief that political machines run the candidates, a skepticism about freedom of speech, and a willingness to suppress certain political and religious liberties.[81]

Authoritarianism, close-mindedness, tough-mindedness, and misanthropy are the traits of a personality which has difficulty dealing with itself and its immediate environment. Threatened from within and without, the person projects his insecurities onto his political world and its salient objects. Lacking a sense of self-esteem he sees other people as out to "get him". Unable to deal with those more powerful than himself he seeks to manipulate those who are weaker; and, when faced with a complex environment he responds by dividing the world into "good" guys and "bad" guys. At the other end of the personality spectrum we find those people who have a sense of "self" and of self-control—they are comfortable with themselves and with others. Able to deal with themselves they are also competent to deal with their political environment. Lane has suggested, "At the base of political man active in American model politics there lies a political personality—the strong, happy, and moral democratic citizen."[82]

Case studies

In addition to the studies of personality traits there have been a number of case studies focused on relating the whole personality to political behavior. One problem is common to these studies, as with studies of personality traits: there is a preponderant concern with pathological cases. The case studies

---

[81]Rosenberg, "Misanthropy," p. 690.
[82]Robert Lane, *Political Life* (Glencoe, Ill.: Free Press of Glencoe, 1959), p. 162.

of political leaders have focused on Woodrow Wilson,[83] Kurt Schumaker,[84] Cermak,[85] Ghandi,[86] and James Forrestal.[87] Although there is an obvious need to understand the psychology of pathological political leaders there is some question as to whether these case studies tell us anything about "normal" personalities and how they relate to their political environment. Lasswell implicitly argues that we cannot avoid studying personality pathology when we study political leaders since most successful leaders have suffered trauma in childhood, sublimated the hostility, and displaced it onto public objects through the pursuit of political power.[88] Two problems arise from Lasswell's theory. First, although political leaders displace their hostility by pursuing public office, not all people who have suffered trauma in childhood seek political power. Some displace their hostility by becoming artists, others seek economic power, and still others never adequately displace it and become emotional cripples in their adult lives. What determines whether a person displaces his hostility onto political objects or not? Opportunity? Second, there is also evidence that Lasswell's initial assumption—political leaders are pathological cases—is incorrect. Studies of state legislators and lobbyists indicate these kinds of political leaders are not much different from the population at large.[89]

Intensive studies of small groups of people have begun to shed some light on the relationship between total personality and public opinion. We now have a number of studies which provide us with some insights. One of the first of these, conducted by Smith, Bruner, and White,[90] began with the assump-

---

[83]Alexander and Juliette George, *Woodrow Wilson and Colonel House* (New York: John Day, 1956); Sigmund Freud and William C. Bullitt, *Thomas Woodrow Wilson* (Boston: Houghton Mifflin, 1967).

[84]Lewis J. Edinger, *Kurt Schumaker: A Study in Personality and Political Behavior* (Stanford: Stanford University Press, 1965).

[85]Alex Gottfried, *Boss Cermak of Chicago* (Seattle: University of Washington Press, 1962).

[86]Erik Erikson, *Ghandi's Truth* (New York: W. W. Norton, 1969).

[87]Arnold Rogow, *James Forrestal* (New York: Macmillan Co., 1963).

[88]Harold Lasswell, *Psychopathology and Politics* (New York: Viking Press, 1960 edition).

[89]See Lester Milbrath, *The Washington Lobbyists* (Chicago: Rand McNally, 1963), pp. 97-108.

[90]Smith, Bruner, and White, op. cit.

tion that personality is the result of a human being with certain needs and goals striving to master its external and internal environment. A person's opinions are the result of this interaction and perform three invaluable functions for the individual:

1. reality testing: a "reality testing" function by which objects in the environment are evaluated in terms of one's needs and goals. Once evaluated they form the basis for the individual's opinion response to them.
2. social adjustment: the holding of opinions which facilitate interactions with people one likes and protects oneself from interactions with people whom one dislikes.
3. externalization: occurs when an individual sees some relationship between some external object and his feelings toward himself. He then projects his attitudes toward himself outward toward the object in his environment.[91]

We hold opinions which are reflections of our evaluation of the world, what other people think of us, and our own psychic inner state. People with weak egos feel the world is a threatening place, respond to it and other people that way, and externalize their inner fears onto the outer world.

One subject, for example, held ambivalent opinions toward Russia because he felt that in Russia working men would be given the best chance to develop their capacity (positive opinion). At the same time,

The *externalization of inner problems* affected his opinions in certain fairly apparent ways. His own passivity, with resentment that his parents had not pushed him, seemed responsible for the special praise he bestowed on the Russian state's pushing of its capable members into trained responsible positions. His feelings of dependence produced an overdrawn picture of individual security in Russia. Finally, the complex of feelings that included fear of his own aggressiveness, fear of the viciousness of others, and the need for firm defense and moral control, seemed to be externalized in his vehement criticism of Russia's attitude toward morality and religion and in his inconsistent advocacy of strong military preparations for a war he believed unlikely to occur.[92]

[91]Ibid., pp. 39-44.
[92]Ibid., p. 195.

Lane's study of 15 men in New Haven substantiates this model.[93] Those men with the weakest egos had the most trouble dealing with themselves, their families, work, and politics. Their dealings with politics reflected their fears—government was run by a cabal of men who were out to deny the birthright of "good" people by denying them access to things which were rightfully theirs. Lane has subsequently shifted from analyzing personality in terms of ego to looking at personality as a series of needs, triggered by stimuli from the environment, which shape or determine the content of subsequent opinions.[94] The shift from ego psychology to need psychology is not easy, since the number of personality theories based on needs are many.[95] Undaunted, Lane has developed his own list of ten needs: cognitive needs, the need to know and understand man's political world; the need for consistency and balance, the need to tie together what man does know about his political world; social needs and values, the need to be liked and be approved of which requires a person to hold views amenable to his friends; moral needs and values, the need to feel moral and to feel that one's political ideas are "just"; esteem needs and values, the need for people to grow in self-esteem by doing what others want them to do; personality integration and identity formation, the need to identify oneself in political and personal terms; the expression of aggression, a need which can easily be met by political expression and participation; autonomy and freedom, the need for freedom and independence is crucial to understand the political thought of man; self-actualization, the need to grow and develop to one's capacity within political institutions which foster such growth; and an instrumental guide to reality, in order to evaluate and make judgments about the political world. Of this list Lane is primarily concerned with four—the

---

[93]Lane, *Political Ideology*.

[94]Lane, *Political Thinking and Consciousness*.

[95]For theories of personality needs see Henry A. Murray, *Explorations in Personality* (London: Oxford University Press, 1938); A. H. Maslow, *Motivation and Personality* (New York: Harper, 1954); and David C. McClelland, *The Achievement Motive* (New York: Appleton, 1953). See James C. Davies, *Human Nature in Politics* (New York: John Wiley and Sons, 1963) for the application of Maslow's need hierarchy to an understanding of politics.

need to be liked, the need to express and control aggression, the need to appear moral, and the need for esteem—which are central to his understanding of the role which personality plays in the formation of political ideas and opinions.[96]

These basic beliefs and needs work themselves out through the individual's political "idea machine" and find their expression in liberal or conservative political beliefs. Unfortunately there is no way of knowing what kinds of stimuli will trigger which needs and how needs, when triggered, will interact with which elements of the "idea machine" to produce which liberal or conservative beliefs. Maslow's model at least has the advantage of being a hierarchy of needs, where the individual seeks to satisfy lower-level needs before higher-level ones; a person's needs for food, shelter, and safety must be satisfied before he can become concerned with his needs for love and self-esteem. Lane does provide us with some unique insights into the needs which form the basis for many political beliefs. For example, the need to be liked, combined with self-doubt and a need for self-validation and self-conscious interpersonal skills, produces vote solicitation on "clean-cut" reform lines, where votes are seen as an affirmation of acceptability.[97] The need for aggression frequently calls forth a counter need to inhibit aggression, which causes anxiety and withdrawal from politics.[98]

The question of which of the two basic models—ego or need—is better overlooks the interrelationship between the two. The development of a stronger ego is the result of the individual meeting basic needs and prepares him to meet higher-level needs. The use of an ego-based model for this work is the result of the author's greater familiarity with ego psychology, more research on ego-related questions, and the utility of Erikson's model of personality development, which is ego-related.

Whichever model is used there is sufficient evidence that opinions are the result of the interplay between the organism and its environment. The organism is viewed as a stimuli-

---

[96]Lane, *Political Thinking and Consciousness*, pp. 31-47.
[97]Ibid., pp. 143-44.
[98]Ibid., pp. 172-89.

processing mechanism, in which environmental stimuli interact with the needs of the personality, values, beliefs, and attitudes, to form opinions. As can be seen from Figure 1-4, a perceptual screen intervenes between the individual and his environment, limiting the elements of the environment with which he must interact and about which he must have opinions.[99]

FIGURE 1–4

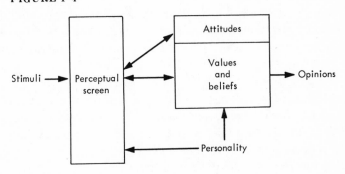

This model assumes that the individual is a stimulus-processing mechanism, in which personality and environment interact to produce opinions, and opinions facilitate the interaction between personality and environment. An individual, however, cannot interact totally with his environment and all stimuli from that environment. Selectivity is necessary. "An organism may shift attention from one stimulus to another rather rapidly, but at any given instant the focus is upon relatively few."[100] In this model the perceptual screen selectively interposes itself between the individual and his environment, excluding some and including other stimuli for processing. Stimuli are the inputs, opinions are the outputs, and the perceptual screen selects which inputs are transformed into outputs.

---

[99]This scheme owes much to Lester Milbrath, *Political Participation;* Smith, "A Map for the Analysis of Personality and Politics," pp. 15-28; and Karl Deutsch, *The Nerves of Government* (New York: Free Press, 1963).

[100]Lester Milbrath, *Political Participation*, p. 33.

As indicated in Figure 1-4, the perceptual screen is a reflection of attitudes, values, and beliefs (and indirectly, personality). Its primary function is to categorize incoming stimuli.[101] To do this, the organism must scan the stimuli to determine their relevance and categorize relevant stimuli so they can elicit appropriate responses. In this sense the perceptual screen can be viewed as analogous to a semipermeable membrane during osmosis—allowing certain kinds of stimuli to pass through and blocking others.

What determines which stimuli shall pass through? Obviously the strength of the stimulus is important. It is possible for us to filter out most of the noise from our immediate environment but we cannot ignore a firecracker detonated at our feet. Stimuli which are new or unintelligible also have easier access through the perceptual screen since the screen has few, if any, means for categorizing them as relevant or not. Once the initial categorization has been accomplished, those same stimuli will have less access. The first time a person sees a surrealistic work of art, he pauses to consider it; having formed an opinion of it he will either pause or not pause the next time he sees such a painting. The painting once classified becomes more or less relevant as a stimuli the next time.

The classical political example is that of the new political candidate seeking to establish name familiarity with the electorate. Even though George McGovern had been a candidate for the Democratic presidential nomination in 1968, early in 1972 he was still a largely unknown quantity to the American electorate, ranking far down the list of candidates that people would support. After convincing wins in seven presidentaial primaries and a substantial amount of media exposure many more people knew who he was and ranked him favorably as a candidate. In order to get that favorable response, however, he had to get their attention.

---

[101]For materials on categorization see Jerome S. Bruner, "On Perceptual Readiness," in Robert Harper et al., *The Cognitive Processes* (Englewood Cliffs, N.J.: John Wiley, 1964; Bruner et. al., *A Study of Thinking;* and Michael J. Shapiro, "Rational Political Man: A Synthesis of Economic and Social-Psychological Perspectives," *American Political Science Review* 63 (December, 1969): 1106-20.

In addition to the strength, newness, or uniqueness of the stimuli, the permeability of the perceptual screen to certain kinds of stimuli is important. This permeability is based on past experience, existing values, beliefs, and attitudes, and current personal needs. Those stimuli are relevant which have been relevant in the past, which pose little or no overt threat to the individual's current values, beliefs, or attitudes, and which the individual consciously defines as relevant. Once a stimulus has been defined as relevant in the past, the threshold of awareness lowers and the perceptual screen becomes more permeable to that stimulus in the present. In this sense, the perceptual screen is perceptually a product of what the individual has experienced in the past, combined with his needs for the present and future.

At this point it would be useful to remember our earlier discussion of the qualities of belief systems and relate these qualities to the function of the perceptual screen. The "openness" of the belief system will be reflected in a perceptual screen which is highly permeable to environmental stimuli. The individual needs information about his environment in order to make decisions about that environment. The more "close-minded" the person the less permeable the perceptual screen and the fewer stimuli the individual will want or need. The individual already has a well-developed framework for responding to his environment—all he needs is a minimal amount of information about his environment.

After the initial scan of the environment and the classification of stimuli as relevant or not, the relevant stimuli are subject to more detailed evaluation. The purpose of the further evaluation is to place stimuli into class categories so that the appropriate responses can be mounted. The stimuli must be categorized so that the relevant attitudes can be combined to form an opinion. "Categorization at the perceptual level consists of the process of identification, literally an act of placing a stimulus input by virtue of its defining attributes into a certain class."[102] Once the stimulus has been defined as relevant, it is

---

[102]Bruner et al., *A Study of Thinking*, p.9.

further defined by one or more distinguishing or "defining" attributes and placed into classes with other stimuli which possess the same or similar attributes.

Categorization performs five important functions for the individual.[103] It reduces the complexity of the political environment by reducing the number of cues a person needs to operate in an otherwise complex situation. Rather than judging political candidates as Jefferson favored, on the basis of comparing their position on issues with ours, we can judge them by their looks, their party label, or whatever. Categorization also allows us to provide a handy set of labels for objects in the political environment, labels which carry all sorts of connotations— Commie, Democrat, Republican, right-winger. Categories cut down on our need constantly to relearn our political environment; once we have labelled Democrats as "good" and Republicans as "bad" those labels and judgments can carry us through a lifetime of elections. In addition to providing labels the categories provide us with cues as to what appropriate action to take. Knowing a man is a Democrat and we are Republican tells us not to vote for him. Categorization also allows the individual to order and relate classes of events just as categories enable him to order types of political objects.

By placing a stimulus into a class of stimuli on the basis of a number of defining criterial attributes, the individual can assume the stimulus to be similar to and possessing other class-based qualities. The knowledge that a person we have just met is a Republican or Democrat allows us to make a number of assumptions about his politics, depending on how clearly we have delineated the class categories of each party. This raises the question of how many and what kind of defining attributes are necessary for categorization. Bruner, Goodnow, and Austin conclude that the more criteria used to categorize a stimulus, the more complete and accurate the categorization; using only one attribute to categorize a stimulus may lead to more errors than using ten.[104] Knowledge of a person's party identification may not tell you whether he is a conservative or a liberal—that

---

[103]Ibid., pp. 4-5.
[104]Ibid.

may require the answer to questions regarding social welfare policy and the expansion of government activities. The more criteria used, however, the longer and more complex the categorization process. And when large numbers of stimuli must be processed, economy is an important factor. The important question for each person is what criteria and how many will he use in categorizing stimuli. What are the fewest number and best criteria which will yield the highest return in accuracy?

The question of the costs of processing information in order to make decisions has become increasingly important to economists and political theorists. Anthony Downs, in a seminal work in this area, argues that political participation is the result of cost-benefit calculations made by individual voters.[105] The voter must determine whether the benefits derived from voting compensate for the costs involved in seeking information on which to make a rational electoral decision. If the voter must determine each candidate's position on a wide range of issues, compare those positions with his own on the same issues, and then vote for the candidate whose position is closest to his own, voting will be worthwhile only for the deeply committed. Downs recognizes that the voter does not have to and does not undergo that vigorous and intellectual process in making his decision; shortcuts are available. Ideology provides the voter with a useful shorthand for interpreting political information from his environment.

> Under these conditions (of uncertainty), many a voter finds party ideologies useful because they remove the necessity of his relating every issue to his own philosophy. Ideologies help him to focus attention on the differences between parties; therefore, they can be used as samples of all the differentiating stands. With this short cut, a voter can save himself the cost of being informed upon a wider range of issues.[106]

For Downs, ideology is a cost reducer because through it the political parties minimize the information which the voter must

---

[105]Anthony Downs, *An Economic Theory of Democracy* (New York: Harper and Row, 1957).
[106]Ibid., p. 98.

process about them. Implicit in this discussion is an assumption that the voter has an ideology which is personal and which allows him to make judgments about the relative merits of the party ideology. Thus, both the party ideology and the voters' ideology play a role in making the political environment more simple.

Campbell et al. suggest that party identification plays a critical role in the categorization of stimuli. "Identification with a party raises a perceptual screen through which the individual tends to see what is favorable to his partisan orientation. The stronger the party bond, the more exaggerated the process of selection and perceptual distortion will be."[107] Party identification is important as a categorization tool because it is one criteria which remains constant from election to election; candidates and issues may change from election to election but the political parties do not. The Democratic or Republican party labels thus become and remain useful devices for making decisions through a whole series of elections. In any given election, however, a person's attitudes toward the candidates and the issues may be a more important dimension of his perceptual screen and serve to distort the voter's perception of the candidate's party affiliation.

When there is consistency of stimuli coming through the perceptual screen, the voter has a clear picture of his political environment and is likely to act in that environment. What happens when there is conflict between stimuli—party identification, candidate orientation, and issue orientation? Campbell, Gurin, and Miller provide data from the 1952 election which suggests that where there is ambiguity or conflict between stimuli, attitudes are frequently inconsistent. For example, ninety-three percent of those people who were Democrats in party, candidate, and issue orientation preferred the Democrat candidate while ninety-eight percent of those people Republican in party, candidate, and issue orientation preferred Eisenhower. The less consistent the cues, the less consistent their preference for one of the two candidates until, for those

---

[107]Campbell et. al., op. cit., p. 133.

people who were nonpartisan in party, candidate, and issue orientation, both candidates were equally attractive. These three stimuli are also positively related to the extent of political participation, straight versus split-ticket voting, consideration of voting for the opposition candidate, and time of voting decision.[108] On this latter point, the more consistent the stimuli, the earlier one made his decision—the consistency of the stimuli made the decision easier—and the less likely he was to consider voting for the opposition candidate.

Perhaps the function of the perceptual screen and its relationship to stimuli and attitudes, values, and beliefs can best be understood by considering a case study. From *Opinions and Personality* we now examine the case of Charles Lanlin.[109]

Charles Lanlin: A case study

Charles Lanlin was one of the ten men intensively studied by Smith, Bruner, and White. An appliance salesman, Lanlin maintained his family in a quiet, middle-class suburb of Boston on his income of $5000 per year. A Catholic but not devout.

> His approach to the world was a smiling one. He laughed and chuckled easily; he was the kind of person who enjoyed a joke—especially when he told it. His aim was to be cordial and pleasant in his contacts with others. Even in repose, his features had a vaguely smiling, if bland, cast. His gesturing, too, was rather vague and loosely knit. Somehow one had the impression that his face was not quite finished.[110]

In common with many other Americans, Lanlin was essentially apolitical; politics played a very marginal role in his life. His family and work were of primary importance to him and it is not surprising that his approach to politics mirrors values which were important to his work. Politics, to paraphrase Clausewitz, is merely an extension of the business ethic. The content of that business ethic was unclear in his mind.

---

[108]Angus Campbell, Gerald Gurin, and Warren Miller, *The Voter Decides* (Evanston: Row, Peterson and Co., 1954), p. 160.
[109]Smith, Bruner, and White, op. cit.
[110]Ibid., p. 115.

Efficiency and economy were its yardsticks, but its content centered on assumptions that business could best be run by reasonable, rational men, acting in pursuit of gain. In politics, as in business, poker, and war, when others threaten trouble, call their bluff—the man with the money, or the cards, or the nuclear warheads, succeeds.

This belief system determined how Lanlin responded to a stimulus like Russia. When asked, "What about the outside world, the world at large? How do you feel about the situation there?" Lanlin responded by mentioning Russia first. Russia was a salient stimulus because it did not fit into the world that Lanlin would have liked. "Here, then, was Russia—bumptious, making unreasonable demands, agitating, and somehow not in the image of the ordinary kinds of people who are not 'hitting the headlines.'" These characteristics of the stimulus made it both salient and classifiable. The Russian leadership was evil because of its subversion and control of the Russian people, who, if left to their own desires, would be friendly to the United States, and because of their attempt to gain world domination. The solution to these problems would be to call their bluff. The inability of the Russian economy to supply consumer goods was evidence enough to Lanlin that Russia did not have the technological capability successfully to challenge the United States. Once their bluff had been called, the Russian leaders would be discredited in the eyes of their people. This fact, combined with an educational program on the part of the United States aimed at educating the Russian people about the U.S., would lead to a lessening of differences between the two countries.

If Lanlin's primary concerns in the world were for his family and work, his response to the political environment was in those terms. The international order was nothing more than a big market place in which reasonable men interacted and one treated belligerent actors in the international market as one treated belligerent adolescents—with firm authority. Having made those decisions, Lanlin did not desire further information about Russia in order to reevaluate his original decision. If Russia became more salient he might do so, but for the present, home and family were more important.

Summary

In order to understand why people hold the opinions they do it is necessary to recognize and understand the attitudes, values, and beliefs which underlie those opinions. It is particularly important to understand what beliefs are and how they are organized to form a cognitive framework with which the individual views his political world. Beliefs, in turn, are related to personality, so that the belief system is both a reflection of the individual's personality and a protection for that personality against a potentially hostile world.

Thus far, however, we have been concerned with the individual—and his attitudes, values, and beliefs—when he is an adult, when those attitudes, values, and beliefs are already fairly well formed and established, as is the individual's personality. What we need to look at now is the process by which the individual develops his own personality and his corollary attitudes, values, and beliefs.

CHAPTER TWO

A developmental model of
opinion formation

A person's attitudes, values, beliefs, and opinions are not fully developed at birth. They are the end product of a complex set of interactions between him and his environment, interactions which allow the child, as he grows older, to deal with an increasingly complex world. In order to understand how people develop their political views we must know about their personal development; we need to focus on the development of children during the critical period between four and fourteen, when they accomplish the bulk of their physical and psychological growth, and to relate their personal growth to the development of their political attitudes.

While political scientists have long been interested in how children learn political values, it was not until 1958 that the first intensive study of the development of political attitudes in children was done by Greenstein, who interviewed over 600 grammar school children in New Haven, Connecticut.[1] His pioneering work did much to legitimize the field of political socialization and was followed by studies by Hess and Torney, Easton and Dennis, and Langton.[2]

---

[1]Fred Greenstein, *Children and Politics* (New Haven, Conn.: Yale University Press, 1965 ed.).

[2]Robert D. Hess and Judith V. Torney, *The Development of Political Attitudes in Children* (Garden City, N.Y.: Doubleday and Co., 1967); David Easton and Jack Dennis, *Children in the Political System* (New York: McGraw-Hill, 1969); and Kenneth P. Langton, *Political Socialization* (New York: Oxford University Press, 1969).

Although there has been a substantial amount of research done a note of caution is in order. The research in general suffers from several defects which must temper too-willing acceptance of the findings. First, much of the research has been done without any theory to guide it, so the topics explored and the findings are not always comparable. Second, the research has focused on samples of largely white, largely middle-class children between the ages of four and eighteen. As a result we know less about non-white, non-middle-class children and we know very little at all about the political development of children prior to the age when they can use paper and pencil. At the same time we know little about the socialization or resocialization process in adults. With these caveats in mind let's examine the literature.

Opinion formation as a process

First, awareness of people in the political environment is based on visibility; the child first becomes aware of those people whom his parents talk about or with whom he has contact— the policeman, the president, the mayor. Seeking a framework for evaluating political figures the child tends to perceive them as omniscient, all-powerful and benevolent versions of his father. As the child grows older his political horizons broaden and he begins to perceive more political figures. Greenstein found that by sixth-grade children were aware of the governor, by seventh grade Congress became salient, and by eighth grade the state legislature and the local Board of Aldermen were relevant dimensions of the child's political world.[3] Easton and Dennis suggest:

> The children's conception of government is, therefore, brought in stages from far to near, from one small set of persons to many people, from a personalized to an impersonalized form of authority, and towards an awareness of the institutionalization in our system of such regime norms as are embodied in the idea of a representative, popular democracy.[4]

---

[3] Greenstein, op. cit.
[4] Easton and Dennis, op. cit., p. 117.

Second, children tend to perceive government as benevolent, just, and fair. As a result children see the output of government, in the form of its laws and regulations, as just and fair.

> The orientations toward the compliance system is fourfold: first, the fund of positive feeling for government, particularly the President, which is extended to include laws made by governmental authorities; second, the core of respect for power wielded by authority figures, particularly the policeman; third, experience in subordinate, compliant roles, acquired by the child at home and school; fourth, the normative belief that all systems of rules are fair.[5]

The role of the citizen in such a benevolent world is an essentially passive one—at least for second graders. By eighth grade the child has a more activist perception of his citizen role, assuming that if the government is benevolent then his participation will be meaningful and fruitful.

From this research we know a great deal about what political perceptions are formed when, but we know very little about how and why. Reviewing the socialization literature Dawson concludes that there are four important research questions yet to be answered:[6]

1. At what age does socialization begin and take place?
2. Is the socialization process continuous or not?
3. Is the learning involved in socialization direct or indirect?
4. How does the learning take place?

In a later work, in conjunction with Kenneth Prewitt, Dawson develops this model in substantially more detail.[7] They argue: "The early basic political learning, then, occurs side-by-side, with other significant social learning. As the child begins to become aware of the political world, he simultaneously forms awareness of other societal groupings and definitions of his self in relation to them."[8] Political socialization is one dimension of

---

[5]Hess and Torney, op. cit., p. 68.

[6]Richard E. Dawson, "Political Socialization," in *Political Science Annual vol. I* ed. *James A. Robinson (Indianapolis: Bobbs-Merrill, 1966)*.

[7]Richard Dawson and Kenneth Prewitt, *Political Socialization* (Boston: Little, Brown, and Co., 1969).

[8]Ibid., p. 47.

the process of growing up and is a reflection of the growth of the child's sense of self and social maturity. The developmental sequence proceeds along two basic dimensions: (1) the growth of a sense of self (or ego strength) and (2) increasing ability to differentiate elements of the environment and engage in more abstract reasoning. No connection is made between the two basic dimensions, and there is no linkage between the major dimensions of this model and the data provided by earlier empirical studies. As we shall see shortly, such a connection is possible. The politically mature person is one who has developed his personality and intellectual skills to the point where he can deal confidently with a complex political environment. The child first learns a "social category system" which he uses to make judgments about the immediate social environment and, later, the more complex political environment. This evaluative system provides the framework which the child begins to fill with political objects, sometime before the third grade, and which becomes increasingly abstract and complex. "Political maturation has been cumulative, evolving through a vague perception of the political world and emotional attachments to it, to more discrete knowledge and differentiation of political roles and objects, to a sense of involvement in the political world."[9] The developmental sequence is linear and reinforcing—the actions of one socialization agent are reinforced by other agents.

There is little data, however, as to how children learn political attitudes or why, and how such learning is related to an individual's personality.[10] Hess and Torney suggest that political learning takes four modes.[11] In the *accumulation model* the child's attitudes and behavior are the result of an accumulation of earlier learning. Learning is a building block process in which everything the child knows is a product of what he has learned before. The *interpersonal transfer model* assumes that the child's interpersonal relations with adults will serve as behavioral models in the political system. An adult's attitudes

---

[9]Ibid., p. 51.

[10]T. Cook and F. Scioli, "A Critique of the Learning Theory Concept in Political Science Research," *Social Science Quarterly* 52 (March, 1972), pp. 949-62.

[11]Hess and Torney, op. cit., pp. 19-22.

toward authority figures, according to this model, are generalized from his experiences with adult authority figures in childhood. Similar to the interpersonal transfer model is the *identification model*, which assumes that the child imitates the values and behaviors of some significant other person(s). The difference between the latter two models seems to rest on what is learned from the relevant other persons; in the identification model the child copies the attitudes and behaviors of someone he admires, while in the interpersonal transfer model he learns attitudes derived from watching adults in interpersonal situations. As a result, the child develops attitudes toward authority with the interpersonal transfer model and party identification with the identification model. The *cognitive development model* assumes that as the child matures he is increasingly able to respond in more abstract and complex ways to his political environment. This model argues that the quality of a child's political world is a result of his personal development—a child in third grade cannot differentiate between the president and Congress because his conceptual skills at that age make it difficult for him to make subtle distinctions of that type in any area of his life.

These four models are not exclusionary alternatives, but different learning models which children can use to adapt to their political environment. Unfortunately, Hess and Torney do not have any data as to which model is used by which children to learn which things. The longitudinal data which Hess and Torney do have seem to fit the cognitive developmental model most closely. While children's initial attitudes toward political authority may be the result of interpersonal transfer, the child's ability to differentiate between different kinds and sources of authority leads me to think that the cognitive development model may do the most for our understanding of political socialization as a process.

Dawson and Prewitt suggest that political "learning" is either indirect or direct. Indirect learning involves the assimilation of politically relevant roles and values which are not transmitted directly or even intentionally, i.e., interpersonal transference (the same concept as that used by Hess and

Torney); apprenticeship, the use of nonpolitical activities to learn skills useful in political roles (learning debate skills which have political, as well as nonpolitical, application); and generalization, where nonpolitical attitudes (toward authority, for example) are extended to include political objects, are modes of indirect learning. They also delineate four kinds of direct political learning, where the transmission is immediate, obvious, and manifestly political: imitation of adults in the immediate political environment (most important for the transmission of party identification); anticipatory socialization, in which the child is trained for specific political roles (whereby parents, teachers, and others tell the child what his role as "citizen" entails); political education, the deliberate and direct attempt to transmit political information and values; and direct learning, which is the result of political experience.

While the dichotomy between direct and indirect learning is useful for further delineation of learning, modes may not be. Learning modes are nothing more than classification schema which enable us to identify certain kinds of behavior but do little to explain such behavior. What is needed is a learning theory which explains how a person learns differently throughout his life and which is related to personality development.

It is clear from the foregoing review of the literature that political scientists know when children learn which political attitudes but they have little idea why. There is a suggestion that political socialization is a developmental process but they can't say what is developing or why. For that reason we will have to propose a developmental model of political socialization and then relate that model to the available research.

A developmental model of political socialization

Several social scientists have been interested in a developmental theory of socialization. Elkin, for example, sees socialization as a continuous process in which the individual goes through a series of developmental stages: "a temporary equilibrium or level of development is reached, then new elements are introduced which lead to readjustments and new equilibria."[12] What "develops" are the child's cognitive skills and personality, which allow him to cope with increasing skill with his environment. Aside from stipulating that development is a stage process involving the development of cognition and ego, Elkin's model is incomplete. The purpose of this section will be to flesh out this model.

I assume that a person is brought into the world *de novo*[13] and that the purpose of human development is to learn how to deal effectively with one's self and the environment. The developmental process can best be viewed in terms of the child's increasing awareness and sense of mastery. When born, the child is initially aware only of himself and his immediate environment; as he masters that initial environment, he becomes increasingly aware of the larger environment outside himself, and he strives to master it. In the process, the child begins to differentiate between himself and others and to develop a sense of self and self-esteem. Murphy has described this process of "coping" during the child's first year in the following terms:

> The child responds (to the environment) with varying configurations of retreat and limitation of the pressure, evoking support, trying to understand, making an effort—with alterations of doubt and confidence—for a considerable period before near-mastery reenforces confidence and leads to the crystallization and integration of perception, feeling and behavior in the actual experience of mastery and the pride accompanying it.[14]

The process of increasing awareness and mastery has been of theoretical interest to psychologists and child development specialists of the past decade. Although focusing on cognitive development and personality development separately, they have developed process models which bear remarkable similarities. It is to these models we now turn.

---

[12]Frederick Elkin, *The Child and Society: The Process of Socialization* (New York: Random House, 1960), p. 21.

[13]Not all developmental theorists accept this assumption. See Zing-Yang Kuo, *The Dynamics of Behavior Development: An Ipigenetic View* (New York: Random House, 1967), Chapter 2.

[14]Lois D. Murphy, *The Widening World of Childhood* (New York: Basic Books, 1962), pp. 185-86.

Cognitive development models

Premier among the cognitive development models is that of Jean Piaget.[15] Central to Piaget's theory is his conception of cognitive development as a continuous and increasingly complex process of generalization and differentiation. During the first two years of life the child develops his sense of physical coordination and mastery; this stage Piaget labels the sensorimotor phase of development. This stage is precognitive in the sense that the child is developing the physical tools which are preconditions to the development of cognitive skills, experiencing stimuli without making much sense of them. When the child's physical growth stabilizes, the child has more time to devote to the exploration of his external world and a greater need to understand it. He begins to make a cause-effect relationship between himself and the world, and to notice similarities between stimuli. Instead of each day being entirely new and different, the child learns that some dimensions of his environment are stable through time and that his actions can elicit the responses he desires. But much of this learning is random and accidental. For that reason Piaget calls it the preconceptual stage. Once the child begins to notice order in his environment and similarities within the environment, he enters the third stage—a phase of intuitive thought—in which he develops categories for labeling and responding to the environment. The process of categorization is critical to cognitive development. "We analyze, compare, and transform, using an activity which starts in perceptive regulation and comparison, but it is integrated in a system of concepts enabling us to give meanings to the elements and relationships thus analyzed."[16] The categories become conceptual schemata for dealing with external stimuli. When faced with an object, the child tries to assimilate it to his present conceptual schemata, with one of two results:

---

[15]Among his works are *Play, Dreams and Imitation in Childhood* (New York: W. W. Norton, 1962 ed.); *The Origins of Intelligence in Children* (New York: W. W. Norton, 1952); and with Barbara Inheld, *The Growth of Logical Thinking* (New York: Basic Books, 1958).

[16]Piaget, *Play, Dreams and Imitation*, p. 77.

1. the object is familiar and can be categorized and fit into the existing conceptual schemata, or
2. the object is unfamiliar and categories must either be combined to create a new conceptual category or the object rejected as not classifiable.[17]

The more complex the environmental stimuli, the more sophisticated the schemata for classification need to be. The child's cognitive development can be traced to his increasing ability to accommodate and assimilate external stimuli within increasingly complex conceptual outlines. Lower-order concepts, when they prove inoperative in dealing with the environment, are combined into higher-order concepts. Intelligence and logical thinking are the outgrowth of this ability to combine, decompose, and recombine concepts. By eight years of age the child begins to generalize from his conceptual schema and to apply it to a wider range of objects—this is the phase of concrete operations. The child is able to operate in and understand his environment; he is curious, quick, and able to grasp new objects and events into his increasingly sophisticated schemata. During his teens the individual begins to extrapolate from the concepts he uses and derive generalizations and propositions. "In other words, the adolescent is the individual who begins to build 'systems' or 'theories,' in the largest sense of the term."[18] The ability to generalize from his experiences and to live within his own conceptual world is the beginning of intellectual development for the child, allowing him to escape the concrete realities of his life.

Piaget's model of cognitive development assumes that the individual goes through a series of stages, progress based on successful completion of the preceding stage, leading through increasingly complex and broad conceptual schema. Each cognitive stage enables the individual to deal with a complex environment and, when the environment becomes more complex or the cognitive stage loses utility, the individual advances to the next stage. The process by which the person moves from one

---

[17]While the principles of assimilation and accommodation are discussed in a number of books, the best statement is found in Piaget, *The Origins of Intelligence.*

[18]Inheld and Piaget, op. cit., p. 339.

cognitive stage to another is through learning to cope with the environment. In a stimulus-response model, the child is confronted with stimuli from the environment; for Piaget the child develops a cognitive style which allows him adequately to handle the environmental stimuli. Once the environmental stimuli have been mastered, something (exactly what is not clear) impels the child to seek more complex cognitive schemata for dealing with the environment. As with much of the socialization literature, however, Piaget neglects the role of personality in the development of cognitive skills and the rates at which children move through the various cognitive stages. It is necessary for us to look at a theory of personality development to see if it offers us any further help in understanding the socialization process.

Personality development model

The number of personality development models is legion.[19] Reviewing them all would be a monumental task and would be of limited utility for this work, where I am interested in a model of personality development which corresponds best with Piaget's cognitive development model and yields an adequate explanation of the research findings developed in the political socialization literature.

Erik Erikson's developmental model of personality offers a useful tool for social scientists.[20] As a post-Freudian, Erikson sees the ego as the basis of personality, seeking a balance between the uninhibited drives of the id and the overrigid moral code of the superego.

Between the id and the superego, then, the ego dwells. Consistently balancing and warding off the extreme ways of the other two, the ego keeps tuned to the reality of the historical

---

[19]C. S. Hall and Gardner Lindzey, *Theories of Personality* (New York: Wiley, 1957).

[20]The best statements of Erikson's theory can be found in *Childhood and Society* (New York: W. W. Norton, 1963 ed.) and its application in *Young Man Luther* (New York: Norton, 1958) and *Ghandi's Truth* (New York: Norton, 1969).

day, testing perceptions, selecting memories, governing action, and otherwise integrating the individual's capabilities of orientation and planning.[21]

Although the id is still the basic drive, the ego assumes importance as it maintains a delicate balance between the undisciplined id and the overdisciplined superego, keeping the individual in control of himself and in touch with the realities of his environment.

Erikson differs from Freud on the role of the family in personality development. While Freud saw the family as all important, leaving a lasting and permanent imprint on the child as he moves to adulthood, Erikson sees the family as only one dimension of an individual's life space. The development process is motivated by the need to come to grips with a social environment, a process in which the family plays an important but not crucial role. Personality development is the result of the individual's conquering psychological obstacles in his life space; the process takes the individual through a series of stages in which he seeks to master broader and more complex dimensions of his environment. After he masters his environment at one level he is then aware of and challenged by a still broader environment. Mastery of each stage then leads to a stronger ego. Two points must be remembered, however: the progression from one stage to another is not automatic; the transition to the development of a sense of identity may result in a crisis in identity, a crisis which some people do not successfully resolve. Because the transition from one stage to another is not automatic, the ages at which each stage occurs must be suggestive rather than definitive. The development of a sense of identity, which Erikson suggests occurs in adolescence, occurred in Luther's twenties and Ghandi's thirties.[22]

The first developmental stage, which occupies the child's first two years, concerns the mastery of his immediate environment and the development of a sense of basic trust while overcoming a feeling of distrust of the environment. As the child's environment stabilizes and he learns it is no longer hostile, he begins

[21]Erikson, *Childhood and Society*, p. 193.
[22]See Erikson, *Young Man Luther* and *Ghandi's Truth*.

to explore the world outside himself. In exploring the world outside himself and his mother (his early immediate environment), the child enters phase two, the acquisition of a sense of autonomy. By age five he views himself as an object apart from his parents and the family, and begins on his own initiative to explore his relations to the world outside the family. Erikson views this period as one where the child develops a sense of initiative. By age eight or nine the child achieves a realistic level of independence from his parents and begins to identify with his peers. In the process he also begins to develop a task orientation which Erikson calls the development of a sense of industry. Parents assume a functional role of providing adult role-models, as well as providing sustenance, housing and clothing. Sometime during adolescence the developing personality goes through the most critical stage in his development—the establishment of a sense of identity. This is the critical transitional stage between childhood and adulthood, in which the child undergoes physical and psychological growth which enables him to assume adult roles and provides him with the ego strength necessary to fill them. The adolescent is different from the child he has been. Physically he is capable of fulfilling an adult sex role. Psychologically he is less concerned with the present, more certain of himself, more aggressive, more confident of his role in adult life and his ability to play that role. He has a well-developed sense of self, both physically and psychologically. Once the individual has developed a sense of identity he can then interact intimately and openly with others; once he knows himself, he can know and understand others. This is the sixth stage in Erikson's model, the development of a sense of intimacy. In adulthood people can move to higher levels of ego development in which they evolve a sense of identification with others—a sense of universality—while maintaining their own sense of integrity and self-worth. In the seventh stage the adult acquires a sense of generativity—a "concern for establishing and guiding the next generation."[23]

---

[23]Erikson, *Childhood and Society*, p. 318. Erikson adds one more state—the wisdom of old age, but since we are primarily concerned with understanding socialization at the preadult level, we shall stop here.

Having achieved mature adulthood, the individual strives to pass on his lessons to his children; in a critical sense the ego expands to include others and the concept of self expands to embrace the family. He has now passed full cycle—from a family in which he is a child to a family in which he is the parent.

Although Erikson's model is useful for understanding the process of personality development, it does very little to aid our understanding of cognitive development. Erikson assumes that the connection exists, but it is not his primary concern.

A synthetic model

Piaget and Erikson are both occupied with human development, seeing it as a continuous process in which a person goes through a series of stages to full cognitive functioning and ego strength. Is it possible to synthesize these two theories? Will such a synthetic model provide adequate explanatory power for the political socialization research?

It would be simple to lay both theories side by side on a time scale and compare the timing of the various stages.[24] That merely tells you, however, that children experience a sense of basic trust and are in the sensori-motor phase of cognitive development (See Figure 2-1) during approximately the same period. A timeline comparison can be useful in mapping the congruence of developmental stages, but what does it tell us of the product of the two developmental processes at that time period? I have attempted to allow both the comparison of developmental sequence in time and a mapping of the total impact of the two developmental processes by using a graph in which the stages of personality development are calibrated by year on the x-axis and the phases of cognitive development are calibrated by year on the y-axis.

A synthesis of the Piaget and Erikson models leads us to view the developmental process as one of growing personal and

---

[24]Henry W. Maier, *Three Theories of Child Development* (New York: Harper and Row, 1965) has developed a useful timeline comparison model in looking at the theories of Piaget, Erikson, and Sears. Much of my thinking about the synthesis of Piaget and Erikson stems from this excellent work.

FIGURE 2-1

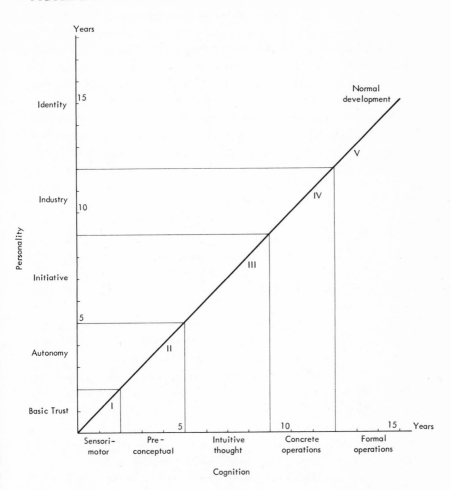

cognitive differentiation and integration, in which the individual learns to cope with himself and his environment at one level before moving on to more complex learning tasks. Stage I finds the child learning the physical skills—touching, walking, and the rudiments of speech—necessary for dealing effectively with his environment. The very acts of developing sensori-motor skills are rewarded by parents and other adults, making the child's immediate environment a more friendly and nonthreatening place. And as the child learns his home is filled with love and trust, he has the opportunity and encouragement to develop his physical skills (as we shall see in the next chapter). Once the immediate environment has stabilized, a happy and trustful place that the child can physically control and manipulate, he can begin to look beyond himself, to see the world as something other than an extension of himself. He has entered Stage II. His immediate objective is to become aware of the world outside himself and to try to make some sense of it. The process of differentiating one's self from others and then attempting to classify the "others" is a critical first step in the development of the child's ego and his need to categorically deal with stimulus objects. The two developmental processes—cognitive and personality—are clearly interrelated; the child finds it hard to dichotomize between himself and others unless he has some means of dealing cognitively with the "others," and he can't categorize "others" until he has the sense of personal autonomy which enables him to make the we-they dichotomy. This period of initial data gathering and mastery of the immediate environment is followed by Stage III where the child begins to explore the world outside his family and begins to make connections between data from his family experience and those from the wide environment. Male figures are thought to be extensions of the father and analogous to him; the same connection is made between the mother and female figures. As the child develops this sense of initiative, he must also begin to form schemata for analyzing data from his everexpanding universe. And as the child forms outlines for understanding his world, he becomes more at ease with it and interested in exploring it even more fully. After a period of time exploration becomes less important than defining a role for one's self in the environment which is known and understood. Stage IV marks the beginning of the child's development of a role concept and standards of evaluating behavior appropriate to that role. The child becomes more goal-oriented, and his cognitive skills are devoted to developing means to attain his goals. Less concerned with understanding his present world, he begins to explore how to manipulate the environment to meet his future role requirements. At the same time he is also developing criteria for evaluating alternative means to the attainment of his goals. The congruence of the formal operation phase and the sense of identity phase in Stage V can be summed up in the question, "Who am I?" which expresses a personal and cognitive question. In this stage it is extremely difficult to differentiate between the cognitive and personality dimensions of the model; the individual needs to abstract himself from his experience in order to answer the question regarding his personal worth, while the question of his identity is one of the most important cognitive questions which he must answer.

The end product of this developmental model will depend on the development along the two axes. "Normal development" will find the young adult who knows who he is, what he wants to be, and where he wants to go, who has a reasonable and realistic idea of the world in which he lives and an idea of how to deal with it. He has a sense of mastery and control over himself and his environment. He has the cognitive and personal flexibility to envision himself in alien situations and to determine the appropriate behavior. Life is no longer episodic, composed of a series of individual events; it is now a fabric of experience in which every event prepares him to deal with the next one.

Do all people develop "normally"? If we view "normal" development as a uniform balance between personality and cognitive development, then most people develop normally, at least within reasonable limits. As noted earlier, Ghandi and Luther both underwent crises in identity after they had achieved the cognitive skills of formal operationalization. Given the interrelationship between the personality and cognitive stages, it should be theoretically difficult to deviate very far from the normal development mode; a person who develops only to the point of concrete operations will find it difficult to establish a well-developed and complex definition of self. Instead, the individual will probably develop a confusion of roles until he can make greater and more sophisticated sense of his experiences. A classic case of arrested personality development and its cognitive impact is that of autistic children, where the underdeveloped, misshapen egos effectively block their ability to deal with their environment in coherent terms.[25] If people cannot cope with themselves, can they be expected to cope with, understand, and evaluate others?

A reexamination of the political socialization research

Having synthesized a model from the Erikson and Piaget frameworks, it is now possible to return to the political socialization research discussed earlier and reexamine it. In the process we will determine the utility of the model and provide some more meaningful insights into the political socialization process.

The unanimity of research which finds that children first develop perceptions of dominant political figures and then, as they grow older, differentiate between governmental institutions is not surprising. For most preschool children the political system is not a salient part of their world. It is too complex to be easily understood and requires personal skills to manipulate which the child at that age does not possess. Those political figures which are salient for the child are those which intrude into the family and which are analogous to figures in the immediate environment. For the children of politically active families, where the child has been encouraged to explore his environment, political interest and awareness will develop at an early age and will be comparatively high. The local precinct captain or policeman may be as relevant a part of the environment as the President. As the child grows older, he becomes more aware of and better able to cope with government in its increasing complexity. The President is no longer an extension of their father when children realize that people other than their father possess power and authority. When the child understands that the President is not a personal friend of the family, his image is depersonalized and his perceived power and authority are reduced to more realistic dimensions. Concomi-

---

[25]See Bruno Bettelheim, *Truants from Life* (New York: Free Press, 1955).

tant with the depersonalization of the President, the child becomes aware that the President must also share his power with others, particularly the Congress. Authority is differentiated by the child, as is function. But the benevolence which the child initially attributed to the President is diffused to include the entire government. When the child's immediate environment is friendly and manageable, it is difficult to perceive as unfriendly an object more distant—in space and attention. When the child's immediate environment is perceived as unstable, threatening, or deprived, the child is less able to build a solid ego and, consequently, political objects are viewed as unfriendly dimensions of that hostile environment.[26] In the same way the class basis of political efficacy can be explained. Black children don't feel politically efficacious because they have learned through experience that black people have little impact on their environment, that they are the manipulated rather than the manipulators.

The data on the development of party identification and ideology is also consistent with the model. With children as well as adults, party identification is an easy shorthand way of dealing with and understanding a remote and complex phenomenon. Party identification means something different for children than it does for their parents; "Democrat" and "Republican" are only labels which young children use to differentiate between political objects—the terms denote nothing else. As the children grow older, the labels begin to accrue meaning and history and serve to do more than differentiate between candidates as people. The child of twelve saying "I'm a Democrat" means something more than a child of six saying the same thing. In much the same way the development of something approaching a comprehensive ideology for dealing with the political world must await the development of a need for such a framework, an appropriate personality, and the necessary conceptual skills for the child to tie together abstract

---

[26]Dean Jaros, Herbert Hirsch and Frederick Fleron, "The Malevolent Leader: Political Socialization in an American Subculture," *American Political Science Review* 62 (June, 1968), pp. 564-75.

principles into a coherent whole. Rokeach found that an adult's openmindedness or closemindedness was related to his perceptions of childhood.

> Low scorers on the Dogmatism Scale, as compared with middle or high scorers, express more ambivalence toward their fathers and mothers, report being more widely influenced by persons outside the immediate family, and report having had fewer anxiety symptoms in childhood. On the other hand, the reports of middle and closed subjects are on the whole similar, and compared with open subjects, they reveal more glorification of parents, a more restricted influence by persons outside the family, and a greater incidence in childhood of thumb-sucking, nail-biting, temper tantrums, nightmares, walking and talking while asleep, and bedwetting.[27]

The more anxiety ridden the parents, the more difficult it is for the child to develop a healthy personality and the concomitant conceptual skills to enable him to deal with his environment.

Rosenberg's research on high school juniors and seniors offers supporting evidence.[28] Low self-esteem (or a negative self-image) could be traced to the child's experiences with his family and their relations with him, particularly in the preschool period. To the extent that the child could not or did not find love and trust in the home he had correspondingly low self-esteem, which resulted in depression, neuroticism, anxiety, vulnerability in interpersonal relations, and alienation. The threatening and hostile environment of the family was generalized to the broader social and political environment, and the high schooler with low self-esteem withdrew from social and political participation. Unable to deal with themselves and others they withdrew, saying, "The world out there is a hostile and violent place."

Lane suggests that the anti-democratic ideologies of some of his working-class men in New Haven were tied directly to the lack of love they received as children, particularly from their

---

[27]Milton Rokeach, *The Open and Closed Mind* (New York: Basic Books, 1960).

[28]Morris Rosenberg, *Society and the Adolescent Self-Image* (Princeton, N. J.: Princeton University Press, 1965).

fathers.[29] For four of Eastport's men, whose fathers had "failed them," the political consequences were low information about and low interest in politics, high authoritarianism, and uncritical acceptance of political leaders, especially strong ones. A childhood rich in love, as Keniston found, can also develop an ego strong enough to challenge governmental policy through student activism.[30]

The evidence is consistent that the warmer the child's initial environment the more likely it is that he will develop a strong ego and the corresponding cognitive skills to deal with an increasingly more complex environment. Lacking the cognitive skills the child as a man is unable to differentiate between governmental officials and policies, and with a weak ego he sees in this confusion confirmation of his feelings that the world is a potentially threatening place.

The Erikson-Piaget model answers one theoretical shortcoming of the socialization research—why political socialization proceeds at the pace it does and why certain things are learned before others. It also enables us to understand why people hold some of the attitudes and opinions they do. Unanswered, however, is the question of *how* children learn what they learn. To what extent is political learning imitative, with the parents performing the unwitting role of model? There is no question from the socialization research that the child endows political figures with superhuman attributes of his or her father. There is less understanding of how much of the role of citizen that the child learns from watching and listening to parents discussing (or not discussing) politics around the dining room table. The research on political recruitment indicates that many political activists first became interested in politics because of a member of their family.[31]

What is still unclear, however, is how children learn. The

[29]Robert E. Lane, *Political Ideology* (New York: Free Press, 1962), pp. 268-82.

[30]Kenneth Keniston, *Young Radicals* (New York: Harcourt, Brace & World, 1968).

[31]See John Wahlke et al., *The Legislative System* (New York: Wiley, 1962), pp. 77-94.

Piaget-Erikson model, although it does not provide a direct answer, suggests some alternative learning strategies, which are related to the age of the child and his level of personal and cognitive development. The interpersonal transfer and identification learning models, where the child learns from interaction with parents or other figures in his immediate environment, would be most appropriate for the earliest forms of political learning. Exposed to a strange dimension of his world the child relies on familiar, loving and trustful figures in his immediate environment to understand the actions of political figures in his more distant political environment. Once he has learned to differentiate between political objects and to cope with them, when he no longer perceives of the president as an embodiment of his father's virtue, the child can piece together and form higher levels of abstraction about the political environment, similar to those learning modes which Hess and Torney label the accumulation and cognitive development modes. The latter most certainly assumes that the child is in the operational stages of his cognitive development, where he seeks to relate his political ideas to each other and to his need to understand the political world.

Summary

The Piaget-Erikson model provides us with a useful conceptual schema for understanding how people develop, personally and cognitively, and from that we can better understand why they develop the political opinions which they do. This model suggests that uneven, irregular, or incomplete personality and cognitive development can seriously handicap the development of interest in politics, the skills requisite for political participation, and the kinds of public opinions which one holds. The studies of Woodrow Wilson, Ghandi, Forrestal, Schumaker, and Boss Cermak, cited in the previous chapter, each indicate that abnormal development does have subsequent political consequences.

Having discussed what several researchers believe to be the process by which children learn political attitudes, values, and beliefs we must now examine the agents which operate on him throughout his life: family, school, friends, and the mass media. From the Piaget-Erikson model it appears that the socializing agents which deal with the child early in his development play a vital role in determining the kind of political person he will be. For that reason we begin by looking at two agents whom the child encounters early in his life and within whose embrace he stays until adulthood—the family and the school.

CHAPTER THREE

Opinion formation: The family and the school

Although there has been a substantial amount of research on political socialization there is little agreement as to which socialization agents have what impact when during the socialization process. There have been studies of the role of the family and of the role of the school, but we know little about the relative impact of each of these agents at any stage in the process. The inability to answer these questions stems from two sources, one methodological and one theoretical. Methodologically, studies of political socialization have focused on children at one point in time, rather than developmentally, and have been unable to unravel the relative impact of the multitude of socialization agents. In studying ten-year-olds, researchers have found it difficult to determine whether the political world of the child at that age is the result of the activities of his parents, the schools, the media, or his friends. Lacking a theoretical perspective researchers have been unable to explain why children learn what they do from some agents and not others.

The cognitive and personality model developed in the preceding chapter provides us with a schema for understanding the role which various socialization agents play in the socialization process. Looking at Figure 3-1 we can see that the family is the

70

primary socialization agent during the child's first two years, while he learns sensori-motor skills and begins to develop a sense of basic trust in his environment. The importance of the family as a socialization agent stems less from the political content of what it teaches the child during these first two years than from the way in which it prepares the child for later learning experiences. Family experiences can serve to facilitate or retard the impact and efficacy of other socializing agents at later points in the socialization process. The educational system becomes a relevant socializing agent only after the child has normally developed a sense of personal security and has the cognitive skills which allow him to deal with the increasingly complex environment which his personality growth allows him to explore. The roles of the school and the family are thus interdependent but different. Schools, peers, and the mass media serve to reinforce or mitigate the effects of the family during the first three or four years and to socialize the child in ways and in areas where the family does not reach. In addition to these formal agents, the environmental milieu into which the individual is born and within which he matures—the social status of his parents, race, and sex—often limit or manifest the influence which other, more formal, socializing agents may have. The environment provides resources and constraints on the kind of political adult the child will be; to the extent that all men are born into different environments they cannot develop the same.

The family

According to Figure 3-1 the family should play a complex role in the socialization process but its impact should be most unquestioned in stages one and two when the child is trying to come to some elemental mastery of his own body and his immediate environment. The family must provide him a stable environment in the immediate postnatal period so that he can begin adequately to develop his personality and cognitive skills. Once past this immediate task the family fulfills several other functions necessary for the development of the child's political per-

FIGURE 3–1

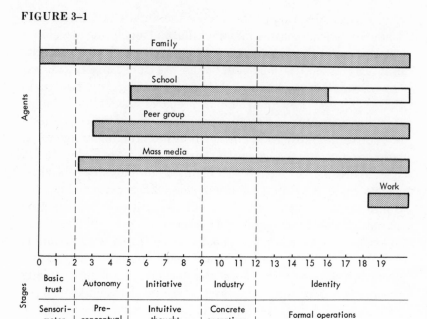

sonality. The family, particularly during stages two and three seems to inculcate in the child basic orientations toward the political system and political objects. At the same time, the family serves as a model for the child to use in evaluating his political environment. When the child first becomes aware of government he does not have the cognitive skills to evaluate the political actors or the performance of the political system. In looking for guidelines the child sees the political system as merely another version of his family, his role in the political system being comparable to his role in the family. Lacking experience in politics the child must look to skills and roles developed from his familial experience. Most of this learning should occur during the first nine years of the child's life, when the impact of the family is at its greatest.

The family provides the first contextual unit for the child and from it he must learn enough to survive in a broader, more complex, and more hostile environment.[1] To prepare the child adequately, the family must perform several basic functions. The parents must provide the offspring with sustenance, love, and shelter, developing in him a sense of trust and providing for him a stable arena within which to grow. This initial function is a crucial one; in his early life, the child must learn that the world is a constant and predictable place, since he has few resources to counter inconstancy and unpredictability. For the first six months of his life, the child's world generally consists of nothing more than him and his mother, and his primary concerns are to stabilize the relationship between the two of them and to master the elemental physical coordination of his body. During this period, the child is almost totally dependent on his mother. She must provide more than physical nurturance and warmth; she must also provide love and affection. Experiments with monkeys indicate that if monkeys are given surrogate mothers, wire models swathed in terry cloth and providing warmth through an electric light bulb, they psychologically wither and die.[2] Spitz's study of children raised in foundling homes showed comparably sad results. Children who had been breastfed by their mothers or human surrogate mothers for three months were placed in foundling homes where they received good physical care, shelter, and food, but little individual care and attention. After normal development for the first three months, the children began to deteriorate psychologically and physically, with approximately thirty percent dying during the first year in the foundling home and the rest showing marked psychological pathologies.[3] In a comprehen-

---

[1]Richard Q. Bell, "A Reinterpretation of the Direction of Effects in Studies of Socialization," *Psychological Review* 75 (March, 1968), pp. 81-95. Bell suggests that by focusing on the family as a socializing agent we overlook the role of the child in socializing his parents. It is undoubtedly true that socialization is an interactive process but our primary concern is with only one side of that process—the family's socialization of the child.

[2]See Harry Harlow, "The Nature of Love," *American Psychologist* 13 (1958): 673-85; and Harry Harlow and Margaret Harlow, "Learning to Love," *American Scientist* 54 (1966), pp. 244-72.

[3]Rene Spitz, *The First Year of Life* (New York: International Universities Press, 1965).

sive study of maternal deprivation undertaken for the World
Health Organization, John Bowlby concluded that "when
deprived of maternal care, the child's development is almost
always retarded—physically, intellectually, and socially—and
that symptoms of physical and mental illness may appear."[4]
The first three years are particularly critical; permanent deprivation of maternal care, temporary deprivation for as little as
three months, or changes from one mother figure to another can
produce pathologies in the child's development. These
pathologies, Bowlby contends, are due to inadequate ego development in the child, understandable if we remember that the
mother fulfills the role of ego and superego during the child's
early formative years.[5] Research on paternal deprivation indicates similar symptoms, particularly among male children.[6]

Morris Rosenberg, in a study of 5000 high school students in
New York State, has found corroborating evidence. In cases
where the mother married at an early age, quickly had a child,
and shortly thereafter was divorced, the adolescent child was
especially likely to lack self-esteem, a manifestation of low ego
strength.[7] For these mothers, a baby is often an impediment to
the resumption of their premarital life and the relationship between mother and child is hardly warm and loving and, lacking
a father with whom to identify, the child (particularly the boy)
"begins to identify with the important 'other' person and to in-
ternalize his (or her) attitudes as well as imitate his behavior."[8]

The research findings on the political manifestations of a
lack of love in the family are few but consistent. Studying the

---

[4]John Bowlby, *Maternal Care and Mental Health* (New York: Schocken
Books, 1966), p. 15.

[5]Ibid.; Leon Yarrow, "Separation From Parents During Early
Childhood," in *Review of Child Development*, ed. Martin Hoffman and Lois
Hoffman (New York: Russell Sage Foundation, 1964), pp. 89-136, after
reviewing the maternal deprivation literature, particularly since Bowlby's
book, concurs with Bowlby. Bowlby's conclusions are not unchallenged,
however. See Mary Ainsworth et al, *Deprivation of Maternal Care* (New
York: Schocken Books, 1966).

[6]For a listing and discussion of this literature, see Kenneth P. Langton,
Political Socialization (New York: Oxford University Press, 1969), p. 31.

[7]Morris Rosenberg, *Society and the Adolescent Self-Image* (Princeton:
Princeton U. Press, 1965).

[8]Langton, op. cit.

reactions of fifty-seven children to the assassination of President Kennedy, Ginsparg, Moriarity, and Murphy found that the study of response to the assassination was related to the child's affective relations with his mother; in families where children were distant from their mothers they tended to be vengeful rather than forgiving toward the assassin.[9] The warmer the family environment, the easier it was for the child to deal with the inconstancies of the external environment. Lane's study of fourteen men in New Haven indicates that a son's early family relations are crucial to his later personal and political development. A healthy and warm relationship leads to the development of a strong ego, while poor father-son relations lead to a lack of faith in people and a low sense of political efficacy—both symptomatic of low ego strength.[10] Keniston's study of Harvard male undergraduates confirms Lane's findings.[11] His alienated students were characterized by their poor relations with their parents, particularly their overdependence on their mothers. Their alienation is manifested in an inability to engage in interpersonal relations or to cope with their external environment. Vietnam War protestors, on the other hand, have well-developed egos and feel highly efficacious, possibly because of remarkably stable and warm family experiences.[12] Adorno et al., after an extensive study of prejudiced and unprejudiced adults, male and female, concluded, "The prejudiced subjects show little evidence of genuine love toward their parents. On the surface, theirs is a stereotyped, rigid glorification of the parents, with strong resentment and feelings of victimization occasionally breaking through on the overt level."[13]

---

[9]Sylvia Ginsparg, Alice Moriarity, and Lois Murphy, "Young Teenagers' Responses to the Assassination of President Kennedy," in *Children and the Death of a President*, ed. Martha Wolfenstein (Garden City, N.Y.: Anchor Books, 1966).

[10]Robert Lane, *Political Ideology* (New York: Free Press, 1962).

[11]Kenneth Keniston, *The Uncommitted* (New York: Harcourt, Brace and World, 1969).

[12]Kenneth Keniston, *The Young Radicals* (New York: Harcourt, Brace, and World, 1968).

[13]T. W. Adorno et al., *The Authoritarian Personality* (New York: Harper and Bros., 1950), p. 357.

Lack of affection in the family during childhood may have serious personal and political consequences. The child's initial relations with his parents are crucial to the development of his ego. The warmer the relationship between parents and child the less threatening the child feels his world to be and the more he feels some sense of control over his environment and himself. That feeling, if reinforced by other experiences, seems to lead to the development of a strong ego. Lack of warmth and affection, conversely, can lead to a lack of ego strength and its concomitant political consequences—a lack of faith in other people, low political efficacy, alienation, a punitive political style, and prejudice. Lack of affection in the home is, of course, not the sole cause of these political maladies. Reinforced by other socialization agents and experiences, a weak ego may never fully develop, and the world—personal and political—may long be a threatening place.

Once the child has begun to develop physically and psychologically, the family begins to fulfill still another function, that of transmitting the basic social and political roles and values which the child needs to survive in his enlarging environment. Key and others argue that this transmission function, particularly of political roles and values, is the most important one since it allows the political system to maintain itself from one generation to another.[14]

The process begins at birth. Research on the impact of childrearing practices on personality development and values indicate a consistent relationship. Miller and Swanson found that trends in childrearing seemed to follow cultural norms through history; in the eighteenth century, during a laissez-faire economy and a hostile physical environment, the stress was on parental dominance and teaching self-control to the child, while in the mid-twentieth century the emphasis has shifted to training the child for self-sufficiency. The values reflected in the childrearing literature were values appropriate for the historical period. Research on the childrearing practices

---

[14]See V. O. Key, Jr., *Public Opinion and American Democracy* (New York: Alfred Knopf, 1961) and David Easton and Jack Dennis, *Children in the Political System* (New York: McGraw-Hill, 1969).

of Detroit mothers found those practices to be related to the occupational class of the parents. Children from entrepreneurial
families (where the father was employed in a high risk job with
no salary guarantee—salesman, small businessman, etc.) were
trained for self-control, while children from bureaucratic families (where the father worked in a hierarchically organized
structure and was often salaried) were trained for active and
independent behavior. Children from the two types of families
were reared differently, learning values appropriate to the occupational class of their parents—values which were not only
appropriate but also critical for survival in their parent's culture.[15] Martha White's study of seventy-four children and their
parents found that the only class-based differences in
childrearing focused on three areas—obedience training,
parental responsiveness, and permissiveness of aggression
against parents. Consistent with Miller and Swanson, she
found that middle-class parents were more permissive of dis-
obedient responses, responded more quickly to the child's
crying, and were more permissive of the child's aggression
against parental authority.[16] On this last point, Kohn's study of
the exercise of parental authority found that middle-class
mothers seem to punish or not punish according to their interpretation of the child's intent, while working-class mothers
are more likely to respond to the child's behavior on the basis of
their evaluation of the consequences of his actions.[17]

What are the consequences of these various childrearing
practices? After reviewing the research on the impact of maternal warmth and the extent of discipline, Becker found that
children who were raised in families which were warm but
which restricted their actions were submissive, dependent,
polite, neat, obedient—quiet and compliant little boys and
girls. Where the parents were warm and permissive, the

---

[15]Daniel R. Miller and Guy E. Swanson, *The Changing American Parent*
(New York: John Wiley, 1958).

[16]Martha Storm White, "Social Class, Child-Rearing Practices, and
Child Behavior," in *Personality and Social Systems*, ed. Neil J. Smelser and
William T. Smelser (New York: John Wiley, 1963).

[17]Melvin Kohn, "Social Class and the Exercise of Parental Authority,"
ibid.

children were active, extroverted, aggressive, independent, creative, and able to take adult roles—children with strong egos and increasing autonomy. Hostile parents and a restrictive family environment produced children with neurotic problems, quarrelsome, socially withdrawn, and maximally self-aggressive—lacking strong egos and autonomy, they withdrew from themselves and their environment. Delinquents were the products of permissive families where the family was hostile to the child—the child had developed a rough sense of autonomy but had no significant ego strength to go with it.[18]

Parents are the product of their cultures, and they transmit segments of it to their children by heeding the advice of cultural leaders in childrearing and by passing on to their children what they have learned about the world in which they expect their children to live. Cohen has postulated:

1. Parents' status positions determine which aspects of a culture they will transmit to their children.
2. Socialization is always future oriented.[19]

Based on their past experiences, parents attempt to prepare their children to live in the future.

While rearing their children in culturally relevant ways, parents also teach them appropriate values and begin to delineate roles for them in the world outside the family. Once the child has become mobile and articulate, two early and critical junctures for the child and his parents, he and his parents spend a large part of the preschool period defining acceptable and nonacceptable roles and actions which are rewarded or punished as appropriate. The child quickly learns he mustn't cross the street alone, touch hot stoves, suck his thumb, or use certain naughty words. In the process of defining acceptable roles within and outside the family, the child may attempt many roles in order to see which role(s) elicit the most favorable responses from his parents. Those role behaviors which are

---

[18]Wesley Becker, "Consequences of Different Kinds of Parental Discipline," in Hoffman and Hoffman, op. cit., p. 198.

[19]Yehudi Cohen, ed., *Social Structure and Personality* (New York: Holt, Rinehart, and Winston, 1961), pp. 64-65.

rewarded, or aren't punished, are internalized and become part of the child's definition of self.

When looking for appropriate roles, it is not surprising that the child looks to his parents. The boy tries to emulate the things that his father does—the way he walks, talks, and treats mother—and the role father plays in and out of the family. Girls emulate their mothers—as homemakers and wives—and because of the frequency of interaction with the role they are modeling, they are more successful earlier than their brothers. With parents as models and behavioral referrents, it is not surprising that children resemble the culture of their parents; having modeled themselves on their parents, they learn skills, attitudes, and behaviors applicable in their parents' world.

Once through the first three years, the family increasingly plays another important function, that of providing a framework for the child's increased development. As the child grows older and begins to explore the world outside his physical being, he learns that he is part of an ongoing social unit—his family. One problem is that of defining the boundaries of his obligations to the growth and maintenance of the unit. The child must learn that he has a role in the family, a role different from that of his parents but similar to that of his brothers and sisters. To help him do this "the spouses must form a coalition as parents, maintain the boundaries between the generations, and adhere to their respective sex-linked roles."[20]

After the first six months, the child becomes aware of other members of the family—a father who offers affection and brothers and sisters who play with him and compete with him for the attention and affection of their parents. Parsons and Bales theorize that, as the child becomes aware of the family, the family differentiates itself on two dimensions: hierarchical organization and power on the one hand, and instrumental and expressive functions on the other.[21] The child learns that all members of the family are not equal, that the family is com-

---

[20]Theodore Lidz, *The Person* (New York: Basic Books, 1958), p. 58.

[21]Talcott Parsons and Robert F. Bales, *Family, Socialization and Interaction Process* (New York: Free Press, 1955).

posed of people of different status and power, and that parents have more status and power than children. The child also learns that there are sex-linked functions; the male's role is that of providing for the material well-being of the family, the woman's role is that of maintaining the social fabric of the family. The father's status role is that of instrumental superior, the mother's that of expressive superior, the male child that of instrumental inferior, and the female child that of expressive inferior.

There is sufficient evidence that the family is, in fact, functionally differentiated. Blood and Wolfe, for example, interviewed almost one thousand married women in the Detroit metropolitan area and found that women make decisions related to the maintenance of the family or the home—decisions regarding whether the woman should work, what doctors to go to, and how much money to spend for food—while the husband makes decisions about how income is to be made and spent—what job the husband will take, what car to buy, and whether to buy life insurance. Some decisions—where to live and where to go on vacation—are shared by the husband and wife.[22]

Further analysis by Blood and Wolfe revealed that the amount and scope of paternal decision making in the family is a function of the father's income. The higher the income, the more influential and the broader the scope of his influence within the family (defined in terms of the number and range of questions on which he made the decision alone). In low-income, often nonwhite, families, the father's role is minimal and decision-making power limited. Unable or unwilling to assume the traditional breadwinning role in the family the father must also abrogate his role as a full and active participant in family decisions. The father's influence in family decisions is the result of his ability to control resources important for the family; to the extent he provides those resources he has influence. The mother, on the other hand, seems to derive her influence in the family from her relations with the child and her husband.

---

[22]Robert O. Blood, Jr. and Donald L. Wolfe, *Husbands and Wives* (New York: Free Press, 1960).

Paternal influence within the family is also related to the ages of the children. The father's influence is at its maximum at the birth of the first child, when the mother must focus her attention and energy on the newborn child, and it slowly declines as the child grows older. Instead of being a drain on the wife's influence, children can and often do become a source of comfort and strength within the family. In families where the father provides adequate sustenance for the family, mother and father are able to divide the decision-making "labor." But if the father cannot fulfill his primary role in the family his influence must wane, particularly as the number of children in the family increases, as they grow older, and as they begin to assume some of the paternal roles and influence.

The decline of the father's influence is not accounted for in the Parsons and Bales model where influence in the family is the result of sexual and generational differentiation and is fairly constant through the lifespan of the family. Caplow, using the family as an example of coalition formation, argues that influence is not constant through the lifespan of the family.[23] In the typical American family the father has more influence than the mother who has more influence than the child. As the child grows older, however, the father is no longer the predominant influence in family decision making; he must form either a coalition with his wife against the child or a coalition with the child against his wife.

> As head of the family, A (the father) has little incentive to form a coalition that subverts the status order and invites conflict with his wife, and he is more likely to choose the parental coalition AB which is strong enough to dominate son C at this stage, and within which A will continue for a while to dominate his wife.[24]

Passing into adolescence, the child increases his influence within in the family and seeks to exercise that influence. In some cases the child may have more influence than his mother

---

[23]Theodore Caplow, *Two Against One* (Englewood Cliffs, N.J.: Prentice-Hall, 1968).

[24]Ibid., p. 66

but less than his father. Such a situation forces the mother into a coalition with her husband to protect her influence and position within the family. Throughout the life cycle of the child, from birth to adulthood, there is a growth in his influence in the family and a decline in his father's influence. One of the critical lessons which the child must learn is how to operate within the structure of the family in order to satisfy his needs and express his wants without alienating his parents.

The situation becomes more complex as the number of children in the family increases. Parents respond differentially to their children, depending on their sex and rank in the family.[25] Each child is thus faced with the task of working out a set of accomodations with his brothers and sisters as well as with his parents. One of the most common coalitions within the nuclear family is that of the children against their parents.[26]

Caplows's formulation of the influence relationships neglects some of the most insightful contributions of Parsons and Bales. Children may form coalitions with or against their parents, but the process of coalition formation is a continuing and constantly evolving one in which children form coalitions with mother for some purposes, father for others, and against their parents for still others. For the male child, the father may be the relevant coalition partner when he wants a camping trip for the weekend, while the mother may be more relevant when he wants pizza for dinner. The critical question for the child is not whether to align himself with his mother *or* father, but under what circumstances should he form *either* coalition.

The coalition formation also may be faulty in its assumption that it is necessary to form a coalition in order to maintain the integrity and authority of the family. The fact that almost fifty percent of American families find both parents making joint family decisions does not mean that the parents have formed a coalition against their children.[27] Using the United States data

---

[25]Robert Sears, Eleanor Macoby, and Harry Levin, *Patterns of Child Rearing* (Evanston, Ill.: Row, Peterson, and Co., 1957).

[26]Caplow, op. cit., pp. 69-75.

[27]Langton, op. cit., p. 44; and James J. Best, "Citizen Support for the American Political System," (Ph.D. dissertation, University of North Carolina, Department of Political Science, 1965).

from the Almond and Verba Five Nation study, the author discovered that people raised in families where family decisions were made by the parents jointly had more influence in family decisions, were more satisfied with their influence in family decisions, and felt more freedom to complain about family decisions than people raised in families where either parent made family decisions alone.[28] By combining data from families where either parent made family decisions and comparing them with families where decisions were made jointly, it becomes clear that when both parents made family decisions the child was an active and meaningful participant in the process. (See Table 3-1.) If the parents coalesce against their children, the children are unaware of the fact. Over half the people who were raised in families where decisions were made jointly felt free to participate in family decisions; for them, the family power structure was open. One of every six people raised in families where either parent made family decisions—and the parent was available to form a coalition with the child—was unable to participate in family decisions. Even though there was potential for a child-parent coalition, the authority structure of the family precluded such a coalition.

What is the relationship between the family power structure

TABLE 3-1. Relation between freedom to participate in
family decisions and who made family decisions

Freedom to participate in family decisions*	Both parents together	Either parent alone
Restricted	16.1%	4.9%
Moderately free	45.9	37.3
Free	38.0	57.3
	(385)	(426)

*Those classified as "restricted" did not feel free to participate in family decisions at all, those classified as "moderately free" felt free to participate in some aspect of family decisions, and those who felt "free" to participate felt they had influence in family decisions, were satisfied with their influence, and felt they could complain about family decisions.

Source: Best, *Support for the American Political System*, p. 60.

---

[28]Ibid., pp. 59-60.

and the child's attitudes toward his political environment? Does the equalitarian power structure in the family provide an effective model for the larger political system? Does it make any difference in the child's political world whether his mother or father was the dominant member of the family?

The Hess and Torney study of grammar school children in the United States reveals that in families where the mother was dominant (she "was the boss in the family"), boys were low in political interest, participation in political discussion, political activities, concern about political issues, and political efficacy (feeling they could participate and have an impact on government). In cases where the father was low in power (he was unable to "make people do what he wants"), both boys and girls scored low on the same set of variables.[29] Langton's analysis of interviews with the parents of U.S. high school students confirms the Hess and Torney findings on the impact of maternal dominance. Boys thrived in a patriarchal environment, while the type of power structure in the family made little or no difference in the political attitudes of girls. Those children raised in egalitarian homes scored lower than those in maternal-dominance families and higher than those in paternal-dominance families on measures of political efficacy, political interest, and political participation. Thus, while the egalitarian power structure was by far the modal type, it did no better nor worse than families where one or the other parent was dominant.[30]

In a large sense, the child's role in the family power structure teaches him far more than how to "get around" his parents. He learns that there are some people who have the authority and influence to make decisions which affect him, that he can have access to those who make such decisions, that there are rules for participating in family decision making, and that he will not always get what he wants from decision makers. The family is the child's first exposure to a system of authority

---

[29]Robert D. Hess and Judith V. Torney, *The Development of Political Attitudes in Children* (Chicago, Ill.: Aldine Publishing Co., 1967), p. 105.

[30]Langton, op. cit., pp. 45-47. This is true for all but lower-class families.

which is duplicated in the political system; it may be that the lessons he learns in the family will have substantial influence on the way he views his role in the larger political system and the legitimacy of that system for him.

In addition to transmitting societal values and mores, the family also transmits political values from generation to generation. Politically, "the family incubates political man. It endows him with the qualities necessary to operate a democratic system and infuses him with the appropriate attitudes and beliefs—or it fails in this respect."[31]

Herbert Hyman's review of the political socialization literature through the mid-1950s found that the family plays an important role in forming the child's political world in at least two areas—the direction of his political party preferences and the nature of his political involvement.[32] There is substantial evidence that children share the same party preference as their parents.[33] Remmers' fourteen-year study of U.S. high school students found correlations between party preferences of family members (parent-child, parent-parent, and child-child) to range from $+.80$ to $+.90$.[34] The correspondence of party identification within the family is true even where husbands and wives have different party affiliations when they first marry; in the vast majority of cases, one of the two, more often the wife, will change party to match the spouse.[35] Langton's analysis of data on parents of high school seniors shows that seventy-four percent of the parents share a common party identification and seventy-seven percent of the children from families where parents share a common party identification match their parents.[36]

[31]Robert Lane, *Political Life* (Glencoe, Ill.: Free Press, 1959), p. 204.

[32]Herbert Hyman, *Political Socialization* (Glencoe, Ill.: Free Press, 1959).

[33]Key, op. cit., pp. 295-96; Herbert McClosky and Harold Dahlgren, "Primary Group Influence on Party Loyalty," *American Political Science Review* 53 (September 1959), pp. 757-76; and Fred Greenstein, *Children and Politics* (New Haven: Yale University Press, 1965), pp. 71-73.

[34]H. H. Remmers, "Early Socialization of Attitudes," in *American Voting Behavior*, ed. Eugene Burdick and Arthur Brodbeck (Glencoe, Ill.: Free Press, 1959), p. 60.

[35]McClosky and Dahlgren, op. cit., Lane, *Political Life*, p. 9.

[36]Langton, op. cit., pp. 61-63.

TABLE 3-2. Relationship between parent and child party
identification with no congruence between parents

Parental party identification		Child party identification			
Mother	Father	Democrat	Independent	Republican	N
Democrat	Independent	51%	37%	12%	20
Independent	Democrat	39	40	21	20
Republican	Democrat	29	38	33	23
Republican	Independent	21	34	45	14
Independent	Republican	43	17	40	15
Democrat	Republican	44	21	35	37

Source: Data from Tables 3-2 and 3-3 in Langton, op. cit., pp. 64-65.

Macoby, Matthews, and Morton discovered that the greatest
intergeneration deviation in party preference occurs in those
cases where the party preference cues from the family are
missing—where politics is not a salient topic in the home or
where party preference cues are ambiguous, i.e., where one or
both parents is an Independent or where the parents do not
share a common party identification.[37] Receiving conflicting political cues, the child is hard-pressed to develop a stable party
identification. In such cases, with whom does he identify—his
mother or his father? Once again, Langton's data is useful.
Table 3-2 shows the relationship between parent-child party
orientations when there is no congruence between parents.
Since much of the literature assumes that the father is the key
political figure in the family, it is surprising that in cases
where there is conflict in party identification between parents
the child follows his mother's lead more than his father's.
Mother's role becomes particularly influential as she becomes
more politically active and holds political opinions more intensely.

What seems to happen is that when her activity levels increase,
the mother becomes a much more visible and salient source
of political information. She reaps corresponding benefits as

[37]Eleanor Macoby, Richard Matthews, and Anton Morton, "Youth and
Political Change," *Public Opinion Quarterly* 18 (Spring, 1954), pp. 23-39.

her relative position improves. . . . As the mother's politicization level becomes relatively high, traditional habits of sex-typing are attenuated. She is seen as having political views in her own right and presumably tests and exercises them in the family circle.[38]

The mother's strong influence is the result of her involvement in politics and her assumption of a manifestly political role in the family, acts which are unusual in American family life. It takes a woman with an ego strong enough to participate in politics and, at the same time, hold opinions different from those of her husband. For many women there is no problem—they assume their role as nonpolitical housewife and leave political decisions to their husbands. Thus the politically active wife has a doubly strong impact on the political socialization of her children; not only is she the source of cues concerning the home and family but she also competes with the father in providing political cues.

As mentioned earlier, the level of political activity in the family is an important determinant of how effective the family will be in transmitting its party identification. Heavily politicized families produce children who are interested in politics and who resemble most accurately the political complexion of the family unit. Not only do the children resemble their parents in party identification and interest in politics, but in later life they are far more likely than average to vote or run for public office.[39] The political activists of one generation produce and train the political activists of the next, insuring a constant supply of people interested in, willing, and able to participate in politics.

With these two variables, consistency of party preference cues from the parents and level of political interest in the home, we can now see under what conditions children are likely to mirror their parent's party identification. In those cases where the parents hold different party identification, it is impossible to transmit a party identification to the child which will match

---

[38]Langton, op. cit., p. 71.
[39]John Wahlke, et al., *The Legislative System* (New York: John Wiley, 1962), pp. 82-84.

that of his parents. The lack of consistent cues combined with a lack of family interest in politics will generally result in a child who is neither politically partisan nor interested. The child from the "mixed" family where politics is salient will be faced with the task of deciding which parental cues to use in finding his way through an important part of his and the family's life. He will recognize the importance of politics and assume the party identification of the most salient figure in the family. Children from homes where the parents agree are in a position to transmit that party identification to their children. The success of the transmission process will be a function of how salient politics is for the family. (See Table 3–3.) If the parents are intensely partisan and active, the child will very likely emulate them in party orientation and interest. If politics is not salient for his parents, the transmission of party label may be

TABLE 3-3. Intergenerational resemblance in partisan orientation, politically active and inactive homes, 1958

Party identification of offspring	*One or both parents were politically active*			*Neither parent was politically active*		
	Both parents were democrats	*Both parents were republicans*	*Parents had no consistent partisanship*	*Both parents were democrats*	*Both parents were republicans*	*Parents had no consistent partisanship*
Strong Democrat	50%	5%	21%	40%	6%	20%
Weak Democrat	29	9	26	36	11	15
Independent	12	13	26	19	16	26
Weak Republican	6	34	16	3	42	20
Strong Republican	2	37	10	1	24	12
Apolitical	1	2	1	1	1	7
	100%	100%	100%	100%	100%	100%
N =	(33)	(194)	(135)	(308)	(187)	(199)

Source: Campbell et al., *The American Voter* (New York: Wiley, 1960), p. 147.

less successful because the child may not be aware of his parent's party affiliation. Parents who don't talk politics at home provide very few cues for their children.

The transmission of party label is an important socialization function for the family because with the party label the child, at an early age, can differentiate between "good" guys and "bad" guys in politics. Party identification is a crucial first element in the child's political perceptual screen.

To what extent do parents transmit their attitudes and beliefs to their children? Earlier we have seen a positive relationship between parental treatment of children, the child's role in the family, and the child's personality and feelings of political efficacy. Intrafamily congruence on party identification is well documented. Do parents inculcate political values and beliefs as well as party identifications?

Remmers' data indicate that the intrafamily agreement on attitude items is nearly as high as that for party identification, ranging from + .80 to + .96.[40] According to Remmers, the American teenager is more responsive to his parents on some matters than others, particularly political questions, how he spends money, and his personal problems.[41] Others dispute Remmers' conclusions. Hess and Torney argue that the family's primary function is the transmission of partisan affiliation and only a few consensual norms of the political system.[42] Jennings and Neimi's analysis of data from U.S. high school students and their parents indicates that while there is a high degree of correspondence within the family on party identification, there is substantially less correspondence on specific issues.[43] Aside from party identification, there is relatively high correspondence on salient, concrete issues; the more abstract the issue, however, the lower the level of agreement within the

[40]Remmers, op. cit., p. 60.

[41]H. H. Remmers and D. H. Radler, *The American Teenager* (Indianapolis: Bobbs-Merrill, 1957).

[42]Hess and Torney, op. cit., pp. 93ff.

[43]M. Kent Jennings and Richard Neimi, "The Transmission of Political Values from Parent to Child," *American Political Science Review* 67 (March, 1968): 169-84.

family between parents and children. "What we begin to discern, then, is a pattern of congruences which peak only over relatively concrete, salient values, susceptible to repeated reinforcement in the family (and elsewhere, perhaps), as in party identification and in certain issues and group evaluations."[44] Attitudes which receive reinforcement inside and outside the family are most likely to be successfully transmitted from one generation to another. Such reinforcement would be most likely in highly politicized families where parents and their children talk frequently about politics and the children are aware of their parent's positions on political issues. Knowledge of parental position serves as a useful reference point for the child —either to emulate or to rebel against.

Easton and Dennis describe the process in these terms:[45]

Child, "There's somewhere."
Father, "I can't park there."
Child, "Why?"
Father, "It's not allowed."
Child, "Who says so?"
Father, "I'll get a ticket."
Child, "Uh?"
Father, "A policeman will stop me."
Child, "Oh."

Government and its officials are generally seen as powerful but benevolent. As Greenstein notes, "The public figure becomes invested with powerful private feelings; response to him assumes some of the qualities of response to family members and others in the face-to-face environment."[46] As the child becomes aware of the world outside himself and his family he seeks some guidelines for this external world. His most logical basis for comparison is the family, and government is thus endowed with many of the qualities of the family—benevolence, wisdom, and the ability to make and enforce rules for the child's benefit. The family assumes sovereignty over the child's immediate environ-

---

[44]Ibid., p. 177.
[45]Easton and Dennis, op. cit., p. 3.
[46]Greenstein, *Children and Politics*, p. 46.

ment and in the larger environment government is the family writ large. "His early experience of government is, therefore, analogous to his early experience of the family in that it involves an initial context of highly acceptable dependency. Against the strongly positive affective background, the child devises his cognitive image of government."[47] Because government is analogous to the family, children do not share their parent's cynicism of politics and government; for the young child, such cynicism would be tantamount to cynicism of the family. As the child grows and begins to differentiate between family and government, he becomes more critical of government and less prone to endow it with qualities of his family.[48]

A benevolent image of government may be a function of social class, however. Jaros, Hirsch, and Fleron caution that much of the research on children's perceptions of authority figures has focused on urban, middle-class children, whose view of authority figures may well be benevolent because they have had no experience with malevolent figures. Their study of grammar school children in Appalachia found that the children's evaluations of the president are substantially less favorable than those of children in New Haven and Chicago. The president is viewed as being less wise, less benevolent, and less powerful than earlier research had indicated children should perceive him.[49] For a child growing up in a barren and destitute environment, it is difficult to assume benevolence to someone who is a part of that external environment. If the child hears his parents blaming "government" for their plight, it should not be surprising that the child has reservations about the most visible figure in "government"—the president.

---

[47]David Easton and Jack Dennis, "The Child's Image of Government," *Annals of the Academy of Political and Social Science* 361 (September, 1965): p. 44.

[48]Greenstein, op. cit.; Jennings and Neimi, op. cit.; David Easton and Robert Hess, "Youth and the Political System," in Lipset and Lowenthal (eds.) *Culture and Social Character: The Work of David Riesman Reviewed* (Glencoe, Ill.: Free Press, 1961).

[49]Dean Jaros, Herbert Hirsch, and Frederic Fleron, "The Malevolent Leader: Political Socialization in an American Sub-Culture," *American Political Science Review*, LXII (June, 1968), pp. 564-75.

The school

The relationship between education and political attitudes has been a constant concern for political scientists. This concern has sprung from two diverse sources: the need to develop youth into active, democratic citizens, and the knowledge that education per se has a marked impact on political attitudes.

Citizenship training: A top priority

The need to develop an alert, informed citizenry was recognized by Plato who stated in *The Republic* that the proper education for Greek citizens should consist of music and gymnastics. "Education, if exclusively musical, tends to produce softness and effiminacy; if exclusively gymnastic, hardness and brutality. The two combined alone produce the desired harmony of the soul, and make it both brave and gentle."[50]

While the question of proper formula for citizenship education dates from Plato, it has been central to American education. Franklin Patterson sees two historic goals of high schools in the United States: to develop mentally, morally, emotionally, and physically each boy and girl as an individual, and to develop each boy and girl as a responsible citizen.[51] How to develop responsible citizenship in America's youth has been the Holy Grail for which American educators have searched.

The first attempt in the twentieth century to develop a coherent program of citizenship education was undertaken by the Committee of Ten of the NEA in 1900. The Committee's report encouraged the study of government as the basis for citizenship education, especially ". . . the simple principles underlying the laws which regulate the relations of individuals within the state."[52] In 1918 the NEA issued another report stating that the purpose of civic education was to develop "those qualities

[50]Plato, *The Republic* (New York: E. P. Dutton Co., 1950), p. xi.
[51]Franklin Patterson, *High Schools for a Free Society* (Medford, Mass.: Tufts University Civic Education Center, 1960), p. 8.
[52]Ibid., p. 19.

whereby he (the student) will act well his part as a member of neighborhood, town or city, state, and nation and give him a basis for understanding international problems."[53] How these purposes were to be accomplished is unclear, although there was an emphasis on the teaching of civics as the prime expedient. By 1952 the "purposes" of citizenship education had grown into a sophisticated list of eleven "objectives."[54]

The continuing problem with these statements of purpose is the unanswered question of how to attain their goals. All too often it has been assumed that the mere transmission of information about the political system from teacher to student would lead to understanding and competence. Somewhat belatedly, educators realized their basic assumption might be in error.

One of the first major efforts in the United States to investigate the impact of citizenship education on student attitudes and behavior was undertaken by Stanley Dimond and his colleagues at Wayne State University in the late 1940s. After an extensive five-year study, Dr. Dimond and his staff concluded that attempts to improve the quality of citizenship education did not result in a corresponding rise in citizenship; the schools were capable of transmitting information about the political system but unable to train students to use that information. In fact, the emotional adjustment of the student, rather than citizenship education per se, was found to be the key to effective citizenship education. The better adjusted and more emotionally mature the student, the more competent he was to use the information gained from civics courses.[55]

H. H. Remmers and his colleagues at Purdue substantiated Dimond's findings on the value of civics courses. For fifteen

---

[53]From the NEA *Cardinal Principles of Secondary Education*, cited in ibid., p. 20.

[54]Ibid., pp. 22-23.

[55]Stanley E. Dimond, *Schools and the Development of Good Citizens* (Detroit: Wayne University Press, 1953); Arnold R. Meier, Florence Cleary, and Alice David, *A Curriculum for Citizenship* (Detroit: Wayne University Press, 1952), and Elmer Pflieger and Grace Weston, *Emotional Adjustment: A Key to Good Citizenship* (Detroit: Wayne University Press, 1953).

years Remmers traced attitudes of high school students toward teenage problems, parents, school, the future, religion, ethics, science, and citizenship.[56] In analyzing the data, he found that civic education in high school has a detrimental effect on political attitudes, i.e., thirty-five percent of those who had a civics course, as opposed to thirty percent of those who had not, agreed with the statement, "The Government should prohibit some people from making speeches."[57]

As Roy Horton has noted:

> The analysis of belief in democratic values, in terms of having taken a school course in U.S. Government or Civics, showed no constructive effect attributable to such school courses. In fact, when differences in response do occur on the items dealing with the freedom guaranteed by the Bill of Rights, those who had a course in Civics tend to be less in agreement with the Bill of Rights. One fairly consistent difference between the groups is that those who have had a course in Civics are less uncertain about their beliefs; their attitudes might be said to be more "crystallized." The lack of evidence for any positive effects of such school courses upon the pupil's beliefs in democratic values may give us pause. It may well be that courses in civics or government concentrate more upon the *mechanics* of government than upon the values of democracy. In considering the teaching of "good citizenship," one may well question the value of instructional objectives that consist of certain dates, names, etc., to be committed to rote memory.[58]

It is sad to reflect that a culture which places such a heavy emphasis on good citizenship and citizenship training does so poorly. Instead of teaching students how to operate within the political system we teach them the "facts" about the system; instead of producing functional future citizens we seem to produce bored ex-civics students, whose response to learning civics "facts" is less rather than more understanding about the political system.

---

[56] Remmers and Radler, op. cit., p. 211.

[57] Ibid., p. 188.

[58] Roy E. Horton, Jr., "American Freedom and the Values of Youth," in *Anti-Democratic Attitudes in American Schools*, ed. H.H. Remmers (Evanston: Northwestern University Press, 1963).

More recent studies of high school students have produced results which differed only marginally from those of Remmers and Dimond. Exposure to civics courses had virtually no impact, positive or negative, on political knowledge, political interest, exposure to political media, political discourse, political efficacy, and civic tolerance.[59]

These findings seriously question the efficacy of civics training in high schools. Three alternative explanations are open for exploration. First, the fault may lie with the teacher. In smaller high schools, social studies are often taught by people untrained to teach them—the football coach, for example. Even more critical are studies which conclude that a substantial minority of teachers and future teachers ". . . have a fear of association with people who are socialistic, a fear of speaking on controversial issues, and a wariness about the extracurricular organizations which they will join."[60] Teachers take the easiest and safest path in the classroom, discussing subjects which are noncontroversial for students and their parents. Zeigler's study of Oregon teachers discovered that the longer a person taught the more conservative he or she became and the less likely they were to express in the classroom liberal opinions which they perceived to be contrary to the dominant ideology of the community.[61] The failure of civics courses may not be the fault of the courses but of the people who teach them. Apparently, the teacher's ability to transmit political values overtly is limited by the role perceptions of the teacher and the teacher's perceptions of community sanctions for certain kinds of classroom activities.

Second, civic educators have concentrated on curriculum rather than pedagogy. The growing recognition that lecture and rote memorization may not be the best teaching techniques has forced civic educators to develop new techniques. These

---

[59]Langton, op. cit., pp. 84-119.

[60]Fay L. Corey, *Values of Future Teachers* (New York: Bureau of Publications: Columbia University Press, 1955), p. 122.

[61]Harmon Zeigler, *The Political World of the High School Teacher* (Eugene: University of Oregon, The Center for the Advanced Study of Educational Administration, 1966), pp. 113-34.

new methods spring from the realization that there are some kinds of political skills and concepts which cannot be learned from listening or reading but which have to be experienced, and that information about the political system can be most useful if it is tied to a student's experiences. As a result alternative teaching techniques, focusing on participation in actual or simulated social and political processes, have gained increasing acceptance in the classroom. Participating in actual political events is difficult since they occur infrequently, do not correspond neatly with the academic schedule, or are inaccessible to most students. For these reasons attempts were made during the 1950s and 1960s to recreate these processes in the classroom.

Beginning in the early 1960s, Harold Guetzkow and a group of political scientists at Northwestern University developed a series of man-man simulations designed to replicate the international system and the development of relations between nations. Fictional countries were created and students were assigned roles in each country; they played the roles of chief policy makers for real and imaginary nations and interacted with one another to formulate and make decisions regarding domestic and foreign policy. Chad Alger, after reviewing the experiences of the Northwestern simulations and others at the high school and college level, concluded: "Although the educational benefits of simulation have not been rigorously measured, numerous testimonials assert that simulation participation has significant educational benefits."[62] Alger contends that the literature indicates four major benefits for the student:

1. Simulation heightens the interest and motivation of students by involving them in quasi-real situations.
2. Simulation offers an opportunity for the student to apply and test the utility and validity of his knowledge.
3. Simulation gives the student greater understanding of the world as seen and experienced by the decision maker.

---

[62]Chadwick Alger, "Use of the Inter-National Simulation in Undergraduate Teaching," in Harold Guetzkow et al., *Simulation in International Relations* (Englewood Cliffs, N.J.: Prentice-Hall, 1963), p. 151.

4. Most simulations provide a miniature world that is easier for the participant to comprehend as a whole than are the real institutions themselves.

Disturbed by the lack of sophistication in examining the impact of simulations, Guetzkow and his colleagues ran one-half of a matched group of students through a course using a lecture-case study teaching technique and the other half through the course using a lecture-simulation format. They found each approach has its advantages. Students exposed to case studies became more interested in the subject matter and did better on fact-mastery tests; students exposed to the simulation became more actively involved in the course (they read more and talked to the instructor) and did better in mastering the basic principles of the course.[63]

One of the advantages of the simulation—the requirement that the student assumes the role of the decision maker—carries with it a built-in disadvantage. While the involvement of the student in the simulation role gives him "greater understanding of the world as seen and experienced by the decision maker," it does little to help him comprehend the process which is being simulated. Each player views the simulation process from his own role perspective, and the collectivity of different role perspectives, does not give a total picture of the process. Players deeply engrossed in their roles are not in a position to generalize about the process in which they are involved. For this reason, simulation as a teaching device has limited utility —it enables the student to experience strains common to decision makers, but it does not allow him to understand the decision-making process.

Alternative teaching styles will work when they fit the needs of the students and the abilities of the teachers who use them. A teacher who believes her role should be one of inculcator of information will not use alternatives, just as students who have never heard of the Middle East will not get much benefit from the Inter-Nation simulation. What needs to be recognized is the

---

[63]James Robinson et al., "Teaching with INS and Case Studies," *American Political Science Review* 60 (March, 1966), pp. 53-65.

multiplicity of teaching techniques which can be used to teach the civic curriculum more adequately.

The content of civic education may also preclude it from effectively performing its function. Civics courses seek to provide the child with information about the political symbol and the inculcation of national symbols. Between first grade and senior year in high school the child is exposed to U.S. History two or three times and Civics at least twice—the differences between the courses is in the amount, not the kind, of information which is taught. During grades three and four information per se may be important for the child but by the time he reaches high school he seeks to develop his own evaluations of the political system rather than taking, without question, those of his teachers. In much the same way reciting the Pledge of Allegiance and singing "The Star Spangled Banner" become less relevant as the child goes through school because he sees less need for the constant reaffirmation of his loyalty. To the extent that the content of the civic education is redundant it is more likely to annoy the student than enlighten him, to alienate him rather than convince him.

High school civics courses, in addition to repeating political symbols, myths, and information learned in the grammar school, also must compete with the mass media as a source of information and opinion about current events. As we shall see later, television has come to play an increasingly central role in determining the quantity and quality of information we receive about the political world. Children of different ages use television for different purposes, however. Young children, while they watch great amounts of television, use it as a fantasy and play device—much as an older generation used radio and comic books. By the time they complete grammar school, children are watching less television and using it more and more for information about the political environment—television news commentators are as well known to thirteen-year-olds as cartoon characters are to six-year-olds.[64] If teachers are afraid to discuss current events in the classroom, students can watch

---

[64]Wilbur Schramm, Jack Lyle, and Edwin B. Parker, *Television in the Lives of Our Children* (Stanford, Calif.: Stanford University Press, 1961).

them unfold on television, interpreted by able correspondents, and make their own judgments. Under these circumstances, civics courses become unreal and irrelevant, something the student studies—like geometry and physics—which has no relationship to or utility in the "real world."

High school: After the "facts" are learned

The research indicates that civic education in the United States occurs at the grammar school level, that much of it involves the transmission of political symbols and myths along with elementary information about the political system, and the subsequent course work at the high school level is redundant and without impact. Does this mean that beyond grammar school the educational process has little or no impact on political attitudes and opinions?

To gain some insight into this question we must go back to our earlier conclusions that awareness of the political system and basic attitudes toward it are well developed by the end of grammar school. The grammar school receives the child from his parents at age five or six, after the child's personality has begun to form and take substance. During his matriculation in grammar school, the child begins to define his concept of self as he comes into contact with people outside his immediate family. He also begins to develop an interest in the world outside himself and sufficient sophistication to absorb as much information as the educational system will give him about that world. This information allows him to differentiate between political actors, teaches him their respective functions, and inculcates in him a set of political symbols and myths, which the child assumes are relevant.

By the time he has completed grammar school, the child has adult like attitudes toward government and politics, attitudes which are congruent with those of his parents and siblings as well as his teacher's.[65] Although the teacher may play an important role in the socialization process the impact is confounded and reinforced by the actions of other socialization

---

[65]Hess and Torney, op. cit., pp. 101-15.

agents working before, simultaneously, and subsequent to the teacher.

High school, then, serves several important functions for the child. It reaffirms symbols and myths learned in grammar school and reinforced in the community. Litt's study of values found in civics texts and dominant community attitudes indicated a high degree of correspondence between values emphasized in text books and values which community leaders felt should be emphasized.[66] While Litt does not argue that high school civics teachers are hired because they concur with community values (although that may be true), it is clear that teachers prefer to teach in environments where they are comfortable and where the values they teach are hospitable to themselves and their students.

With the correspondence between community values, teacher's values, and textbooks it is not surprising that children are socialized through the schools into roles which are relevant for the community or which the community wants them to fulfill. In the process they are exposed to values which are functional for the society which they will enter or which they are supposed to enter. Lower-class children are not to aspire to upper-class jobs just as upper-class children must learn the values appropriate to their station in life. One area where there has been a disjunction between the values of the school and the values of the community has been in urban ghetto schools, where black students increasingly complain that the values of white, middle-class teachers and their texts are irrelevant and unreal. These values would not be unreal if all blacks strove to become successes in the dominant white culture—but the rosy glow of the Horatio Alger myths now clash with the reality of the urban ghetto.[67]

Second, high school serves as a useful training ground for the

---

[66]Edgar Litt, "Civic Education Norms and Political Indoctrination," *American Sociological Review* 28 (February, 1963), pp. 69-75.

[67]Edward S. Greenberg, "Black Children and the Political System," *Public Opinion Quarterly* 34 (Fall, 1970), pp. 333-46; and Schley R. Lyons, "The Political Socialization of Ghetto Children: Efficacy and Cynicism," *Journal of Politics* 32 (May, 1970), pp. 288-305.

student to develop potentially useful political skills and interests. The student finds himself in an authority structure more diffuse and yet more structured than that of the family; instead of one or two authority figures, he has a new one for every class, and several more in the main office. His relations with his teachers in and out of the classroom, school administrators, and school peers provide continuing cues regarding how and under what circumstances the student can control and manipulate his school environment. Such experiences reinforce or mitigate lessons learned in the family.

Friedenberg's challenging study of the authority structures of nine high schools graphically illustrates the relationship between students, teachers, and school officials. Millburn High, for example, is described in the following terms:[68]

> Between class periods, the corridors are tumultuously crowded; during them they are empty; but they are always guarded with teachers and students on patrol duty. Patrol duty does not consist primarily in the policing of congested throngs of moving students, though it includes this, or the guarding of property from damage. Its principal function is the checking of corridor passes. Between classes, no student may walk down the corridor without a form, signed by a teacher, telling where he is coming from, where he is going, and the time, to the minute, at which the pass is valid. A student caught in the corridor without such a pass is taken to the office where a detention slip is made out against him, and he is required to remain at school for two or three hours after the close of the school day. He may do his homework during this time, but he may not leave his seat or talk.[68]

The purpose of these rules, which Friedenberg deplores, is to impose upon the adolescent student an awareness of his status within the school authority structure. In the process, the school produces people who accept uncritically decisions which are made by others and authority which others exercise.

The program of extracurricular activities also plays an important role in socializing the student. While participation in

---

[68]Edgar Z. Friedenberg, *Coming of Age in America* (New York: Random House, 1963).

these activities has little relation to attitudes toward politics, it does have two benefits.[69] First, extracurricular activities provide an opportunity for the student to develop an interest in politics and develop skills, such as debating or public speaking, which are useful adjuncts for a political career. Model U.N.s and mock political conventions, to the extent that they simulate reality, provide stimuli for political interest and exercise in the utilization of political skills. While political attitudes and cognitions are developed in grammar school, the first participation in politics occurs during the high school period, either in extracurricular events or using school-derived skills.

Second, Zilblatt found that participation in extracurricular affairs had an impact on political attitudes in a rather indirect way: the more frequently students participate in such activities, the more they were integrated into the social framework of the school. The more integrated into the social structure of the school, the greater their prestige and social trust. The greater their social trust, the more positive their attitude toward politics.[70] In other words, the more they participated, the more they were accepted by their peers; the more accepted, the greater their ego strength; the greater their ego strength, the more positive they felt toward politics. Whether low ego strength is the result or cause of nonparticipation is not clear. Rosenberg argues that

> ... students with low self-esteem are less likely than those with high self-esteem to be active participants in formal groups, to be active and frequent participants in informal discussions, to be informed opinion leaders, and to be formal group leaders. Whether the group is formal or informal, voluntary or involuntary, the person with low self-esteem tends to be a relatively impotent social force.[71]

Lastly, high school offers the student a culture and a set of norms which are increasingly universal for his age group but which are independent of those of his family. The school is an

---

[69]David Zilblatt, "High School Extracurricular Activities and Political Socialization," in *The Annals of the Academy of Political and Social Science* 361 (September, 1965): 20-31.

[70]Ibid.

[71]Rosenberg, *Society and the Adolescent Self-Image*, p. 202.

ongoing social system in which the student learns what kinds of behavior yield appropriate rewards from the authority structure and from his peers. Good grades may endear a student to parents and teachers but have very little payoff in the social structure of the school where athletic prowess is more prestigious than academic excellence.[72] High school is one of the first places a person learns that there may be more than one set of standards or rules—one for parents and teachers and one for friends. And since the high school period is one of physical and emotional development, where the student's concerns are primarily personal and social, it is no wonder that the student culture becomes more important than that of parents and the formal school structure. Acne or Friday night's date are more important than the number of congressmen for high school freshmen and sophomores.[73]

The student who receives his diploma from high school is, for the most part, a larger, more mature, and socially competent version of the grammar school graduate. The high school has served as a relatively stable environment, not much different from the home in atmosphere and values, within which he can develop a sense of personal identity and interpersonal competence. Politically, the high school provides him with redundant information and the reinforcement of political values, as well as providing an institutional framework within which he can develop political interests and potential political skills. Political attitudes and perceptions formed during the preteen period are seldom challenged by the high school experience; high school acts as a leavening agent rather than a catalyst in the political development of the adolescent citizen.

The college experience

The high school graduate who goes on to college differs from his peers who don't. His parents are higher status, expect him to go to college (often to the same one they attended), and he

---

[72]James Coleman, *The Adolescent Society* (New York: The Free Press, 1961).
[73]Remmers and Radler, op. cit.

has higher grades than those who do not go on.[74] In comparing the political attitudes of those with college education and those who have completed only high school, Langton argues, we may be confounding the effects of selection with that of socialization. "For example, do the highly educated feel more politically competent because of their college socialization experiences or were they significantly different in this respect from their non-college-bound peers before they entered college?"[75] His analysis of the Jennings' data indicates that college-bound students do differ significantly from those not going on to college. They are more likely to be knowledgeable about politics, to be more politically interested, politically efficacious, to support First Amendment freedoms, and to read and discuss politics with friends, qualities normally attributed to the impact of a college education.

For many students, college will be their first extended experience away from home and family. Free from parental control, the student must depend on the values and beliefs learned in the family and school. There will be no more parents looking over his shoulders, asking questions, and making judgments. And no more rules about what to do and what not to do. But are values and beliefs developed in the family and reinforced by the schools relevant for the college environment? Without constant reinforcement from parents, school, and community, can the student maintain his values and beliefs?

The college or university which the student enters is a unique place. Regardless of whether it is a small liberal arts college in New England, a church-affiliated school in the South, a junior college in California, or a metropolitan university in New York, it offers a frustrating combination of freedom and restraint, asking the student to think critically but acting *in loco parentis* to him. While the rules are irksome or trivial and the procedures cumbersome, the school is an institution which, like the U.S. Senate, has a tolerance for all but the most deviant behavior. The higher the academic standards of the school, the

[74]Langton, op. cit., p. 116.
[75]Ibid., p. 114.

more likely they are to be tolerant of idiosyncratic personal and intellectual behavior.[76] The "Hutchins Plan" at the University of Chicago, for example, allowed students to receive credits for courses they didn't take if they knew the course materials and required only that students pass the final exam to receive full credit for the course. For some students, the lack of structure and sanctions is detrimental. Left to their own devices, they cannot muster the personal resources to plot their own goals or move toward their achievement. Alternately, some students have values which provide them with guidelines, but guidelines which are inimical to the college environment. As Newcomb found in his study of Bennington College, the most conservative girls in a liberal environment who did not become more liberal became social isolates.[77]

Not everyone attends Bennington or the University of Chicago and not all students who do attend these types of institutions are equally affected by them. Many, and perhaps most, college freshmen attend a college whose intellectual, social, and political climate is not inimical or challenging to their own values. For many college students the "crisis in identity" will occur within an ambience which is supportive of the type of person they were and will serve to reinforce rather than drastically alter political values. In looking at the amount and type of change in political attitudes which is accomplished in college we must recognize that attitudinal change is the result of many factors—the type of college, the political "ambience" of the school, the type of students, and the attitudes, values, and beliefs which students bring to the college environment and the strength with which they hold them. To the extent that the socialization experience has been consistent and reinforcing the student may find that college has very little impact. For the student whose beliefs are not firmly held and who finds himself

---

[76]See Seymour Martin Lipset and Phillip Altback, "Student Politics and Higher Education in the United States," in *Student Politics*, ed. Seymour Martin Lipset (New York: Basic Books, 1967), pp. 199-252.

[77]Theodore M. Newcomb, *Personality and Social Change* (New York: Holt, Rinehart, and Winston, 1943).

in a nonsupportive environment there may be substantial change in attitudes, values, and beliefs.

The colleges and universities also bring together people who have undergone radically different life experiences. Catholics, who may never have questioned Church dogma, find themselves defending it against the onslaught of Protestants, Muslims, theists, and atheists. Republicans, Democrats, socialists, syndicalists, and anarchists argue the merits of republican government. The son of a house painter has coffee after class with the daughter of a plant manager. At the same time, the university forces the student to be critically aware of his environment. As a result, the student is forced to test his beliefs and values; keep some, discard some, and develop others; and reintegrate the new complex of values, beliefs, and attitudes into a personally meaningful whole. The college years, then, become the period between adolescence and adulthood which the student uses as a trial period, seeking to define who and what he is and how he is related to the adult society which he will enter. Intellectually he is given skills which are societally useful, but he must decide what role he will play in that society and with what impact. College is an exposure to the diversity of society combined with the freedom to explore that diversity without sanction. The recognition that college is a place to "sow wild oats" is universal, often with the understanding that college is the last fling before adulthood.[78]

The period between adolescence and adulthood is called by Keniston "the stage of youth."[79] In a society which requires more and more education for admission to the work force, adulthood is being postponed for greater numbers of American youth. Keniston argues that the Peace Corps, VISTA, the New Left, and the hippie movement provide meaningful expressions of this postadolescent and preadult stage.[80] Such activities, while the most visible, are not the only ones for the transition

---

[78]Daniel Goldrich, *Sons of the Establishment* (Chicago: Rand McNally, 1966), finds that the radicalism of Latin American students is excused by their parents on these grounds.

[79]Keniston, *Young Radicals*, pp. 263-64.

[80]Ibid., p. 266.

through the "youth" life stage. College itself provides a less visible but socially more acceptable incubator for this phase, allowing college students the opportunity to "defer their entry into established society, examine their relationship to it, and continue the process of personal change."[81] While political activists may be critical of American higher education as an extension of the societal "Establishment," they must also remember that much of their activity occurs within and under the protective umbrella of the college or university. The role of college student confers certain immunity from governmental sanctions; the college provides a sanctuary from which students can criticize both the college and the society of which it is a part.[82]

It is not surprising, therefore, that American colleges are increasingly becoming the centers of the American "counterculture," where societal values are challenged and alternative life styles are developed and tested. In a series of surveys of college students between 1967 and 1971 Yankelovitch found that the main themes of the developing life style are:

1. Increasing non-acceptance of traditional authority, particularly institutionalized authority such as the police, and in areas which the young feel are their own personal domain—dress and the use of drugs.
2. The search for substitutes for traditional religious values.
3. A new sexual morality, in which men are more accepting of sexual freedom than women.
4. A questioning of war as an instrument of policy. In 1971 there was only one reason that more than fifty percent of college students saw as justifying our entrance into war—counteracting aggression.
5. Dissatisfaction with marriage in its traditional form with a growing emphasis on having children and being part of a family being more important than the institution of marriage itself.

---

[81] Ibid., p. 266.

[82] It is interesting to note that the European and Latin American concept of the university as a sanctuary from civil authorities is being increasingly invoked by student activists in the United States. One of the thorny issues between students and administration has been the use of civil, as opposed to campus police, to control or quash student disorders.

6. A shifting away from the external signs of success (money and status). Making money is a less relevant career value.
7. A search for cooperative life styles, emphasizing a belief in love and friendship as dominant personal values.
8. Increasing emphasis on living in closer harmony with one's friends and with nature.[83]

These values emphasize a different life style for the college student of the 1970s, a life style which stresses interpersonal honesty and a desire for self-fulfillment, often within a communal context, and envisions a world where the individual is the supreme arbiter of his own life but where people with shared values can live together in harmony. It is also a nonpolitical, almost apolitical world, in which the style of political participation is as important as the content of the issue.[84]

The purpose of the college experience has obviously changed. Where instilling technical and intellectual skills was once the primary goals of college, developing personal and societal awareness is now equally important. College is less relevant as a "gateway to a job" and more relevant as a place where a person can find himself. And in the process the student increasingly seeks to relate himself to the larger world of which he is a part. No longer willing to accept that world as it is the college student today sees himself as an agent of social and political change—whose job it is to use his college years and the college as an institution to accomplish that change. The role of the college and university subsequently has broadened. For some students, particularly those using college as a means of attaining or maintaining social status or occupational mobility, the purpose of a college education may remain that of instilling skills for the economic marketplace. But for others— "psychologically, socially, and economically privileged, and often possessed of unusual talent and vitality"[85]—college will be a period and place of experimentation, self-development, and expression, a place where they can determine the defects of the

---

[83]Daniel Yankelovitch, Inc., *The Changing Values on Campus* (New York: Washington Square Press, 1972), pp. 25-49.
[84]Keniston, *Young Radicals.*
[85]Ibid., p. 273.

political system and from which they can work to change or destroy the system.

Summary

One of the surprising dimensions of the literature on the role of the family and school in political socialization is how little the child learns directly about politics from these two agents. One of the primary roles of the family is to foster a strong ego in the child—an ego that will enable him to deal with his environment which will be analogous later in his political life. Learning how to deal with parents may not be much different from dealing with the boss or the city council. Those political cues, such as party identification, the child learns indirectly from his parents.

The ability of the school to socialize the child seems to depend on a mix of factors—the political culture of the school, the perceptions of the teacher, the political culture of the community, and the ego strength of the school. Like the family the school seems to do the job of political socialization by indirection; it places the child in a social milieu from which he can learn appropriate opinions and behaviors, as well as factual information about the political system. Although the school teaches its pupils about the political system it doesn't teach them how to operate within it. That they must learn for themselves, with the school serving as an occasionally useful microcosm of the larger political system.

CHAPTER FOUR

Opinion formation: Other socialization agents

Although the family and school are normally assigned primary importance in the socialization process it must be remembered that the child encounters other socializing influences as he moves toward adulthood. As we saw in Figure 3-1 in Chapter Three the mass media and peer groups begin to play a role between the ages of two and five and, together with the family and school, provide the complex matrix within which the child learns to live in his political environment. Once the individual reaches adulthood the family and school are replaced by the work environment as a socializing factor. In this chapter we will examine each of these agents.

Peer groups

About the time the child starts grammar school he also begins to spend more and more time outside the home with children his own age. His first peer group[1] is composed of age-mates with whom he plays and goes to school. Since physical propinquity is a basic prerequisite for early peer group forma-

---

[1]For the purposes of our discussion peer groups will be defined as those nonfamily members with whom the person interacts regularly and with some intimacy. For an excellent discussion of groups see George C. Homans, *The Human Group* (New York: Harcourt, Brace, and World, 1950).

tion, the child's first friends are similar in many ways; the social class homogeneity of most residential neighborhoods insures that playmates will have similar home experiences and receive common cultural cues. Their cultural heroes will be defined by what they watch on television and their behavior shaped by their parents. Given the homogeneity of children's television programming and the class base of childrearing practices it is not surprising that children have little difficulty "getting along" with other neighborhood children; the homogeneity of their environment makes it comparatively easy for the children to interact with one another and to reinforce cues they receive from home and culture. From this perspective the neighborhood peer group is nothing more than an extension of the family.

The child's peers enable him to define sex-linked roles in "play acting" fantasies. Playing "house" the boy seeks to emulate his father and the girl her mother in defining and working out the roles of mother and father, as perceived by the child and checked with the perceptions of other children. By moving outside the family, but into a cultural setting similar to the family, the child begins to check his sense of increased identity against external referents. By seeing how other children behave the child develops a belief system and values which have relevance beyond the immediate environment of the family. He begins, in other words, to develop beliefs and values which are universal rather than particular. In testing beliefs and values in a larger social arena the child also checks on the efficacy of the family as a socialization agent. How well have they prepared him to deal with situations outside the family; attitudes and behavior which are appropriate in the family setting must face the severe test of exposure to nonfamily members. Children who manipulate their parents often find they cannot manipulate their playmates, and a bloody nose is often the first sign of failure in the socialization process. The family, correspondingly, acts as a check on attitudes and behaviors learned in the peer group. Parents slowly recognize that the peer group now provides another set of standards for the child, not totally or even very alien from that of the parents, to which the child can appeal when the occasion demands. The appeal for a new bicycle "because everyone else has one" is a common and powerful one. The child has learned that there are more than one set of rules, that rules are not absolute, and that some rules can be manipulated, lessons valuable for later adult life.

As the child grows older the peer group becomes an increasingly important factor in the socialization process. As the child's universe expands he finds the family is less central to it and he spends less time with his family and more time in school and with friends. While the peer group becomes increasingly important with age, it also becomes sexually segregated. Once past the stage of playing "house" boys and girls form separate and exclusive friendship cliques. The process of sexual differentiation is manifested in the high school where, Coleman found, the social structure is composed of sexually segregated cliques which interact and share some common values. Status within each of the cliques is different; athletic ability is important to boys where good looks, clothes, and dates are relevant for girls.[2]

Coleman also found that social class is an important variable in structuring the school social system. The peer group structure of the school is then differentiated by both sex and social class. Class-related values are reinforced by the education system.

> If you take a College Preparatory Course you're better than those who take a General Course. Those who take a General Course are neither here nor there. If you take a Commercial Course, you just don't rate. It's a funny thing, those who take College Preparatory set themselves up as better than the other kids. Those that take the College Preparatory run the place. I remember when I was a freshman, mother wanted me to take Home Economics, but I didn't want to. I knew I couldn't rate. You could take typing and shorthand and still rate, but if you took a straight Commercial Course, you couldn't rate. You see, you're rated by the teachers according to the courses you take. They rate you in the first six weeks. The teachers type you in a small school

---

[2]James Coleman, *The Adolescent Society* (New York: The Free Press, 1961).

and you're made in classes before you get there. College Preparatory kids get good grades and the others take what's left. The teachers get together and if you are not in College Preparatory, you haven't got a chance.[3]

Participation in each course of study is a function of sex and class. Very few boys take the commercial course (except college preparatory boys who take typing) and very few lower-class children, boys or girls, are found in the college preparatory courses. Social class determines which academic programs are attractive to which students, students with similar social backgrounds take the same program, and people who take the same courses form friendship cliques based on similarity of interests and social class. The education system serves to structure academically the social distinctions which students make on the basis of sex and social class. The school social structure, conversely, influences expectations of teachers and students about academic performance and grades. Boys are thought to do better in math and science and girls in home economics and typing and they do.

There is also evidence that social status of peers influences one's values and political attitudes. Lower-status students frequently defer to upper-status students and seek to emulate them, particularly when there are heterogeneous peer groups.

> From this, we might hypothesize that the primary function of homogeneous class peer groups in the political socialization process is to reinforce the way of life and associated political orientations of the lower classes, and thus, to maintain the political and cultural cleavages which may exist between classes. On the other hand, heterogeneous class peer groups function in an important way to re-socialize the attitudes of working class members in the direction of those held by higher class peers.[4]

Langton's study of Jamaican students found that working-class students in heterogeneous peer groups had substantially different political attitudes than their working-class counterparts who were members of working-class peer groups: they

---

[3]W. Lloyd Warner and Associates, *Democracy in Jonesville* (New York: Harper and Brothers, 1949), p. 207.

[4]Kenneth P. Langton, *Political Socialization* (New York: Oxford U. Press, 1969), pp. 125-26.

were less committed to economic aggrandizement at the expense of political liberty, more disposed toward fulfilling their voting obligation, and less intolerant of minority groups.[5]

Where the peer group culture is homogeneous and corresponds to the values which the educational system emphasizes, very few discontinuities occur in the socialization process. Such a correspondence heightens the impact of the educational system by reinforcing the school's social system. If both the school and one's peers place a premium on getting good grades then grades will become an important goal. When the peer group culture and the values of the educational system do not correspond, but do not conflict—the two value systems are concerned with different dimensions of the student's existence— each agent works independently of the other and in its respective area of competence. The student looks to the school for cues about the value of grades and his friends to cues about hair styling. The differentiation between school and peers may be viewed in terms of the school socializing the student into the political system while peers socialize him into the larger social system. Discontinuities in the socialization process arise when there is conflict between the peer group culture and the values of the educational system. As in other settings where socialization cues are inconsistent, the impact of the school as a socialization agent is lessened. Forced to choose between the values of his peers and those of the school the student will adopt those which seem most relevant and rewarding to him. In an era when the school is being criticized as being irrelevant for the needs of its students, it may find itself less efficacious as a transmitter of the societal culture. To the extent that what he learns in school is irrelevant the student will look to others for relevant values, often to his friends who share his dilemma.

Mass media

The widespread use of the mass media, particularly television, for news, entertainment, and education has led many peo-

---

[5]Ibid., pp. 126.31.

ple to fear the possible ill effects on a nation's youth raised with "Batman" and *Bonnie and Clyde*. Saturday morning television cartoons and violence on television and in the movies are condemned, while Walt Disney films and educational television are praised. Reactions to the mass media are based on three assumptions, clearly stated by The National Council on Crime and Delinquency:

1. Motion pictures and television are a new and powerful educative force affecting the young.
2. The amount of time and number of television programs involving crime, horror, and violence is conspicuous.
3. There are bases for concern about what children are learning through movies and television.[6]

The obvious question is whether there is any relationship between what children (or adults for that matter) see on television or in movies, or read in newspapers and magazines, and their attitudes toward the world. The lack of research, however, is surprising. And the research which has been done is far from consistent or conclusive.

What is clear is that people make extensive use of the mass media, especially television. Television has, in a relatively short span of slightly more than thirty years, become as widespread as the telephone as a means of communication; over ninety percent of homes in the United States have at least one television set. At the same time television has assumed preeminence as a source of news and entertainment for the family.

The use of television begins at an early age, probably during the period when the child becomes aware of others and begins to conceptualize at a rudimentary level. Schramm, Lyle, and Parker found that children at the age of three watched an average of forty-five minutes, at age six watched an average of two hours, and by sixth grade were watching an average of three hours of television each day. As a result, "During the first

---

[6]National Council on Crime and Delinquency, "Summary Report on Findings and Recommendations of the Conference on Impact of Motion Pictures and Television on Youth," in *Problems and Controversies in Television and Radio*, ed. Harry J. Skornia and Jack W. Kitson (Palo Alto: Pacific Books, 1968), pp. 279-83.

sixteen years of life, the typical child now spends, in total, at least as much time with television as in school."[7] Although parents may object to the amount of time which their children spend before the television set, three-fourths of parents with children under age fifteen feel that children are "better off with television."[8] Parents see the benefits for both themselves and their children; television serves as an educational tool for the child and as a babysitter for his parents.

While children are heavy consumers of television, their consumption varies with age as does the content of what they watch.[9] Television usage is heaviest between second and sixth grade, but declines through high school; television viewing consumes fifteen hours per week for second graders, over twenty hours per week for eighth graders, and sixteen to eighteen hours for twelfth graders. Matching the decline in television viewing is an increase in radio listening and newspaper and magazine reading. In essence, the teen-ager is developing adult media tastes which rely less on one media and combine print with audio and visual media. There are several important factors which influence the amount of media consumed at any age. In terms of television viewing, children follow patterns set by their parents; if the parents watch little television, the children do likewise. Television consumption is thus a family trait rather than an individual trait, just as decisions on what shows to watch are family rather than individual decisions. One other factor influencing media consumption is IQ. Children with high IQs seem to discover television more quickly than their age-mates, use it more heavily, and then switch to other media earlier than children of comparable age. Schramm, Lyle, and Parker argue that television ceases to challenge them and they turn to the print media.[10] An alternative explanation is that the high IQ children begin to develop an interest in non-

---

[7]Wilbur Schramm, Jack Lyle, and Edwin B. Parker, *Television in the Lives of Our Children* (Stanford, Calif.: Standford University Press, 1961), p. 12.

[8]Gary A. Steiner, *The People Look at Television* (New York: Alfred A. Knopf, 1963), pp. 79ff.

[9]Ibid., pp. 12-97.

[10]Schramm, Lyle, and Parker, op. cit., pp. 35-37.

fantasy programs earlier than their age-mates and there is less of that on television than in the other media. In other words, their intellectual development is faster and their media needs change at a proportionately earlier age; they may, in fact, watch as much television as other children—they watch it at different rates and at different ages. As a result different children will use different media for different types of information at different points in the socialization process. The shift from visual to print media with increased cognitive skills also means that as the child becomes more aware of the world outside himself he is less likely to use television to form basic beliefs and attitudes about that world. Not only do media-use patterns change, but the types of things children seek from the media also change as the child grows older.

What do children watch on television? For young viewers television is an expansion of their fantasy world; the programs "usually have animals, animated characters, or puppets as their chief characters . . . although sometimes children themselves play the sympathetic parts. They are in story form, are full of action (often slapstick), and often have a heavy component of laughter. The traditional time for these programs is late afternoon or Saturday morning."[11] But children watch television more than just late afternoon and Saturday morning. As a result they are exposed to adult television fare as soon as they can stay up late enough in the evening to watch it. By the age of ten the child is spending at least half of his television time watching "adult" programs. Understandably, the child who watches "adult" programs prefers those which are closest to the "children's" programs he normally watches. Situation comedies and game shows rank high on the list. Crime and adventure stories, serious drama, and public service programs are less appealing for young viewers. They are watched if their parents watch them and there are no other attractive alternatives. Schramm, Lyle, and Parker conclude:

> So far as these figures tell us what is a "child" program and what is an "adult" program, they seem to say that at one end

---

[11] Ibid., pp. 37-38.

of a continuum we have the serious dramas and the sophisticated analyses of public affairs, in which the view of life is
too complicated and subtle for most children. At the other
end of the continuum we have cartoons, animal and puppet
shows, and adventure programs in which the behavior is
mostly ritual, the emotions are uncomplicated, and the interpretation is simple and direct. Between them is a world of
adventure, Westerns, crime mysteries, and popular music
programs which are attractive, in almost equal measure, to
children and adults.[12]

As the child matures, his television viewing tastes move
through the continuum from the "child" to the "adult" program end. By the end of high school, the teenager is not only
watching less television but he is watching less fantasy-
oriented and more reality-oriented television. The Saturday
morning cartoons have been replaced by the six o'clock news as
a prime consumption item on television. By high school the
viewing patterns of teenagers are suspiciously similar to those
of their parents; they are interested in and watch the same programs. In a highly politicized family they might watch news
specials and little else.

What impact does television have in the socialization
process? Schramm, Lyle, and Parker suggest that it provides
an additional fantasy world for the child, replacing other fantasy materials such as comic books, in which the child can
displace his frustrations and aggressions. He learns from television but his learning is incidental. Reality-oriented learning
does not occur from television viewing; television is used for
entertainment by both parents and children. The charge that
television, with its emphasis on violence, leads children to
become violent misunderstands why children watch television.
In a classic comment, Schramm et al. conclude:

> For *some* children, under *some* conditions *some* television is
> harmful. For *other* children under the same conditions, or for
> the same children under other conditions, it may be
> beneficial. For *most* children, under *most* conditions, *most*
> television is probably neither particularly harmful nor par-
> ticularly beneficial.[13]

---

[12]Ibid., p. 44.
[13]Ibid., p. 1.

Joseph T. Klapper, after an extensive inventory of research on the impact of the mass media, concluded that they serve to reinforce already held attitudes, values, and beliefs.[14] The world which is portrayed through the mass media is a white middle-class world; the audience is perceived as being white and middle-class. Klapper argues that competition between the media and within any one medium constrains them from transmitting values which are not culturally acceptable. Thus, the opportunity for socialization into anything other than the dominant culture would be next to impossible. Gerson's study of blacks in the San Francisco area indicates that they use the media for reinforcement and norm-acquiring of the values of the dominant white culture. Hence they learn behavior which is socially acceptable to whites.[15] The media can serve as an instrument of innovation under very specific situations. The media can produce attitude change when the individual is predisposed to change his attitude, if the person is "persuadable," or if the person has no attitude in the first place. In the latter case the media are not changing attitudes so much as creating them. This role of the media will be explored in a later chapter.

Bandura's findings are in disagreement with those of Klapper and Schramm, Lyle, and Parker. Unlike Klapper, Bandura is interested in the impact of media on behavior and, unlike Schramm, Lyle, and Parker, seeks to discover that relationship in an experimental setting.[16] In his best known experiment children were exposed to a simulated television program, in a puppet fantasy format, featuring a character pummeling a life-size doll with fists and hammer. Children exposed to this "program" and others who weren't were then placed in a room with a life-size doll identical to the one pummeled on the program. Those children exposed to the program were far more likely than the others to pummel the doll as they had seen on

[14]Joseph T. Klapper, *The Effects of Mass Communication* (Glencoe: The Free Press, 1961).

[15]Walter M. Gerson, "Mass Media Socialization Behavior: Negro-White Differences," *Social Forces* 45 (September, 1960), pp. 40-50.

[16]A. Bandura and R. H. Walters, *Social Learning and Personality Development* (New York: Holt, Rinehart, and Winston, 1963).

television, with the girls more physically aggressive than the boys. Bandura concludes that children can and do use television to provide models for aggressive behavior and that violence on television is translated by children into the acceptance of violence as condoned behavior.[17]

The Bandura studies are not as conclusive as they may seem. The children were asked to view a program they had never seen before and in a context different from their usual television viewing. They were then placed in a room with a doll, which they attacked. Did the uniqueness of the experimental situation and the program they were watching influence their subsequent behavior? Why interpret the children's aggressiveness toward the doll as being indicative of how television influences their behavior toward other people? Schramm, Lyle, and Parker might well argue that television performed the very useful function of showing how to deal with feelings of aggression in nonhuman ways, i.e., attacking a doll.

And the debate endures.[18] From the preceding discussion it is clear that the mass media serve as an important transmission line between the dominant culture and the child, reinforcing values and beliefs the child is learning elsewhere. If the media are teaching children to be violent, it may well be because violence is a prominent value of the dominant culture which condones and encourages it. The relative impact of the mass media, however, is a function of the roles played by other socialization agents. While the child may be an insatiable consumer of television he spends far more time with his parents, friends, and in school, in contact with agents that play a preeminent and predominant role in the socialization process.

Parents, teachers, and peers: Their relative impact

There is very little direct or conclusive evidence as to the relative impact of these three socialization agents. It is most often

---

[17]One of the major drawbacks of television, according to parent, is that it shows to much violence to their children, Steiner, op. cit., pp. 90ff.

[18]While this book was being written the federal government commissioned an extensive study of the impact of television violence on children.

assumed that the family is the most important because it molds the child, unaffected by other socialization agents. Langton argues that parents are the most important agents;[19] Hess and Torney argue that the school is the most important agent; Longstreth argues that if we are concerned with the socialization process as an interaction process, then after the child enters school the role of the parents declines dramatically, that of the teacher increases, and the peer group predominates.[20]

Direct comparisons between family, school, and peer groups are virtually nonexistent. Langton, using causal modelling techniques, concludes:

> The family accounted for almost four times more movement along the entire efficacy scale than either peer group or school. In fact, it was the only agency that moved students along the entire range of the efficacy scale. The family also exceeded significantly the other two agencies in creating a medium level of efficacy, although this relative influence was reduced among the upper classes. The same pattern was visible at the high efficacy range. Among working and middle classes the politicized family accounted for the placement of more highly efficacious respondents than either peer group or school. But among the upper class the family succumbed to the dominant influence of the peer group.

> Although the family influences movement along the entire efficacy dimension, the peer group and school operate at different ends of this scale. The broader, less intimate school environment moves students from low-to-medium efficacy but has almost no influence at the high efficacy range. The face-to-face peer group, on the other hand, concentrated almost exclusively on what may be a more difficult socialization task —moving students from medium-to-high political efficacy.[21]

While the family may play an important role in developing political efficacy in the child it also shares that role with the peer group and school. One wonders what the relative impact of each agent would have been on the formation of attitudes

[19]Robert D. Hess and Judith V. Torney, *The Development of Political Attitudes in Children* (Chicago: Aldine Publishing Co., 1967), p. 105.
[20]Langdon Longstreth, *Psychological Development of the Children* (New York: Ronald Press, 1968).
[21]Langton, op. cit., pp. 158-59.

toward government, or voting, or writing letters to Congressmen—other dimensions of the political system of which political efficacy is only a part.

Further research may reveal that the impact of each socialization agent is differential. If the argument that socialization is a function of personality development is valid then the impact of each socialization agent may be determined by the point at which it influences the maturing individual. The family, aside from helping protect and nurture the child's ego, may play a predominant role in developing his attitudes toward authority structures and develop in the child some rudimentary skills in coping and dealing with authority figures. At the same time the family begins to establish basic ground rules for behavior, some of which are applicable to the political world, and overtly teaches political cues such as party identification. The primary role of the school may be to provide information about the political system which is a prerequisite for operation within it. Transmission of political symbols from generation to generation may also be a vital function of the school. The primary function of the peer group is less clear cut, in part due to the difficulty of extricating its impact from that of school and family. The role of the peer group may be largely supportive—reinforcing attitudes developed earlier in life and forming a post-family or ancillary-family reference group for testing attitudes toward political objects. At a minimum the peer group allows the individual to make decisions about his environment which are relevant to the groups to which he belongs.

Adult socialization

Much of the research on political socialization has dealt with how children learn political orientations and develop political cognitions. Like Freud, many social scientists have assumed that the important socialization processes have been completed by the time the individual reaches puberty. The adult *Homo Politicus* is merely the child writ large. In a perceptive essay on socialization through the life cycle, Brim develops the idea that the content of adult socialization differs from child socialization in a number of important ways.[22] In some cases adult socialization may be viewed as "resocialization," remedying the defects of socialization which should have occurred in childhood. For those people who were successfully socialized in childhood, "The most important change, perhaps, is the shift in content from a concern with values and motives to a concern with overt behavior."[23] Having sufficient information about the political system the individual must tie together beliefs and attitudes into opinions which are relevant for his role in society. Having developed political beliefs he learns which beliefs can be related to which political objects to form what political opinions. Adult socialization is less concerned with socialization into the dominant society than with socialization into a specific role within that society and the teaching of political opinions appropriate to that role.

With this in mind we can now examine the role played in adult life by several important socialization agents: work, primary groups, and the mass media.

The work environment

Since man spends approximately forty percent of his adult life "on the job," the people with whom he works form an important peer group. The work group performs several important functions. Colleagues set formal and informal work standards and make important personal and professional judgments on the basis of those standards. To the extent he is aware of the work standards and accepts them as legitimate he will enjoy his work and his colleagues. The work group also serves as an informal communications network, often operating faster, more efficiently, and with less distortion than the official communication channels of the organization. Colleagues will

---

[22]Orville G. Brim, "Socialization Through the Life Cycle," in Orville G. Brim and Stanton Wheeler, *Socialization After Childhood* (New York: John Wiley, 1966), pp. 1-50.

[23]Ibid., p. 25.

often explain to a new member of the work group how to cut through the red tape of organization procedures and how to understand what directives really "mean." The work group may also play a third role for the individual, outside the work setting. For those occupations which have a strong sense of organization loyalty, friendships developed in the work group provide a basis for the workers' social life outside the job. Lipset, Trow, and Coleman's study of typographers in New York City found that the typographers bowled together, their families socialized together, and the union provided an important source of nonwork leisure time activity for the worker and his family.[24]

The influence of the work group on a person's opinions is a function of the importance of the job to the worker and the extent to which the job permeates his daily existence. If, as is the case with the typographers, there is little distinction between work and nonwork, in terms of whom one associates with, then the work group becomes an important factor in determining an individual's attitudes toward his political environment. On the other hand, if the job is nothing more than a place to spend eight hours with people one doesn't see again or care to see again, then the work group is of marginal importance.

The social fabric of the work situation may not be the key determinant of how people respond to their political world. The kind of work a man does may be as important as who he works with. Lipsitz argues that men who are dissatisfied with industrial work which calls for low skill levels and in which the work pace is set by the machines, not the worker, are also dissatisfied with other dimensions of their life.[25] Alienation from work is generalized to alienation from society and politics by the worker.

Robert Blauner, in an excellent study of workers in four different kinds of technology, found that automobile workers, who had the least control over the product and process of their

---

[24]Seymour Martin Lipset, Martin Trow, and James Coleman, *Union Democracy* (Glencoe, Ill.: The Free Press, 1956).

[25]Lewis Lipsitz, "Work Life and Political Attitudes: A Study of Manual Workers," *American Political Science Review* 58 (December, 1964), pp. 951-62.

work, were the most dissatisfied with their job.[26] Textile workers, however, who have little control over the pace of their work, little variety, and a lack of physical movement on the job, are less alienated than automobile workers. Blauner found two basic reasons for this: textile workers, because of poor education and limited background, have lower aspirations and find routine work less boring and monotonous; and the common background of community ties among textile workers (they live together in segregated corporate communities and share a strong common religious tie), which is rare in other technologies, provides a degree of social integration which counters the more tiresome dimensions of the work process. Thus, while the work process for automobile and textile workers may be equally boring, monotonous, and devoid of physical freedom, the textile worker can draw on the social context of the work situation to defray the more onerous aspects of the job. Textile workers are working with friends and neighbors who live for the time they can spend together away from the machine.

Why is it important that the worker feel some connection with the process and product of his work? How do his feelings about work relate to his feelings about the political system? The data, while skimpy, are consistent. Voting research indicates that political participation, political efficacy, and a sense of civic duty increase as one moves up the occupational hierarchy, from blue-collar to white-collar to managerial and professional occupations.[27] Lipsitz also found that the more control the automobile worker had over his job the more efficacious he felt in the political world.[28] The assumption generally made is that the harder one has to work at his job the less control he has over that job, the more oppressive and the

---

[26]Robert Blauner, *Alienation and Freedom: The Factory Worker and His Industry* (Chicago: University of Chicago Press, 1964). Blauner compares four different jobs: automobile assembly line work, textile weaving, typesetting, and petroleum refining. He found that the refinery personnel, in highly skilled jobs which provided maximum freedom and responsibility, felt the least alienated from their jobs.

[27]See Robert Lane, *Political Life* (New York: Free Press, 1959); and Lester Milbrath, *Political Participation* (Chicago: Rand McNally, 1965).

[28]Lipsitz, op. cit.

more time-consuming the job the less energy and the fewer the resources available for participation in the political system.

Such an assumption overlooks the possibility that people who can participate in a number of areas, including politics, gravitate toward jobs where they can and do exercise control. An alternative hypothesis is that people who lack resources to participate in politics also lack the necessary resources to obtain high skill and participatory jobs. A third alternative would be that participation is the result of a third variable, such as education or personality.

Work then has an impact on the worker in two significant ways. The social structure of the work situation acts as an important peer group for the individual. To the extent that his work is a consequential part of his life the people with whom he works constitute an important peer group. At the same time the work process has some impact on how the worker perceives his political world and his ability to participate in that world. In work settings which are oppressive the worker finds himself without sufficient resources to participate in the political world. In such a setting the worker may find that his coworkers reinforce this nonparticipatory ethic.

Peer groups

Outside of work the individual belongs to many groups, which constitute "a network of group affiliations."[29] The impact of each group on the individual is a function of the importance of the group to the person and the degree of conflict between the values which each group holds dear. The more important a group to him, the more a person will adhere to its values, and the more he adheres to the group's values the more important the group becomes. While this statement may seem tautological it embodies a significant social dynamic. Once a person decides that a group is important to him he begins to as-

---

[29] Georg Simmel, *Conflict and the Web of Group-Affiliations*, trans. Kurt Wolff and Reihard Bendiz (Glencoe, Ill.: The Free Press, 1955).

similate the group's values; the more he assimilates the values of the group, the better socialized he becomes, the better able he is to function within the group and the more vital the group becomes to him.[30]

The more important a person is to the group the harder the group will work to maintain him within it; subsequently, group leaders—because they are leaders and define the group's values—can be more deviant than marginal members. Describing the Senate, White has said, "The easiest and somewhat oversimplified way to express the real situation is simply to say that the great ones do about as they please, short of action so outrageous as not possible to be overlooked."[31] Deviance, whether by group leader or marginal member, is likely to be tolerated in order to maintain the solidarity of the group. Deviant members are rarely expelled from the group; most frequently they are ignored.[32] If deviance from group norms becomes so widespread that the cohesion of the group is threatened then the group must respond. The problem for any social aggregation is to allow some deviance but not enough to threaten the existence of the group.

The impact of the group is also the result of the extent to which the group's values conflict or reinforce values of other groups to which the individual belongs. Many people belong to the National Rifle Association and consider themselves to be good Democrats, active in the party and working for the party's candidates, without experiencing any conflict. The NRA supplies ammunition and sanctions shooting matches while the Democratic party contests elections. So long as the person doesn't perceive the groups as being in conflict or if the issue is

---

[30]For a discussion of the small group research see Sidney Verba, *Small Groups and Political Behavior* (Princeton, N.J.: Princeton University Press, 1961).

[31]William S. White, *Citadel* (New York: Harper and Brothers, 1956), p. 122.

[32]For an excellent discussion of deviance see Howard S. Becker, *Outsiders: Studies in the Sociology of Deviance* (New York: Free Press of Glencoe, 1963). An excellent discussion of punishment for deviance from group norms can be found in Richard H. Rovere, *Senator Joe McCarthy* (New York: Meridian Books, Inc., 1959).

of minimal importance there will be no problem. Dissonance occurs when the NRA and the Democratic party take contradictory stands on gun control legislation and seek to mobilize their respective memberships. It is at that point that the Democratic shooter must decide which of the organizations he values most highly.

Value conflicts between groups and the resultant crosspressures on members may not occur very frequently. While the United States may be classified as "a nation of joiners" only a very small proportion of the population belong to a large number of organizations; for most Americans there is little organized group association outside the family, church, and work.[33] The possibility of value conflicts, consequently, are greatly reduced. Those Americans who do join a wide variety of organizations do not experience many crosspressures because the groups to which they belong form a homogeneous value system for the joiner. Very few people wish to, or do, belong to both the John Birch Society and the Americans for Democratic Action. One belongs to a group because he agrees with the values of the group and, assuming that a person does not consciously crosspressure himself, the groups to which he belongs should, more or less, reflect his personal belief system. In such a homogeneous milieu the possibilities of conflicting values are few.

In addition people who belong to multiple groups also find their involvement is differential, i.e., groups are perceived as more or less important and people participate in them accordingly. When conflicts between group values do occur the individual can decide which of the groups is the more important and what action to take in order to reduce the conflict.

Normally, however, the groups to which an individual belongs serve as a guide for understanding the environment. We look to different people and different groups for guidance on matters of fashion, religion, and politics. As Katz and Lazarsfeld discovered, the individual finds himself in the center

---

[33]Angus Campbell et al, *The American Voter* (New York: John Wiley & Co., 1960), pp. 295 ff.

of only partially overlapping circles of influence; the person we listen to or go to for advice on political matters is only marginally relevant for other decisions. Each leader serves as a "gate-keeper" for his group's sphere of influence, filtering and evaluating the available information for the members of the group.[34]

The mass media

There is no question that the mass media play an important role in the everyday American life. In addition to providing us with light entertainment they are also the major sources of trustworthy information about our political environment.[35] The ability of the mass media quickly to transmit news from locales around the world has greatly expanded the world view of today's citizen. An earthquake shakes Chile and we read about it in the next morning's newspaper. A riot occurs and the local radio stations provide live coverage from the scene. Astronauts walk on the moon and we see them on our television sets. As a result Americans now know more about more things than was ever possible in the past. The mass media have provided us with the information necessary for us to form opinions about objects in our political environment.

One of the factors which prevents the news media, particularly newspapers, from giving complete coverage to news events is the media's conception of what constitutes "news." For most media, news is defined episodically, i.e., those events which are seen as most important on any given day are treated as news. An issue which takes time to develop will rarely be covered by the media until it has been perceived by the media as important and, once recognized, its continued coverage will depend on how important it is compared with other news

---

[34]Elihu Katz and Paul Lazarsfeld, *Personal Influence* (New York: Free Press of Glencoe, 1955).

[35]Roper periodically asks samples of the population whether they trust the mass media as a source of information and which media is the most trustworthy. Newspapers, radio, and television have traditionally emerged as trusted and objective sources of information. See also Steiner, op. cit., p. 266.

depend on how important it is compared with other news events on any given day. As a result, news events have a curious half-life; they are rarely anticipated and hardly ever covered completely. The public is made aware of the high points of an event, without corresponding knowledge of how it arose or its outcome. The problem is clearly most acute for newspapers and television which must cover the news on a continuing day-by-day basis (although television can and does cover an occasional issue in depth and completely), and less critical for magazines whose format precludes episodic coverage and encourages completeness and analysis.

Because television and newspapers focus only on "hot" news they are subject to manipulation by people who understand their requirements. Senator Joseph McCarthy, while investigating alleged Communist infiltration of government, would often gain the headlines on Monday morning by announcing, late Sunday afternoon, that he was subpoenaing an important witness to testify before his Senatorial committee. Since Monday is often a slow news day McCarthy could be reasonably sure of getting the Monday morning headline.[36] During the 1968 Democratic National Convention in Chicago the Yippies often used television newsmen to their advantage, staging incidents to insure that they would be filmed and shown on television.[37] Newsmen are aware of the dangers inherent in trying to cover news episodically. The counter-argument is that longitudinal news coverage is expensive and there is no guarantee that it would produce better news coverage. A reporter assigned to cover an issue might spend three weeks on it before he discovered it would never be "news," and during that same three-week period he might have had to pass up a half-dozen stories which were "news."

An additional difficulty is that media personnel also define news on the basis of their own expectations. Lang and Lang studied the media coverage of the 1952 television coverage of

---

[36]See Richard Rovere, *Senator Joe McCarthy* (New York: Harcourt, Brace, 1959).

[37]See Daniel Walker, *Rights in Conflict* (New York: Bantam Books, 1968).

the return of General MacArthur to Chicago after being dismissed from his command by President Truman by monitoring the television coverage with on-site reports from researchers.[38] They found that camera angles and broadcast descriptions were based on expectations of what the public's response would be rather than what it actually was. Rather than emphasizing small crowds, camera shots were chosen which emphasized gatherings of people; emotion was imputed to people watching the parade which the on-site inspectors found hard to detect. The same authors, studying the 1952 Democratic convention, found that each television network focused on different dimensions of the convention—leaving viewers with different and not necessarily compatible pictures of what had "really" happened.[39] The differential foci were the result of the capabilities of each of the network staffs, network decisions as to what was important, and the announcers' values as to what was "news."

The media do more than merely provide information, however. Since they cannot provide all the information nor cover all the news stories available to them they must make judgments as to what it is that the public wants to hear, see, and read about. By deciding that some stories are more important than others the media perform an "agenda setting" function for the media consumer and the society of which he is a part.[40] By defining a story as "newsworthy" the media also confer salience —the object of the story is one that should be the object of an opinion.

Although the media can provide information about and define the salience of political objects, does this mean that the media create public opinion? McGinnis' description and analysis of the Nixon media campaign in the 1968 Presidential race is based on the assumption that Presidential candidates, like underarm deodorants, can be "sold" to the public.[41]

---

[38]Kurt and Gladys Lang, *Politics and Television* (Chicago: Quadrangle Books, 1968), pp. 36-77.

[39]Ibid., pp. 78-149.

[40]The "agenda setting" function will be discussed in more depth in Chapter Seven.

[41]Joe McGinnis, *The Selling of the President, 1968* (New York: Trident Press, 1969), p. 29.

Television seems particularly useful to the politician who can be charming but lacks ideas. Print is for ideas. Newspapers write not about people but policies; the paragraphs can be slid around like blocks. Everyone is colored gray. Columnists—and commentators in the more polysyllabic magazines—concentrate on ideology. They do not care what a man sounds like; only how he thinks. For the candidate who does not, such exposure can be embarrassing. He needs another way to reach the people.

On television it matters less that he does not have ideas. His personality is what the viewers want to share. He need be neither statesman nor crusader; he must only show up on time. Success and failure are easily measured; how often is he invited back? Often enough and he reaches his goal—to advance from "politician" to "celebrity," a status jump bestowed by grateful viewers who feel that finally they have been given the basis for making a choice.

Viewing the electorate as passive and disinterested consumers, more interested in being entertained than enlightened, the role of the media becomes clear in a political campaign—concentrate less on the issues of the campaign and more on the personalities of the candidates. If the electorate wants to use television for entertainment, then present a candidate who is entertaining. The cardinal rule of "media-politics": "Style becomes substance. The medium is the massage and the masseur gets the votes."[42]

The "McGinnis rule" is contrary to much of what we know about the impact of the media, particularly television, on public opinion. Klapper's review of the mass communication research, although dated, indicates that the mass media are most influential for reinforcement of existing opinions or the creation of new opinions where none had existed before, rather than the conversion of opinion from one side of a question to the other.[43] The early voting studies indicated that during the course of a presidential political campaign very few people changed their opinions as a result of information received from the mass media.[44] In-

---

[42]Ibid., p. 30.

[43]Klapper, op. cit.

[44]Paul F. Lazarfeld, Bernard Berelson, and Hazel Gaudet, *The People's Choice* (New York: Duel, Sloan, and Pearce, 1944).

stead, the process of selective exposure was operative. Republicans tended to listen to and read information about the Republican candidate while Democrats did the same with their candidate. Although the media impartially conveyed information about both candidates the media were monitored in a partisan way, to reinforce preexisting opinions about the two candidates.

Much the same process occurred during the much publicized and researched Kennedy-Nixon debates in 1960. The four debates created a great deal of interest in the election and engendered enormous audiences for a series of political broadcasts but, in the long run, they changed very few votes from one side to the other. Katz and Feldman, after reviewing the substantial survey research on the public's response to the debates, concluded that the debates had benefitted John Kennedy because they had allayed the fears of many of his supporters who might have deserted to Nixon.[45] For these people the debates performed the valuable function of reinforcing their initial decisions. Robinson and Burgess found much the same process in response to Edward Kennedy's 1969 speech to the nation after he drove his car off a bridge near Martha's Vineyard, Massachusetts.[46] Following the accident and in light of the ambiguous circumstances surrounding the death of Mary Jo Kopeckny, Kennedy's popularity as a Democratic presidential candidate plummeted. Shortly thereafter Kennedy appeared on television to explain what had happened and to seek to recoup some of his lost popular support. Robinson and Burgess found that almost everyone interviewed in Columbus, Ohio (the site of the study) was aware of the accident and that news of the accident had seriously undermined public confidence and support for him. At the same time Senator Kennedy's television speech did much to recoup his original supporters who had deserted him after hearing of the accident. The

---

[45]Elihu Katz and Jacob Feldman, "The Debates in the Light of Research: A Survey of Surveys," in *The Great Debates*, ed. Sidney Kraus (Bloomington, Ind.: Indiana University Press, 1962).

[46]Michael J. Robinson and Phillip M. Burgess, "The Edward M. Kennedy Speech: The Impact of a Prime Time Television Appeal," *Television Quarterly* 9 (Winter, 1970): 29-39.

authors do agree with McGinnis' contention in part, however. They recognize that part of Edward Kennedy's success in recapturing his former supporters was due to his style, rather than the content of his speech, and the fact that he was able to make his speech without immediate and contradictory evidence to rebut it.

We can conclude that any man with some public notoriety who puts his case humbly before the television audience, *and puts it there knowing that nobody is going to pan him after the performance,* can only come out ahead, *regardless of what he has to say.*[47]

Two caveats are in order, however. A public statement by a public figure will have the greatest impact on those supporting or included toward the figure making the statement and have the least impact on those opposed to him. He may have difficulty even getting those opposed to him to listen to the speech. Secondly, there are very few political situations where a man "with some public notoriety" is going to find himself saying something "knowing that nobody is going to pan him." The more public a person he is and the more political the occasion the less likely this is to happen. Robinson and Burgess can find only three such occasions—Nixon's Checkers speech, Edward R. Murrow's *See It Now* program on Senator Joe McCarthy, and Kennedy's speech.

Television can have an impact in creating opinions regarding unfamiliar political objects or events—with the evening news, it has brought the war in Vietnam into every living room. When a government is overthrown in Latin America or Africa it is the mass media which provide us with the information on which we base our opinions. The ability to describe and interpret new events as they occur may be the focal power of the media in their ability to form opinions; if we are "other directed" as Riesman suggests we must rely on others to interpret our political world for us, particularly when some element in that political world is novel or unique. Television news

---

[47]Ibid., p. 38.

announcers and newspaper editorialists and columnists serve
to explain what the world really looks like and means.

The media are not totally free to disseminate all information
to their customers. The Federal Communications Commission's
"Fairness Doctrine" requires that the electronic media give
equal time to candidates for public office and, in some instances, to groups who hold opposing views on issues. This has
carried over to the television networks who are reluctant to air
programs which are politically controversial, for fear of losing
viewers and/or sponsors, or because they may have to yield
equal time to the opposite side.[48] The public uproar and
subsequent Congressional investigations of the media analysis
of the Pentagon's public information programs and the publica-
tion of the *Pentagon Papers* must force the media to think quite
seriously about presenting controversial issues to the public.

One consequence, of course, is that the analysis of news often
comes long after the event has passed, controversy has cooled,
and opinions have been formed. Another result is that the
media do comparatively little public service broadcasting and
news analysis, far less than hoped for and envisaged by leading
proponents of public service broadcasting.[49] Even when the
media do analyze the news such analysis is too little publicized
or presented in such a way or time that many people miss it.
Why are the interview shows "Meet the Press" and "Face the
Nation" presented on Sunday, outside of prime time? To insure
broad reception? To educate the public?

Summary

The political socialization process continues throughout
one's whole life, from birth to death. As the person grows older,
however, it becomes increasingly difficult for socializing agents
to have any impact, for the socialization process at age forty

---

[48]Bernard Rubin, *Political Television* (Belmont, Calif.: Wadsworth,
1967), pp. 7-10.
[49]Fred Friendly, *Due To Circumstances Beyond Our Control...* (New
York: Random House, 1967).

means unlearning what one knows and learning new material. For that reason the socialization which occurs during the early years of one's life is more determinant of what the adult will be like than are the things he experiences as an adult. We need only remember the discussion of cognitive dissonance in Chapter One to realize that an adult, with already formed attitudes, values, and beliefs, will normally not place himself in a position where those attitudes, values, and beliefs are called into question or conflict. For the child, however, cognitive dissonance may not be a problem since his attitudes, values, and beliefs are largely unformed. As a result he is more likely to be socialized than the adult who must be resocialized.

CHAPTER FIVE

The distribution of public opinion

Thus far we have focused on public opinion at the micro level, as the product of an individual's interacting with his environment, whose attitudes, values, and beliefs allow him to deal with and understand that environment and whose opinions represent his response to it. It is important that we now look at public opinion at the macro level, i.e., the composite of the opinions of all those who hold opinions on a subject and are willing to express them.

Although everyone has opinions, until people verbalize their attitudes, values, and beliefs in the form of opinions it is difficult to know what "public" opinion on any issue "really" is. Indeed, we must rely on the skills and talents of public opinion pollsters and polling organizations who periodically interview nationwide samples of the population in order to aggregate their opinions; in this sense public opinion is "whatever Gallup and Harris say it is." Reliance on professional pollsters to gather and express the opinions of the American public is not without a price. Because Gallup and Harris are in the process of measuring the American pulse for a profit, we rarely know the public opinion on all issues at all times. Instead, we know how the public feels about those issues which are felt to be important at that point in time. As a result, we know a great deal about opinions on issues that are current and controversial, but substantially less about those which are remote or resolved.

Our knowledge of public opinion is thus segmented—we know what public opinion on an issue is while the topic is "hot," but nothing about public opinion before or after that point in time. Lacking this information we must focus on those opinions which are more enduring, which focus on how the political system should operate and evaluations of its operation as well as orientations toward the proper role and scope of government. In essence we need to know what the public thinks of the institutions and procedures by which policy decisions are made, what political scientists call the "political culture."[1] Governmental institutions are thus imbedded in a political culture or set of attitudes held by members of the political system regarding how governmental institutions should perform. If the citizenry expects their elected officials to be corrupt and accept bribes, and so offers bribes to those officials, they should not be surprised when the actions of governmental officials conform to their expectations.

In one of the first empirical studies of national political culture, Almond and Verba operationalized the concept by measuring citizens' attitudes toward the political system as an object, the operation of the system, the policy outputs of the system, and the citizen's role in the policy-making process. They asked:

1. What knowledge does he have of his nation and of his political system in general terms, its history, size, location, power, "constitutional" characteristics, and the like? What are his feelings toward these systemic characteristics? What are his more or less considered opinions and judgements of them?

2. What knowledge does he have of the structures and roles, the various political elites, and the policy proposals that are involved in the upward flow of policy making? What are his feelings and opinions about these structures, leaders, and policy proposals?

3. What knowledge does he have of the downward flow of policy enforcement, the structures, individuals, and

---

[1]See Gabriel Almond and Sidney Verba, The *Civil Culture* (Princeton: Princeton University Press, 1963), pp. 12ff; and Gabriel Almond and G. Bingham Powell, *An Analytic Study of Comparative Politics* (Boston: Little Brown, 1966), pp. 42-72.

decisions involved in these processes? What are his feelings and opinions of them?

4. How does he perceive of himself as a member of his political system? What knowledge does he have of his rights,
powers, obligations, and of strategies of access to influence? How does he feel about his capabilities? What
norms of participation or of performance does he acknowledge and employ in formulating political judgements, or in arriving at opinions?[2]

They found that Americans, compared to Mexicans, British,
Germans, and Italians, exist in a highly political environment;
Americans are more aware of their political system, take pride
in it, feel an obligation to participate, do participate, and feel
their participation does have an impact on the policy-making
process. This activist orientation they have labelled the "participant political culture."

This is not to say, however, that all Americans feel allegiance
to the American political system, perceive it as being relevant
for them, or feel a need to participate in it. Almond and Verba
suggest that the American political culture, although heavy in
emphasis on participation, encompasses people who view their
role in the political system in substantially more passive terms.
Overall, and in comparison with the other four nations, Americans have a greater need to participate and a greater sense that
participation will be beneficial. One of Almond and Verba's
U.S. respondents remembers the preceding Fourth of July,
"when the whole family was together and everyone discussed
Cuba, Communism, and the presidential campaign, with
special reference to the religion of the candidates. Everyone
talked; parents, sons, and daughters-in-law. Opinions varied,
but the discussion was amiable."[3]

Taking a somewhat different approach, although still concerned with the concept of political culture, Devine has examined the American public's acceptance of basic values
regarding their sense of identity with the United States as a political system, belief in fundamental libertarian political
beliefs, acceptance of the democratic procedures which govern

---

[2]Almond and Verba, *Civil Culture*, pp. 16-17.
[3]Ibid., p. 446.

the operation of the political system, and those things which serve as abstract symbols for the political system—the Constitution, the flag, and the national anthem.[4]

Like Almond and Verba, Devine found high levels of support for the American political system. Unfortunately, the data may not be as convincing as would appear in Table 5-1. The ninety percent support level for the national anthem is in response to the question: "Do you think people should stand when 'The Star Spangled Banner' is played in public?" *asked in 1939*, while the behavioral measurement of national identity is based on responses to the question, "If you were free to do so, would you like to go settle in another country?" *asked in 1948 and 1971*. Lacking comprehensive data from one point in time Devine is faced with piecing together a national political culture over time.

Regardless of the methodological problems involved, Devine's work confirms the findings of Almond and Verba; the political culture of the United States is participatory and sup-

TABLE 5-1. Percentage of support for major regime values

Identity system		*Rule system*	
National (behavioral)	91%	Popular rule	76%
National (attitudinal)	96	Elections	88
Sense of community	77	Institutional rule	85
		Legislative predominance	61
Belief system		Federalism	73
		Decentralized parties	57
Liberty	83		
Press freedom	79	*Symbol system*	
Free speech	96		
Education	81	Constitution	64
Equality	78	Flag	90
Property	81	National anthem	90
Achievement	61		
God	96		
Religion	71		
Altruism	86		

Source: Taken from Table VII.4, Devine, *The Political Culture of the United States*.

---

[4]Donald J. Devine, *The Political Culture of the United States* (Boston: Little Brown, 1972).

portive of liberal democratic values. Americans, through time, have been and continue being supportive of the American political system and their continued role within it. As we shall see below, however, there is not necessarily the unanimity implied from Devine and Almond and Verba.

Other political scientists have sought to examine the political cultures of individual states within the United States. Elazar, for example, suggests that it is useful to divide the political cultures of the states into three subcultures—the individualistic, the moralistic, and the traditionalistic, depending on what the citizens in a state perceive as the legitimate ends and style of the state government.[5] Political culture thus becomes an indicator of the dominant ideology within a state, representing a consistent statement by the people of the state regarding how their government should be run.

The individualistic political culture sees government as handling only those functions which cannot be handled by the private sector. Government then becomes a business, whose job it is to see that a marketplace can function effectively.

> Since the I (Individualistic) political culture eschews ideological concerns in its "business-like" conception of politics, both politicians and citizens look upon political activity as a specialized one, essentially the province of professionals, of minimum and passing concern to laymen, and no place for amateurs to play an active role.[6]

The moralistic political culture, on the other hand, starts from the assumption that the role of government is the attainment of the public good and protection of the public interest. The measure of governmental effectiveness is the extent to which it furthers these goals. As a result, government may interfere in the private sector when it feels that the public good is being jeopardized.

> Since the moralistic political culture rests on the fundamental conception that politics exists primarily as a

---

[5]Daniel J. Elazar, *American Federalism: A View from the States* (New York: Thomas Y. Crowell, 1966), pp. 85-116.

[6]Ibid., p. 88.

means for coming to grips with issues and public concerns of civil society, it also embraces the notion that politics is ideally a matter of concern for every citizen, not just those who are professionally committed to political careers. Indeed, it is the duty of every citizen to participate in the political affairs of his commonwealth.[7]

The traditionalistic political culture combines some of the qualities of the moralistic and individualistic political cultures, but is a throwback to an earlier, preindustrial period. It accepts a positive role for government but relegates government to protecting the vested interests of the elite.

Having identified the three subcultures, Elazar then proceeds to classify the states according to the dominant subcultures within each state. Looking at the pattern of distribution he concludes:

In general, the states of the greater South are dominated by the traditionalistic political culture; the states stretching across the middle sections of the United States in a southwesterly direction are dominated by the individualistic political cultures; and the states of the far North, Northwest, and Pacific Coast are dominated by the moralistic political culture.[8]

In addition, the number of states where the traditionalistic political culture is dominant are declining and the bulk of the states are either moralistic or individualistic. The distribution of political subcultures in the U.S., according the Elazar, is the result of regional, ethnic, and mobility patterns.[9] Regardless of their cause each of the three political cultures serves to effect the state's response to policy problems which confront it and have an impact on the American federal system.

Although Elazar's trichotomy is appealing and seems to fit intuitively, there is not data to verify his divisions empirically. The categories may be valid and useful for looking at federal-state political relations but they still await empirical validation.

Patterson, borrowing concepts from an earlier work by

---

[7]Ibid., p. 91.
[8]Ibid., p. 109.
[9]Ibid., pp. 94-115.

Easton and data from the Almond and Verba study, suggests that it is useful to look at the political system in terms of attitudes toward major dimensions in the political system, the government, the regime and the community.[10] The government refers to those people who occupy the official seats of power and have the power to make decisions; the regime refers to the written and unwritten rules of the political system which govern how policy decisions are made; and the political community refers to those people who identify themselves as members of the political system. In addition, Patterson suggests that political cultures have a "style" component which defines the ways in which the basic beliefs of the system are articulated.

The Almond and Verba data, analyzed by region of the U.S., provides the empirical base for his analysis of the political culture of the American states. From the Almond and Verba data he finds regional differences in the percentage of respondents who say they are proud of their governmental and political system; from Survey Research Center data he finds regional differences in feelings of political efficacy; and from Harris data he finds that Mississippians and Southerners differ from the rest of the nation in their ration of President Lyndon Johnson's job rating. These are unfortunately weak reeds upon which to build a theory of state political culture. Patterson's division of political culture into attitudes toward government, regime, and community provide us with a useful tool for aggregating existing data about political culture in the U.S.

The regime

For any government to exist there must be a consensus on the "rules of the game"—the processes by which decisions are made and the rules which govern their operation. Beginning in the early 1950s political scientists began to explore people's attitudes toward basic rights guaranteed in the U.S. Constitution. Their primary concern was with whether Americans accepted or rejected the democratic "rules of the game." The first

[10]Samuel C. Patterson, "The Political Cultures of the American States," in Norman Luttbeg, *Public Opinion and Public Policy* (Homewood, Ill.: Dorsey Press, 1968), pp. 275-92.

of these studies, conducted by Samuel Stouffer and his associates, sought to determine the extent to which the activities of Senator Joseph McCarthy (1950-1954) had influenced people's tolerance of social, religious, and political deviance.[11] Two nationwide samples of the population were interviewed along with a special sample of community leaders drawn from communities with populations between ten and one-hundred-fifty thousand.

From his interviews Stouffer found that the American public was not very tolerant of nonconformists—Socialists, atheists, accused Communists, and avowed Communists. The degree of tolerance did vary, however, in two basic ways. Americans were the most tolerant of nonconformists when they could not be seen or heard or were not perceived as being influential, i.e., people were more willing to tolerate an accused Communist selling shoes than one working in a defense plant or teaching grammar school. People did differentiate, however, between various kinds of nonconformity. They were more tolerant of the rights of a socialist and an accused Communist to teach than they were in granting that right to an atheist or an avowed Communist.

While Americans as a whole are not overly tolerant, certain subgroups within American society are more tolerant than others. Throughout his study, Stouffer found his sample of community leaders to be substantially more tolerant than either a cross section of the community they represented or a cross section of the total population in the United States.

> Attitudes toward curtailing the civil liberties of the four kinds of nonconformists or suspected nonconformists can be combined in a single summary measure. This is a general scale of willingness to tolerate nonconformity.... On this scale, all categories of community leaders, including commanders of the American Legion and regents of the D.A.R. tend on the average to be *more respectful of the civil rights of those of whom they disapprove* than the average person in the general population, either of the same cities from which the leaders come or of the nation as a whole.[12]

---

[11]Samuel Stouffer, *Communism, Conformity, and Civil Liberties* (New York: Wiley, Science edition, 1955).
[12]Ibid., p. 27.

The fact that community leaders are *more* tolerant than the people in their communities does not mean that they are tolerant in an absolute sense. Sixty-six percent of the community leaders (as opposed to seventy-seven percent of the national cross section) agreed that an admitted Communist should have his American citizenship taken away from him. Tolerance, Stouffer found, is a relative thing. In addition to community leaders, the young, well-educated men in the sample were also comparatively more tolerant. Those most tolerant of people who deviate from the norms of the political system were the men who had benefitted the most from the system, had the skills to operate within the system, and knew that the operation of a democratic political system requires tolerance. And operation in the political system requires that participants believe in the democratic rules of the game to act accordingly.

A later study by Prothro and Grigg found that people in Tallahassee, Florida, and Ann Arbor, Michigan, expressed a high degree of consensus in support of the principles of majority rule and minority rights.[13] Ninety-five to ninety-eight percent of those interviewed agreed that elections should be decided by majority rule with every citizen having an equal chance to influence government policy, with the minority having the right to criticize the majority and to try to become the majority. This consensus on abstract democratic principles broke down, however, when the questions focused on the application of democratic principles to concrete situations, i.e., whether a Communist should be allowed to run for Mayor, and, if he won, whether he should be allowed to take office. The greatest deviation from democratic principles occurred, as one might expect from reading Stouffer, on the questions regarding a Communist running for and holding political office. A similar disparity occurred in the Tallahassee sample when people were queried concerning a black running for and holding public office. Lack of consensus is not uniform throughout the population. The more highly educated the respondent the greater the correspondence between his adherence to democratic principles

---

[13]James W. Prothro and Charles M. Grigg, "Fundamental Principles of Democracy: Bases of Agreement and Disagreement," *Journal of Politics* 22 (1960), pp. 276-94.

in the abstract and in practice, leading Prothro and Grigg to call this highly educated subgroup the "carriers of the creed." These findings have been more recently validated by McClosky.

The data . . . confirm that the influentials not only register higher scores on all the pro-democratic scales (faith in freedom, faith in democracy, procedural rights, tolerance), but are more likely to reject anti-democratic sentiments as well. Although they are themselves an elite of a sort, they display greater faith in the capacity of the mass of men to govern themselves, they believe more firmly in political equality, and they more often disdain the "extreme" beliefs embodied in the Right Wing, Left Wing, totalitarian, elitist, and authoritarian scales.[14]

The political influentials are also less cynical about politics and have a higher sense of social responsibility than the general electorate. The areas of highest agreement between leaders and the general electorate occur in support of freedom in the abstract. As with Stouffer, and Prothro and Grigg, it is the well-educated, higher income community influentials who are the carriers of the democratic creed.

If there is a lack of tolerance for political nonconformists and an equal lack of agreement on the specific rights of nonconformists among the general public, what keeps the Constitution, which guarantees the rights of all citizens, from being anything more than a sham for those who live under it? First, there is an obvious gap between what people say (their opinions) and what they do (their behavior). As Prothro and Grigg note, "Fortunately for the democratic system, those with the most undemocratic principles are also those who are least likely to act."[15] Political leadership is thus abdicated to those people who are most supportive of the democratic political system and have the time, energy, resources and skills to work within the system. Apathy on the part of the least democratic citizens insures the continuance of the democratic political system. Second, there is very little opportunity for individual citizens to take actions which directly affect the rights of political nonconformists. The ques-

---

[14]Herbert McClosky, "Consensus and Ideology in American Politics," *American Political Science Review* 58 (June, 1964), pp. 366.
[15]Prothro and Grigg, op. cit., p. 294.

tions posed regarding the firing of defense workers and high school teachers who were admitted Communists or denying a Communist from assuming public office were largely rhetorical, since very few people had ever been confronted with such decisions. For that reason their answers were unreal conjectures regarding their responses to a set of hypothetical situations. It may well be that Americans can be intolerant of people with whom they have had little real contact but whom they perceive as posing a threat. Third, McClosky argues that adherence to democratic rules of the game is not a prime determinant of loyalty to the regime; the political system can tolerate a certain amount of "slack" so long as there is an active minority who do act according to the rules. "So long as no urgent reason arises for bringing such differences (between leaders and followers) to the surface, most men will be satisfied to have them remain dormant."[16]

Several conclusions can be drawn from the research on regime norms. Discussions of democratic rules of the game can occur at a theoretical level and amongst apparent unanimity. The public will tolerate deviation from democratic norms when faced with concrete situations; it is the community leaders, those who must act in concrete situations, who are the most supportive of those democratic norms. And community leaders would rationalize their actions in terms of abstract democratic principles—principles with which they share agreement with their constituents. The community leaders

> ... as participants in political roles, the actives are compelled (contrary to stereotype) to adopt opinions, to take stands on issues, and to evaluate ideas and events. As *articulates* they are unavoidably exposed to the liberal democratic values which form the main current of our political heritage. The net effect of these influences is to heighten their sensitivity to political ideas and to unite them more firmly behind the values of the American tradition.[17]

We thus have the anomaly of community leaders and followers agreeing on abstract principles but when faced with

---

[16]McClosky, op. cit., p. 378.
[17]Ibid., p. 375.

concrete situations the citizenry is far more willing to tolerate undemocratic action than the leadership is to act undemocratically. As citizens we may be willing to have the police use rubber hoses to extract confessions but as community officials we are unwilling to make use of that discretion offered us.

The government

Not only are Americans ambivalent about the democratic rules of the game but they are also ignorant of who mans the machinery of government. Almond and Verba found that in the United States sixty-five percent of the population could name four or more party leaders and thirty-four percent said they could name four or more cabinet members.[18] It is not surprising that public opinion polls continually find substantial numbers of people who do not know the names of their elected representatives in the state or national capitols. On the other hand, awareness of the national government is quite high in the United States, particularly when compared with countries like Mexico and Italy where political interest and awareness is minimal.

Evaluation of political leaders tends also to be quite high. We never completely lose our image of the president as a benevolent leader. Traditionally, the first polls taken after a presidential election show that the winning candidate has a large majority of the population behind him and willing to give him a chance to prove himself. Regardless of the margin of victory the public endorses the victor. Mueller's study of presidential popularity for Truman, Eisenhower, Kennedy, and Nixon shows that this initial honeymoon period is followed by a gradual erosion of support except for occasional reinvigorations due to events or presidential actions.[19] The way to prevent or control the erosion in public popularity is to engage in some sort of energetic action, particularly in the international arena, which

---

[18]Almond and Verba, op. cit., p. 96.
[19]John Mueller, "Presidential Popularity From Truman to Johnson," *American Political Science Review* 64 (March, 1970), pp. 18-34.

can serve as a rallying point for public sentiment. The public, as Neustadt suggests, is not concerned with the content of the action; they want to see the president in his role as leader and problem solver.[20] But the public may also become jaded, over time, at presidential activity which produces few tangible results. Few would deny that Herbert Hoover was trying to reverse the Depression during the period 1929-1932. His fault lay in being unsuccessful.

Political community

Although we are all members of the American political system, we are differentially allegiant to it. Morton Grodzins suggests that there are very few Americans who are totally patriotic or totally traitorous: we are all "tratriots" to one degree or another.[21] Although the study of political alienation has increased in scope, Almond and Verba found that Americans are, by and large, satisfied with the output of government—at least in terms of treatment by government officers—and with their role in the political system. They are aware of avenues of access to governmental policy makers and feel they could have some influence in the policy-making process if they desired. Comparatively few, however, have become involved.

In many ways, then, the belief in one's competence is a key political attitude. The self-confident citizen appears to be the democratic citizen. Not only does he think he can participate, he thinks that others ought to participate as well. Furthermore, he does not merely think he can take a part in politics: he is likely to *be* more active. And perhaps most significant of all, the self-confident citizen is also likely to be the more satisfied and loyal citizen.[22]

There is a minority of the citizenry who feel that people should participate in government, who are satisfied with the operation of the political system, and have the resources to

---

[20]Richard Neustadt, *Presidential Power* (New York: John Wiley, 1960).
[21]Morton Grodzins, *The Loyal and the Disloyal* (Chicago: University of Chicago Press, 1956).
[22]Almond and Verba, op. cit., p. 257.

TABLE 5-2. Percent of U.S. respondents who report satisfaction with their voting participation, believe that elections are necessary, and believe that the ordinary man should be active in his community, among three groups of subjective competents

	Levels of Subjective Competence		
	High	Medium	Low
Satisfied with voting participation	78% (400)	72% (183)	41% (109)
Elections are necessary	81 (506)	74 (251)	58 (212)
Ordinary man should be active in his community	61 (506)	54 (251)	23 (212)

Data from Tables 3, 6, and 7 of Chapter 9 of Almond and Verba, *The Civic Culture*, op. cit.

operate within the system—a minority which is well-educated, active and democratic.[23] Those who score lowest in subjective competence and are lowest in satisfaction with voting don't believe that elections are necessary and do not feel that the ordinary man should be active in his community. In addition, subjective competence is related to education; those people with the highest levels of education have the highest levels of subjective competence and are more likely to support liberal democratic values.

It should not be forgotten that the political culture of the United States is mixed; comparatively few members of the population are totally alienated from or totally allegiant to the political system. In addition, those who are satisfied with their role are also the most likely to participate in the system. The "carriers of the creed" not only endorse the democratic rules of the game but, as can be seen in Table 5-2, also participate in a constant reaffirmation of those rules.

Who are the people at the opposite end of the scale—who are unaware of the political system, have no attachment to it, and

---

[23]Twenty-one percent of the U.S. sample were ranked at the top of the subjective competence scale, although the top two scale positions, combined for analytic purposes in Table 5-2, constitute fifty-two percent of the population, while those with the two lowest scale scores, combined into the "Low" subjective competence category, constitute twenty-one percent of the population.

are critical of its policies and of their role in it? Demographically, they have low incomes and are poorly educated. Their lack of attachment to the political system may stem from two basic sources. For the man earning barely enough to live on and having to work to his limit for that meager sustenance, politics is too time-consuming an avocation for his attention. When he has free time he wants to escape from his world, not analyze the reality of it; his extracurricular interests are baseball, beer, and bowling, not public policy debates. Allegiance to the political system requires that the citizen devote at least a minimal amount of time, attention, and energy to monitoring it. Some people don't have the available resources or would rather use those resources for other, more pleasant, purposes.

On the other hand, alienation from the political system may be a rational response to one's current social, economic, and political position. Comparing their plight with that promised by "the American Dream" they find the gap to be everbroadening. The poor, having more experience with government—particularly its social welfare agencies, police, and fire departments—have found it unresponsive to their needs. Who can say that their alienation from the political system is not a rational response to their political environment? They have tried working within the system, it has failed to meet their needs, and they have rejected it.

We thus have the curious dilemma of democratic government: those who benefit the most from government are its most active participants and adherents while those who could stand to benefit from governmental activity are the least likely to seek (or to obtain) governmental benefits.[24] The abnegation of political responsibility to those interested enough to participate is often applauded by democratic theorists, so long as there are safeguards on the rights of those who do not participate. They rarely go the next step and inquire why people hold undemocratic attitudes, feel alienated from the political system,

---

[24]This point is made by Thomas R. Dye and L. Harmon Zeigler, *The Irony of Democracy* (Belmont, Calif.: Wadsworth, 1970), pp. 127-44.

and don't participate. Instead, the focus is on control. As Key notes, "Groups of persons not involved in democratic processes but possessed of intense discontents may occur in any order. The practical question is how large such blocs of sentiment need to be and what circumstances need to exist for them to become destructive of the normal democratic processes."[25] Implicit in such a statement is the assumption that the only "good" public opinions are of those who are allegiant to and who participate in the political system.

Projecting these conclusions into the future, two developments seem possible. With the increase in the educational level of the population, more and more people will perceive they have a role and a stake in the political system and will seek to act within that system. Thus, the proportion of "democratic" citizens in the general population would be expected to increase; at least for the foreseeable future. Regardless of how large a group of "democratic" citizens there are there will be a substantial segment of the citizenry who will be antithetical to regime norms and who provide the potential for those ideologies and mass movements which can mobilize them. Hoffer's argument that this group constitutes a fairly consistent base for mass political movements of the Left and Right in the United States fits with the data.[26]

Liberalism versus conservatism: The American ideology

Ever since Riesman's attempt to tie national character and political style into a neat and digestable package,[27] American social historians and political scientists have been concerned with the ideological orientation of Americans. Although we have seen earlier that ideology alone is not an important determinant of voting behavior, people do have a more or less complete belief system which they use for dealing with the political environment. What are the dimensions of that belief

---

[25]V. O. Key, Jr., *Public Opinion and American Democracy* (New York: Alfred A. Knoff, 1961), p. 548.

[26]Eric Hoffer, *The True Believer* (New York: Mentor Books, 1951).

[27]See David Riesman, *The Lonely Crowd* (New Haven, Conn.: Yale University Press, 1950).

system and to what extent do people favor retaining the status quo or expanding the role of government, the usual definitions of conservatives and liberals?

Herbert McClosky has constructed a twelve-item measure of conservatism based on the respondent's agreement with statements derived from the writings of conservatives such as Edmund Burke and Russell Kirk.[28] This measure was administered to a random sample of respondents in the Minneapolis-St. Paul area, who were slightly more conservative than liberal and more moderate than extreme in their ideology. McClosky found he could differentiate between liberals and conservatives on the basis of their education (liberals were more likely to have a college education), knowledge (liberals were more aware and intellectual), and personality traits (conservatives scored lower on social responsibility and self-confidence while scoring higher on anomie and pessimism). Using another measure of liberalism-conservatism, designed to measure expansion or contraction of governmental services, he interviewed random samples of voters and party leaders attending the 1956 presidential conventions.[29] He found that Republican and Democratic party leaders took comparatively extreme positions on his scale, with the voters being substantially more moderate. In other words, he found that Democratic and Republican party activities were far more "liberal" and "conservative," respectively, than the voters they were trying to influence, who saw themselves as being primarily "middle-of-the-road." Republican voters, in fact, were ideologically closer to the Democratic leaders than they were to the leaders of their own party. In 1964, when the Republican leaders nominated a presidential candidate whose ideology mirrored their own, it was not surprising that large numbers of Republican voters defected to vote for the Democratic candidate.

Given the disparity in measures used, McClosky's data does

---

[28]Herbert McClosky, "Conservatism and Personality," *American Political Science Review* 52 (March, 1968), pp. 27-45.

[29]Herbert McClosky, "Issue Conflict and Consensus Among Party Leaders and Followers," *American Political Science Review* 54 (June, 1960), pp. 406-27.

indicate that comparatively few people give answers which indicate that they hold extremely liberal or conservative views although education, knowledge, party activity, and personality
variables serve to differentiate between liberals and conservatives and the more extreme from the less extreme.

Eldersveld has found that ideological differences occur
within as well as between political parties.[30] His analysis of the
ideology of party members in Wayne County, Michigan, indicates the following hierarchy within the parties:

Most liberal	Democratic chairmen
	Democratic secondary cadre
	Democratic precinct workers
	Republican secondary cadre
	Republican precinct workers
Least liberal	Republican chairmen

As we have noted earlier (Chapter One), the more involved one
is in politics the greater the ideological commitment. We can
now see that the greater the involvement in the party the more
likely one is to take liberal or conservative positions, depending
on the party.

Interestingly, there have been relatively few attempts to
measure liberalism-conservatism in the electorate at large.
Using 1960 nationwide data from the Survey Research Center,
Converse has attempted to relate people's ability to label themselves as Conservatives or Liberals with their ability to assign
the correct meaning to those terms, and to relate those terms to
the correct political party.[31] Table 5-3, which shows the percentage of respondents who can correctly make the three connections, is misleading. Almost half of the people in the United
States are unable to either label themselves, attach a meaning
to the label, or attach the label to either party. In addition, only
seventeen percent of the population attach a broad philosophy
to the terms liberal and conservative; instead, Americans seem
to define these concepts in economic terms. Almost half of those

---

[30]Samuel Eldersveld, *Political Parties: A Behavioral Analysis* (Chicago:
Rand-McNally, 1964), p. 188.

[31]Phillip E. Converse, "The Nature of Belief Systems in Mass Publics,"
in Apter, op. cit., pp. 206-61.

TABLE 5-3. Association of ideological label with party and meaning

Ideological label	Meaning	Party	Proportion of those giving some answer
Conservative Liberal	Conservative Liberal	Republican Democrat	83%
Conservative Liberal	Liberal Conservative	Republican Democrat	5
Conservative Liberal	Conservative Liberal	Democrat Republican	6
Conservative Liberal	Liberal Conservative	Democrat Republican	6
			100%

Source: Converse, "Nature of Belief Systems," p. 221.

who attached a meaning to the ideological labels "indicated in essence that the Democratic Party was liberal because it spent public money freely and that the Republican Party was more conservative because it stood for economy in government or pinched pennies."[32]

In a more recent study by Free and Cantril three different measures of liberal-conservative ideology were used.[33] Using nationwide public opinion data gathered in the mid-1960s they first constructed an "Operational Spectrum" measure of ideology, designed to tap opinions regarding acceptance of ongoing governmental programs in the fields of education, medical aid, housing, unemployment, and poverty. Using this measure sixty-five percent of the American population are liberal, fourteen percent conservative, and twenty-one percent "middle-of-the-road."

In brief, as of 1964 a large majority of Americans were congenial to the practical operations required to attain and improve the welfare state. In this sense, at the operational level of Government programs, President Johnson was correct when he indicated that the argument over the welfare

[32]Ibid., p. 222.
[33]Lloyd A. Free and Hadley Cantril, *The Political Beliefs of Americans* (New York: Simon and Schuster, 1968).

state had been resolved in favor of Federal action to achieve it.[34]

Free and Cantril next constructed an "Ideological Spectrum" composed of five questions designed to tap ideological conceptions of the proper role and sphere of government and about the nature and functioning of the political system. To their consternation they found that Americans are predominantly conservative on the Ideological Spectrum. This does not mean, however, that people who are conservative on one measure are liberal on the other; the data indicate that the liberals on the Ideological Spectrum are also liberals on the Operational Spectrum but the conservatives on the Ideological Spectrum are not conservative on the Operational Spectrum. Those least likely to exhibit this "schizoid combination" were the college educated, the well-to-do, people with upper-status occupations, people living in large cities, Jews, and blacks—the people most likely to be interested in politics, to be affected by politics, and to need a coherent belief system for dealing with their political environment. As one respondent noted:

> I would like things to be more simple, not so complex—not to be burdened down with bills, like freeways, not for the U.S. to be involved in so many things. They shouldn't be so concerned about Vietnam and poverty. It makes for more complex government. I'd like to see a simple government, not having so much to think about.[35]

In addition to classifying people on the basis of their answers, the respondents were asked to classify themselves as being liberal, conservative, or middle-of-the-road. If the population is schizoid in response to questions concerning the Operational and Ideological Spectra, they are even more so on the Self-Identification Spectrum, where approximately equal proportions of the population perceive themselves as being liberal, conservative, and middle-of-the-road. Comparing the distribution of the population on the three scales (Table 5-4) leaves one with the distinct impression that, while Americans may hold opinions, those opinions are not consistent.

---

[34]Ibid., p. 22.
[35]Ibid., p. 40.

TABLE 5-4. Operational and ideological spectrums and self-identification as liberal or conservative

	Operational spectrum	Self-identification	Ideological spectrum
Liberal	65%	29%	16%
Middle-of-the-road	21	38	34
Conservative	14	33	50
	100%	100%	100%

Source: Free and Cantril, *The Political Beliefs of Americans*, p. 46.

To paraphrase Gertrude Stein, a liberal is not a liberal is not a liberal. The disparity between the Operational and Ideological Spectra can be explained, at least in part, if we keep in mind the questions used to construct each measure. The Operational Spectrum was constructed from questions tapping opinions regarding current public policy in areas such as housing, unemployment, and urban renewal, where governmental activity was once controversial but is now readily accepted and supported by public opinion. Taking a "conservative" position on these policy questions would require a response supporting the *status quo ante*. One could argue that a supportive response to these questions is in fact the conservative response, i.e., it stipulates the acceptance of current governmental policy. Thus, the liberals on the Operational Spectrum may be conservatives supporting the current level of governmental involvement. This does not resolve, however, the conflict between the distribution on the Operational and Ideological Spectra and Self-Identification; Americans do not perceive themselves as ideologically extreme as their answers to public opinion questions indicate. When someone says he is a moderate there is little way of telling his opinions regarding the operation of government at the abstract or real level. Self-Identification does not carry with it a common denotation of what the labels used mean to the people who use them. The term "moderate" or "middle-of-the-road" may be used by people to disguise a multiplicity of often conflicting opinions.

Recognizing the incongruity of the distribution of opinion

found in Table 5-4, Free and Cantril argue that although most Americans are ideologically liberal and operationally conservative any conflict between the two is resolved in favor of the Operational Spectrum.

This conflict is resolved in a typically pragmatic American fashion: the practical is given precedence over the theoretical. At the operational level of government, the great majority of Americans are more concerned about practical problems than they are about abstract conceptions on the ideological problems than they are about abstract conceptions on the ideological level. They want government to work.[36]

Rather than resolving this conflict most Americans are probably unaware of its existence; Americans may well use different criteria when evaluating their world in ideological terms, using one ideological set when evaluating what the government currently is doing and another for evaluating what government should do. Some people may very well hold conflicting belief systems without problem because the relatively low salience of politics does not produce dissonance. The conflict between ideology measured by responses to questions and self-identification may be more of a problem for the political scientist than for the respondent. Respondents who take liberal or conservative positions but call themselves "middle-of-the-road" experience little ideological dissonance because their statements define what they mean by "middle-of-the-road." The fact that one person's definition of his ideology conflicts with someone else's does not bother him, unless there is some need for them both to agree that they are both "middle-of-the-road."

The Free and Cantril findings must be arrayed against Converse's findings that only fifty percent of the population are able to match their own ideological self-identification with a definition of that label and attach both to the proper political party. American citizens, by and large, do not think in broadly philosophical terms as liberals or conservatives. As we have seen, they support basic liberal democratic values regarding

---

[36]Ibid., p. 51.

how the political system should run and respond almost pragmatically to questions about how the system currently operates. Assuming the support for liberal democratic values and the relatively high level of subjective competence, it is not surprising that the population endorses the policy decisions made by their government; they approve of the principals which underlie the operation of that government, and they are reasonably satisfied with the role they play in the operation of the government, so it is not surprising that they endorse the output of government. And, as Free and Cantril note, Americans are far more concerned about how the political system does work than about how it should work.

Changes in the distribution of opinion

In order adequately to understand the role which public opinion plays in the policy process, we must know not only what public opinion is at any one point in time but how public opinion changes through time. The research cited in the preceding chapters, showing that early attitudes, values, and beliefs form the basis of adult opinion and are difficult to change, would argue that we should not be concerned about changes in public opinion since they would be glacially slow and of minimal proportion. Public opinion is not immutable, however; on topics about which people have no opinions, opinions can be formed, and where people hold their opinions weakly, those opinions are liable to change. One of the first findings from the voting studies was that very few people totally changed their preference from one presidential candidate to another during the course of a political campaign.[37] At best the campaign served to move a small proportion from support for one candidate to the point where they were undecided between the two or from a position of undecision to that of support for a candidate.

We can thus talk about the distribution of public opinion at one point in time and the potential for change in that distribu-

---

[37]Paul E. Lazarfeld, Bernard Berelson, and Helen Gaudet, *The People's Choice* (New York: Columbia University Press, 1948).

tion over time. The latter quality of public opinion—its potential for change—I will call *fluidity*.[38] To measure fluidity it is necessary to know the number of people who hold an opinion on an issue and the strength with which those opinions are held. Situations where relatively few people hold opinions and hold them with little conviction (Figure 5-1) would have a highly fluid public opinion, a high potential for change as more people begin to hold opinions and those already holding opinions begin to strengthen them.

FIGURE 5–1　　　　　　　　**FIGURE 5–2**

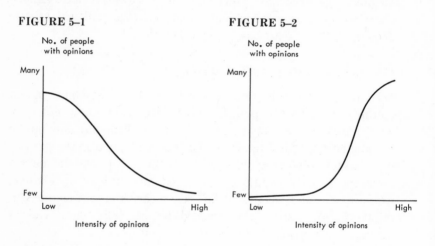

Figure 5-1 illustrates the distribution of opinion on an issue, such as international control of deep sea fishing, of which the general public is unaware or unconcerned. Their response is loose and unclear, more a "mood" than a clear-cut response to the issue.

A characteristic response to questions of foreign policy is one of indifference. A foreign policy crisis, short of the immediate threat of war, may transform indifference to vague apprehension, to fatalism, to anger; but the reaction is still a mood, a superficial and fluctuating response.[39]

---

[38]The concept of fluidity differs from V.O. Key's concept of viscosity, since the latter refers to the amount of, rather than the potential for, change in the distribution of public opinion. See *Public Opinion and American Democracy* (New York: Knopf, 1951), pp. 234-42.

[39]Gabriel Almond, *The American People and Foreign Policy*.

Using Almond's definition of mood one would say that public opinion on foreign policy questions tends to be highly fluid, with relatively few people holding opinions without much feeling. If foreign policy questions do become salient for the American public, that mood can crystallize into firmly and widely held public opinion. Americans have historically been slow to reach consensus on entering a war, but once war has been declared the public rallies behind their nation, creating a situation of low public opinion fluidity (Figure 5-2) where large numbers of people hold opinions strongly, with very little potential for the creation of or change in opinion. When public opinion crystallizes it does not have to form a consensus around only one alternative. Public opinion on the war in Vietnam, for example, has crystallized into support for a wide range of policy alternatives, from complete withdrawal to a full-scale U.S. military intervention short of nuclear war.[40]

The fluidity of public opinion about an issue will vary from issue to issue and depend on the salience of the issue for the public. When the issue is new and unfamiliar very few people will have opinions and even fewer will hold their opinions strongly. As the issue becomes more salient for more people opinions begin to form and more people become committed to taking a position on the issue. At its height the issue will find everyone holding some opinions on it with some intensity. To say that everyone will hold an opinion does not imply that there will be unanimity in their opinions. Dahl, for example, suggests that where people have opinions on issues, they can be classified into four categories:

1. Strong consensus with strong preferences. Most people prefer one policy alternative and they do so with some intensity of feeling.
2. Strong consensus with weak preferences. Most people prefer one policy alternative, but they do not feel strongly about it.
3. Opinions about equally divided on policy alternative with no strong preferences.

---

[40]Sidney Verba *et al*, "Public Opinion and the War in Vietnam," *American Political Science Review* 61 (June, 1967), pp. 317-33.

4. Opinions about equally divided with those favoring one alternative or the other holding strong preferences.[41]

Categories number one and four are cases of low fluidity; the population is committed to one or more alternatives and opinions are strongly held. Categories two and three are very fluid, with people not holding strong preferences even when they favor one position or another. Under those circumstances public opinion can still crystallize—it can still change or be changed. Category four, as Dahl so aptly notes, is where the people are divided against one another with everyone holding strong opinions which pose dangers for democratic stability, a distribution reminiscent of that regarding slavery prior to the Civil War.

Most public issues do not divide the population as slavery did the American population of the 1850s. Public opinion tends to crystallize around one of the policy alternatives and after the issue has been resolved public opinion tends to become supportive of the solution, creating a "halo effect" for successful solutions to difficult problems. Successfully resolved, an issue tends to be less salient for the public so that, although they support the solution to the problem, they no longer feel as strongly about the problem. Medical care for the aged was a controversial issue during the later 1940s and 1950s, but once the problem had been resolved by federal Medicaid legislation in the 1960s medical care for the aged became far less salient as an issue for the American public.

The salience of issues

Because the political environment is complex, people must decide which issues are the most important for them and to which they will pay the most attention. For that reason we can talk about the salience of issues for the American public in terms of which issues are salient and for what proportion of the public.

---

[41]Robert A. Dahl, *A Preface to Democratic Theory* (Chicago: University of Chicago Press, 1956), pp. 90-119.

It is Lippmann's contention in *Public Opinion* that people are more likely to be concerned about and have rational opinions about issues which they can see and have experienced than about those which are beyond their experience or perception.[42]

There is evidence, for example, that people do not necessarily have consistent attitudes toward domestic and foreign policy issues and that there is greater consistency within the set of attitudes toward domestic issues than within the foreign policy set.[43] Those issues with which the American public is most familiar are those they are most likely to have opinions about. Foreign policy issues, being further away in time and space, find it harder to penetrate our perceptual screens to become salient.

> For example, a study conducted by the Survey Research Center of the University of Michigan for the Council of Foreign Relations in the late spring of 1964 showed that one-fourth of the American people were not even aware that mainland China was ruled by a Communist government. The same study revealed that, as of then, about one-fourth of those interviewed had not heard anything about the fighting in Vietnam.[44]

Increased U.S. involvement in Southeast Asia and the media coverage of that involvement have made it the most salient issue for many Americans. A survey of Gallup polls over the past five years finds that the war in Vietnam has been seen by the American public as the most important problem facing the country. Although Vietnam has remained salient throughout the period, other foreign policy issues have declined in importance; the threat of war, the spread of world Communism, and our prestige abroad—important issues in 1965—had diminished in importance by 1970, to be replaced by crime and lawlessness, poverty, and college demonstrations as salient issues. The increase in the salience of domestic issues during this period, even though Vietnam remains a predominant

---

[42]Walter Lippmann, *Public Opinion* (New York: Macmillan, 1960 ed.).
[43]See Converse, op. cit.
[44]Gabriel Almond, pp. xi-xxx.

foreign policy issue, may be the result of several factors.

Key argues that foreign policy questions become salient when the country enjoys a period of economic plenty and the number of domestic issues is limited; with "a full chicken in every pot" and two cars in every garage, the public can turn its attention to the international arena. When serious domestic issues develop and become salient they force public opinion "toward withdrawal into our national shell."[45] The emergence of national or international issues into public consciousness is not due to chance. One of the goals of participants in the political system is to structure which issues will be considered when by public decision makers. Much of the political effort in the political system is devoted to making some issues more or less salient for both the public and public officials. One of the primary functions of a political campaign is to make the right issues salient for the right segments of the population in order to build a winning electoral coalition.

A second factor would be that as foreign policy questions occur more frequently—the Dominican Republic crisis is replaced by one in the Middle East to be replaced by one in Cambodia—or as foreign policy issues persist through time, the public becomes anesthetized to them, accepting them as givens of the political environment. As the international environment becomes heavily politicized the public becomes aware of it, but it is an awareness with little knowledge or understanding of how to resolve the issues involved. For this reason foreign policy issues, particularly if they are dramatic or traumatic, engage the attention of the public but little more. What can John Q. Citizen do about the Arab-Israeli conflict? School bussing may be less important but is is an issue where, if he does have an opinion, he can express it and hope to have some effect.

The stratification of opinion

From the foregoing discussion it should be clear that some people have some opinions on some issues some of the time.

---

[45]V.O. Key, Jr., *Public Opinion and American Democracy* (New York: Knopf, 1961), p. 163.

Most people, if they have opinions, are concerned about a narrow range of issues which are of personal interest to them; only a small segment of the population is interested in and have opinions on a wide range of issues all of the time.

The variable distribution of opinions within the political system has led Rosenau to classify the opinion-holding public into three groups: the mass public, the attentive public, and the opinion makers.[46] The bulk of the public on an issue are members of the mass public—they have neither the opportunity nor the inclination to participate in the policy-making process. They are uninformed, disinterested, and without structured opinions.

As a passive mass, in other words, the mass public lies virtually outside the opinion-policy relationship. Its only function is that of setting, through the potentiality of its more active moods, the outer limits within which decision-makers and opinion-makers feel constrained to operate and interact.[47]

Although the mass public does not have opinions on an issue it has the potential for forming opinions. Thus, the constitution of the mass public depends on the salience of the issue for the public and the stage of the policy-making process. For example, when an issue first comes into public view the numbers involved in the mass public are quite large. As the issue develops, debate ensues, and as policy makers begin to consider the issue, the members of the mass public begin to form opinions on the issue.

The attentive public are informed, interested, and have structured opinions, but do not have access to the policy-making process. Concerned and attentive, but lacking access, they serve as the audience for the opinion makers. "If the latter 'mass public' sets the outer limits beyond which the policy choices cannot be made, then the former (the attentive public) can be said to determine the inner limits within which the opinion-policy relationship operates."[48] The attentive public are the

---

[46]James M. Rosenau, *Public Opinion and Foreign Policy* (New York: Random House, 1961).

[47]Ibid., p. 36.

[48]Ibid., p. 41.

consumers of public policy, serving to translate that policy to the mass public and providing a sounding-board for opinion makers and governmental policy makers. They force the opinion-policy process to be conducted in public and in specific terms.

Opinion-makers are those people who have opinions and access to the policy-making process which allows them "to transmit, either locally or nationally, opinions about any issue to unknown persons outside of their occupational field or about more than one class of issues to unknown professional colleagues."[49] Opinion makers differ in their geographic (local or national), issue (single or multiple), and occupational (governmental, associational, institutional, or individual) base for their opinion-making power. These are the opinion elite. They have opinions and the positions, prestige, and resources to transmit those opinions to relevant people in the policy-making process. Because of their position and visibility, they are looked to as spokesmen for the mass and attentive publics who lack the access to the policy-making process. ". . . While the mass and attentive publics set the outer and inner limits of the opinion-policy relationship, the opinion-making public determines its structure and content within these limits."[50]

Who are the members of the mass public, the attentive public, and who are the opinion makers? In reviewing the distribution of public opinion on foreign trade, Bauer, Pool, and Dexter found that in the post–World War II period the public was not very concerned about foreign trade as an issue: between 1946 and 1962 only forty to fifty percent of the American public was concerned.[51] Among those for whom trade was an issue there was consistent support for lower tariff levels and the Reciprocal Trade Agreement. It is also possible to differentiate between the mass and attentive publics on the basis of education and economic level. The higher the educational and oc-

---

[49]Ibid., p. 45.

[50]Ibid., p. 72.

[51]Raymond Bauer, Ithiel de Sola Pool, and Lewis Anthony Dexter, *American Business and Public Policy* (New York: Atherton Press, 1963), pp. 80-104.

cupational level the more likely an individual was to be informed about and interested in the tariff question. Equally important, there were differences of opinion between those who constituted the mass and attentive publics. Those who were the least interested in the issue tended to be protectionist while those who had the greatest interest were in favor of reciprocal trade. The opinion makers, characterized in the Bauer, Pool, and Dexter study by their political activity, were the most vigorous adherents of reciprocal trade. As a result:

> The public may be thought of as an iceberg. Visible at the top are the active, the alert, the influential few who are always in the open air of political activity. Invisible below water are the generally apathetic many who appear only on rare occasions, such as in election campaigns, when strong tides of politics expose them. On some issues, and trade is one, distribution of attitudes at the top and bottom of the iceberg differ. The appearance of public opinion changes when something raises the iceberg higher out of the water.[52]

In order drastically to change the distribution of public opinion the issue must become more salient for more people and a number of people must move from the mass to the attentive public.

We must recognize that there are a number of mass publics, attentive publics, and opinion makers, depending on the number of issues. As a result, the same person might be a member of the mass public on one issue, the attentive public on a second, and an opinion maker on a third. The Assistant Under-Secretary for Latin American Affairs may be an opinion maker for Western Hemisphere foreign policy, a member of the attentive public for Middle Eastern foreign policy, and a member of the mass public on the question of mass rapid transit.

Party identification and voting

Although the American public has difficulty making the linkage between an ideological position and a political party label

---

[52] Ibid., p. 95.

TABLE 5-5.   Distribution of party identification, 1952-1966

	1952	1956	1960	1962	1964	1966
Strong democrat	22%	21%	21%	23%	26%	18%
Weak democrat	25	23	25	23	25	28
Independent democrat	10	7	8	8	9	9
Independent	5	9	8	8	8	12
Independent republican	7	8	7	6	6	7
Weak republican	14	14	13	16	13	15
Strong republican	13	15	14	12	11	10
Apolitical	4	3	4	4	2	1

Source: The data were collected in October of each year by the Survey Research Center at the University of Michigan and reported in John H. Kessel, *The Goldwater Coalition* (New York: Bobbs-Merrill, 1968), pp. 302 and 307.

it is important to remember that political party label, regardless of the ideology (or lack thereof) behind it, is one of the major determinants in any given election of how a person will vote, interacting with the voter's perception of the candidates and issues involved in that election.[53] Since a party label is one of the first and most enduring things a child learns from his parents it is not surprising that the party identification in the electorate has been remarkably stable over the past twenty years, with approximately forty-five percent of the population identifying themselves as Democrats, thirty percent as Republicans, twenty percent as Independents, and the remainder being apolitical (Table 5-5). With the exception of 1964, when the percentage of Democratic party identifiers climbed to fifty-one percent, there has been little variation from one election year to the next. Even when we compare the congressional election years of 1962 and 1966 with the presidential election years there is little difference. Why did the Republicans win the presidency in 1952 and 1956 and barely lose it in 1960?

Analysis of survey research data from the 1952 and 1956

[53]Angus Campbell et al, *The American Voter* (New York: John Wiley, 1960). Party identification is measured by asking people in interview situations which party they identify with, and how strongly. Independents are asked if they lean toward the Republican or Democratic party and, if they do, they are labeled as Independent Republicans or Democrats.

elections indicates the stronger one's party identification the more likely he is to be interested in the campaign, be concerned over the outcome, and to vote. Campbell et al. found:

> Independents tend as a group to be somewhat less involved in politics. They have somewhat poorer knowledge of the issues, their image of the candidates is fainter, their interest in the campaign is less, their concern over the outcome is relatively slight, and their choice between competing candidates, although it is indeed made later in the campaign, seems much less to spring from discoverable evaluations of the elements of national politics.[54]

Flanigan, analyzing the same data, concludes that while Independents may be less interested in the more partisan dimensions of politics, this does not mean that they are not well informed or capable of making reasonable choices.[55] During the period 1952-1964 Independents have tended to vote for the winning presidential candidate in every election except 1960. Whether Independents are informed or not, the point to be stressed is that they are mobile in their voting patterns, especially important in elections where partisanship is an important influence in voting behavior.

A careful examination of the data in Table 5-5 can give some interesting insights into American electoral politics. It is clear, for example, that if presidential elections were waged solely on the basis of appeals to party identification the Republicans would stand scant chance of success. In that type of election the Democrats would merely have to retain those people who identify themselves, however strongly, as Democrats. The Republicans cannot wage a campaign based on partisan appeals since they must hold Republican party identifiers and appeal to Independents and even weak and Independent Democratic party identifiers. It is not surprising to find that presidential campaigns are waged in which the Democrats emphasize heavily the party label of the candidate while the Republicans argue, "Vote the man, not the party."

---

[54]Ibid., p. 143.
[55]William Flanigan, *Political Behavior of the American Electorate* (Boston, Allyn & Bacon, 1972 ed.).

The success of the Republicans in 1952 and 1956 can be attributed to the voting behavior of Independents and the defection of weak Democrats, whose party identification was weak enough to allow them to vote for an attractive Republican candidate who took stands on issues which they felt were important. At the same time Republican partisans were intensely loyal to their party's candidate—over ninety percent of those identifying themselves with one party or the other in 1952 and 1956 voted for the candidate of their party; Eisenhower's victories are accounted for by the defection of a higher proportion of Democrats to Eisenhower than Republicans to Stevenson. The 1964 landslide for Johnson is accounted for by the higher-than-average defection of Republicans to vote for Johnson, and a preponderance of Independents who voted for Johnson.

The process of the campaign can make one or the other variable more salient for the electorate as it seeks to make up its mind. Analysis of Gallup poll data for the 1968 presidential election campaign indicates that Nixon's campaign, from mid-August until election day, served to stabilize and solidify his support among Republican partisans. Humphrey's support among Democrats declined precipitously prior to the Democratic convention but became stronger as the campaign progressed. The effect of Humphrey's campaign was to remind Democrats of their party identification and to swing Democratic voters for Wallace back to Humphrey. Among Independents, a similar phenomenon occurred. Although Nixon's percentage of the Independent vote remained remarkably stable from August until November the post-convention campaign served to increase Humphrey's and decrease Wallace's support among Independents. Humphrey was thus able to reduce and almost eliminate the vote difference between himself and Nixon by siphoning Democrat and Independent support away from Wallace.

This analysis does not imply that party identification is the only variable that was important for the 1968 election. The 1968 campaign does serve to remind us of the fluidity of public opinion in a political campaign, particularly among those whose attachment to candidate or party is weak. Although over eighty percent of the electorate may identify with and vote for their party's candidate that still leaves a substantial proportion of the electorate to be moved to make a decision by the political campaign.

Summary

From the preceding discussion it seems clear that Americans are, and have been, highly supportive of the American political system and the basic principles which underly its creation and operation. This high degree of consensus gives remarkable stability to the system and prevents sudden changes in the structure and operation of the system. Stability makes the American political system attractive for those who work within it—they need not worry about an instantaneous revolution because one candidate rather than another has won the presidency. That same stability is infuriating to those who wish to reform or revolutionize the political system and cannot understand the lack of positive response from the bulk of the citizenry. As I shall point out in the last chapter, however, failure to heed those seeking change, regardless of how few in number, can be dangerous.

While Americans may agree on what the political system is and how it should operate they are not very well informed or highly opinionated. On most issues the mass public consists of the vast bulk of the population while the attentive public consists of a very small, select set of people. At the same time those people who do hold opinions on issues do not necessarily hold ideologically consistant opinions. As a result politics in the United States lacks much of the ideological flavor and fervor that one finds in other parts of the world. This is not to say that Americans cannot hold strong and consistent opinions; instead, on many issues public opinion is very fluid. When an issue first arises there is often great potential for the creation of new opinions. After the issue has been in the public eye for some time opinions harden and public opinion is substantially less fluid. Questions such as party identification are thus quite firm while opinions on questions like the siting of nuclear power plants may be far more fluid.

CHAPTER SIX

Opinion articulation and aggregation

Knowing that people in the political system have opinions is of little use unless we understand how public opinion, of the great mass or of the elite few, is transmitted to policy makers. Given the distribution of public opinion on a salient issue, how is that opinion expressed to the policy maker? What are the linkages between the people and their government which allow them to communicate with one another? Are some means of communicating public opinion "better" or more effective than others? The primary concern of this chapter will be with what some theorists have labelled as "interest articulation" and "interest aggregation" functions for the political system, i.e., the ways in which opinions are publicly stated and combined into support for alternative policy proposals.[1] In focusing on these two processes we shall focus on three dimensions: the *structures* which serve as vehicles to gather and express public opinion, the *channels* which serve as the transmitters of public opinion, and the *style* or manner in which opinions are communicated.

The styles of opinion aggregation and articulation

In order to understand the procedure by which opinions are fed into the policy-making process we must recognize that we

---

[1] See Gabriel Almond and G. Bingham Powell, *Comparative Politics* (Boston, Mass.: Little, Brown & Co., 1966).

are talking about a *communication* process. The choice of structures and channels will be predicated on an understanding of the communication process which will determine the style of communications by any structure through any channel. For public opinion to have any impact the decision maker must be listening; if he is listening he must be able to hear and understand what public opinion is saying to him. The style of opinion aggregation and articulation thus play a major role in determining whether he can or will hear and understand what public opinion is saying.

Communication theorists tell us that there are a number of variables which determine the efficacy of a communication process.[2] Communication is initially dependent upon the ability of the communicator accurately to translate his message into something which is intelligible to another person. To the extent that the sender and receiver (the lobbyist and the legislator, respectively) have a common lexicon the communication process can proceed effectively. But if the one says "pigs," meaning policemen, and the other hears "pigs," meaning a fat farm animal which produces ham, communication cannot occur. To the extent that the people in a communication process share a common culture they also share a common lexicon. For that reason it is not surprising that lobbyists and legislators have many of the same background characteristics, and belong to the same clubs, play golf on the same courses, and attend the same operas.[3] The easier it is for men to communicate with one another the more likely they are to do so. One of the first requirements of an effective opinion articulation style is that the articulator share a common language with his communicants.

Opinion must be transmitted with sufficient strength to be

---

[2]Two of the better statements of this communication theory are found in Claude E. Shannon and Warren Weaver, *The Mathematical Theory of Communication* (Urbana, Ill.: University of Illinois Press, 1964), pp. 1-28; and Melvin DeFleur, *Theories of Mass Communication* (New York: McKay, 1970 ed.)

[3]Lester Milbrath, *The Washington Lobbyists* (Chicago, Ill.: Rand-McNally, 1963); and Harmon Zeigler and Michael Baer, *Lobbying* (Belmont, Calif.: Wadsworth, 1969).

heard and understood; a whisper will not do when a shout is required. In some circumstances a quiet presentation of the case will be sufficient. Wahlke et al. say that the legislator's orientation toward lobbyists end pressure groups will determine how loud the message must be in order to be heard.[4] The "facilitator"—who feels that lobbyists have an important role in the legislative process—will be more responsive to the opinions which lobbyists present; the "resistor," on the other hand, may not listen under any circumstances even when the opinion is expressed through the ballot box. The required strength of the message is also a function of the channel which is being used and the number of other people using that channel at the same time. A lobbyist trying to communicate with a policy maker at a crowded cocktail party when others are talking to him runs the risk of not being heard; it is the wrong channel and there may be no way of making the message strong enough in that channel to get him to listen. The fewer the number of people using the channel and the more appropriate the channel for communicating, the softer the message can be.

At the same time the transmitter must be perceived as a relevant source of information by the receiver. Dr. Benjamin Spock may be universally recognized as "baby doctor" for the nation but a number of people do not give credence to his opinions on American foreign policy. An experiment conducted by Hovland and Weiss investigated the credibility of various sources of information on topics read to college students.[5] On the question of selling antihistamine drugs without a prescription the *New England Journal of Biology and Medicine* was perceived as more credible than a mass circulation pictorial magazine; Robert J. Oppenheimer was more credible than *Pravda* on the possibility of building a nuclear submarine; the *Bulletin of National Resources Planning Board* was more credible than an

---

[4]John Wahlke et al., *The Legislative System* (John Wiley & Sons, Inc., 1962), pp. 311-42.

[5]C.I. Hovland and W. Weiss, "The influence of Source Credibility on Communication Effectiveness," *Public Opinion Quarterly* 15 (1951), pp. 635-50.

antilabor, anti–New Deal, "rightist" newspaper columnist on whether the steel industry is to blame for a steel shortage; and *Fortune* was more credible than a woman movie-gossip columnist on whether there would be a decrease in the number of movie theaters. Not only were some sources more credible than others, but source credibility was also related to perceived trustworthiness and subsequent attitude change. Credible sources were perceived as being trustworthy and influential in changing attitudes. We should not overlook the fact that source credibility is a matter of specialization. Although Hovland and Weiss did not investigate the matter, it is doubtful that Robert J. Oppenheimer, who was perceived as credible and trustworthy on the question of constructing nuclear submarines, would carry any credence whatsoever on the question of whether there will be fewer movie theaters. Katz and Eldersveld have found that source credibility and influence is segmental; women who are influential in determining community fashions are not influential in voting decisions.[6] In much the same way both Francis and Best have found that legislative influence is only marginally transferable from one policy area to another.[7] Not only must the transmitter have the capacity but he must also be perceived as legitimate by the receiver.

Regardless of what the sender does, the receiver must be willing and able to engage in the communication act before the communication process can exist. A television show without an audience, a newspaper without readers, and a radio broadcast without listeners is not communicating. The secret of the communication process is in the sender's ability to get the receiver to listen to what is being said. To do so requires that the receiver perceive the message as being worth listening to and at a price that he can afford. The process is made all the more difficult by the number of messages which are sent over a variety of

---

[6]Elihu Katz and Samuel Eldersveld, *Personal Influence* (Glencoe, Ill.: The Free Press; 1955).

[7]Wayne L. Francis, "Influence and Intervention in a State Legislative Body," *American Political Science Review* 56 (December, 1962), pp. 953-60; and James J. Best, "Influence in the Washington House of Representatives," *Midwest Journal of Political Science* 14 (September, 1971), pp. 27-48.

channels to the receiver. Why should a legislator listen to one lobbyist as opposed to another, read one newspaper rather than another?

Governmental decision makers listen to those people whom they think will provide them with information which they want or with which they agree. Milbrath lists a number of elements which contribute to effective communication between lobbyists and legislators, elements which are common to all communications of public opinion. The communicator should be pleasant and nonoffensive; the communication process should not be a costly one for the policy maker. The policy maker must be convinced that it is important for him to listen, not only to cut his cost but to show him positive benefit from listening. The communicator should be well prepared and informed, regardless of whom he is communicating with in what way. Policy makers are willing to listen to people from whom they feel they can learn something. When using public opinion in attempting to influence public policy the communicator must be convinced of the position he is espousing and the people he represents. Perhaps most important, the message communicated must be concise, well organized, and clear if it is to have a desired impact. If the policy maker must decipher what he has heard, organize it for his own purposes, and then decide what to do with the information, he is not very likely to want to listen.

Structures

Two institutions have traditionally assumed primary responsibility for communicating public opinion from the public to governmental decision makers—political parties and pressure groups. V.O. Key states unequivocally that political parties "perform the function of the articulation of the interests and aspirations of substantial segments of the citizenry, usually in ways contended to be promotive of the public weal" while pressure groups "perform a representative function by communicating the wishes of their members to public authorities."[8]

---

[8]V. O. Key, Jr., *Politics, Parties and Pressure Groups*, (5th ed., New York: Thomas Y. Crowell, 1964), pp. 9, 11.

Sorauf takes a broader view:

> These political organizations ... stand athwart complex
> political systems as intermediaries between the millions of
> political individuals and the distant seats of governmental
> authority. They bring together into large and powerful
> aggregates the many individuals whose political influence is
> miniscule and insignificant when it stands alone. By at-
> taching the loyalty of individuals to sets of interests, pro-
> grams, symbols, and leaders, the organizations establish
> powerful political aggregates and bring them to bear on the
> selection of policy-makers and on the process of policy-
> making. By working between the political individual and the
> policy-making machinery of government, they aggregate po-
> litical influence as it moves from individual to government,
> they codify and simplify information about government and
> politics as it moves back to the individual. Political organiza-
> tions are the informal agents of representation in the
> complex and enormous representative democracies of our
> time. In a practical way they permit the individual and small
> groups to participate in the selection of their representatives
> and in the formation of the decisions of a usually remote gov-
> ernment. They are in the broadest sense both the builders
> and agents of majorities.[9]

It is clear that political parties and pressure groups serve as
intermediaries between the citizenry and their government,
serving to explain the actions of government to the people and
to communicate the wishes and desires of the populace to relevant government officials. Serving as intermediaries, as
Kornhauser notes, political parties and pressure groups
prevent the public from imposing their will directly and
abruptly on the institutions of government and, at the same
time, prevent the institutions of government from manipula-
ting the public to meet the government's ends.[10] In the process
of acting as intermediaries political parties and pressure
groups seek to define public opinion on issues of interest to
them and to serve as the vehicles of communicating those
opinions to others within the political system.

---

[9]Frank J. Sorauf, *Party Politics in America* (Boston: Little, Brown and
Co., 1968), p. 3.
[10]William Kornhauser, *The Politics of Mass Society* (Glencoe: Free
Press, 1959).

Political parties

There are a number of ways of defining what constitutes a political party, at least three of which are relevant to our discussion. There is the "party in the electorate"—those members of the voting public who identify themselves with one or the other political party. Second, there is the "party as electoral machine"—the legally recognized entities which seek to gain control of government by electing their members to public office. Third, we have the "party in government"—those elected officials who identify themselves with a political party. Each of these "political parties" plays an important but different role in aggregating and articulating public opinion.

The party in the electorate

The distribution of people who identify with one or the other political party has remained remarkably stable over the past twenty years. As we have seen in Chapter Three, a large proportion of the population (approximately forty percent) consider themselves to be Democrats, a smaller proportion identify themselves as Republicans, and a still smaller segment have no party identification. Who are the people who identify themselves as Democrats and Republicans, members of the party in the electorate?

An analysis of the social backgrounds of partisans indicates that both parties have been very adept at constructing electoral coalitions which have appealed to a broad spectrum of the population. Flanigan concludes that "on most social characteristics Democrats, Republicans, and Independents are very heterogeneous."[11] Nonetheless, the parties do draw differential support from various segments of the population and different parts of the country. Republicans are more likely to be from small towns or medium-sized cities, be Protestant, white, and have white-collar and professional occupations. Conversely,

---

[11]William Flanigan, *Political Behavior of the American Electorate,* (Boston, Mass.: Allyn and Bacon, 1972 ed.), p. 51.

Democrats tend to be from large cities, Catholic, belong to racial or ethnic minorities, and hold blue-collar positions. In a broad sense the higher the person's socioeconomic status the more likely he is to consider himself a Republican.[12] But these are merely modal descriptions of party identifiers.

> There are poor Republicans and wealthy Democrats. There are urban Republicans and small-town Democrats; manual laborers are Republicans; doctors and lawyers are Democrats. There are Catholic Republicans, Southern Republicans, just as there are well-educated Democrats, Midwestern Democrats, and Protestant Democrats.[13]

To the extent that a voter has a consistent set of demographic characteristics he is more likely to identify with a political party, vote a straight party ticket, be interested in and informed about politics, and know how he is going to vote. (See Table 6-1.) This is true of partisans in both parties.

TABLE 6-1. Relation of strength of party identification to interest in campaign, 1956

	Strong party identifiers	Weak party identifiers	Independents
Very much interested	42%	23%	25%
Somewhat interested	38	42	43
Not much interested	20	35	32
	100%	100%	100%
N =	(624)	(651)	(415)

Source: Campbell et al, *The American Voter*, p. 144.

Independents, contrary to popular mythology.

> . . . tend as a group to be somewhat less involved in politics. They have somewhat poorer knowledge of the issues, their image of the candidates is fainter, their interest in the campaign is less, their concern over the outcome is relatively slight, and their choice between competing candidates, although it is made later in the campaign, seems much less to

---

[12]See Angus Campbell et. al., *The American Voter* (New York: John Wiley & Sons, Inc., 1960).

[13]Flanigan, op. cit., pp. 51-52.

spring from discoverable evaluations of the elements of national politics.[14]

The stronger the party identification the more likely that a person will vote in a partisan election and that he will vote for his party's candidate. The strong party identifiers constitute what Shadegg calls "yellow dog" Democrats and Republicans —they would vote for yellow dog if it were their party's nominee for office.[15] It is these strong party identifiers who form the hard core of the party in the electorate, always supporting their party's candidates and always voting. But elections are not decided by the hard-core party faithful; although they constitute a substantial portion of the electorate their constancy means that any given election is won by a coalition of party identifiers and "others."

Given the distribution of party identifiers in the United States, it is clear that Republican presidential candidates would have a difficult time winning if people voted only on the basis of the candidate's party. The Democratic campaign strategy would be to get their partisans to the polls and to appeal to some of the Independents. The Republicans, in addition to maintaining their partisans in the fold, would have to appeal to Independents and some Democrats. According to Kessel, Johnson's strategy in 1964 was aimed at holding together the traditional Democratic coalition of Westerners, Southerners, blacks, and urbanites, together with whatever moderate Republicans could be convinced to vote for him. Goldwater's strategy, on the other hand, was to lure party loyalists, conservative ideologues, foreign policy hard-liners, and Southerners into a common cause.[16] As a result, the two parties must wage different types of campaigns in order to appeal to their different parties in the electorate. The political necessity that the two parties and their candidates talk at and past one another in order to appeal to different segments of the electorate is one

---

[14]Campbell et al., op. cit., p. 143.

[15]Stephen Shadegg, *How to Win An Election* (New York: Taplinger, 1964).

[16]John H. Kessel, *The Goldwater Coalition* (New York: Bobbs-Merrill, 1968).

that many people find so annoying about American politics. The candidates never seem to talk to one another or talk to the electorate about the same thing!

The stability of party identification in the American electorate is by no means permanent. Key has suggested that the United States has seen a series of "critical elections" in 1800, 1828, 1860, 1896, and 1932 which marked basic shifts in the political orientations of the American electorate.[17] As Burnham so succinctly identifies them,

> . . . eras of critical realignment are marked by short, sharp reorganizations of the mass coalitional bases of the major parties which occur at periodic intervals on the national level; are often preceded by major third-party revolts which reveal the incapacity of "politics as usual" to integrate, much less aggregate, emergent political demand; are closely associated with abnormal stress in the socioeconomic system; are marked by ideological polarizations and issue-distances between the major parties which are exceptionally large by normal standards; and have durable consequences as constituent acts which determine the outer boundaries of policy in general, though not necessarily of policies in detail.[18]

One of the major impacts of the realignment of the Democratic party after 1932 was the inclusion of large numbers of Catholics and blacks who had earlier been heavily supportive of the national Republican party. The campaign of William Jennings Bryan in 1896 polarized the electorate by forming a Democratic party of farmers and the urban poor behind a Populist program of opposition to big business interests.

Several recent works have argued over whether the 1968 election marked another critical election in American politics. Phillips suggests that there is a thirty-six year periodicity in American politics, which means that 1968 is the election in which the next critical election should have occurred. He also argues that the coalitional base of Nixon's 1968 victory signalled the end of the New Deal Democratic coalition.

---

[17]V. O. Key, Jr., "A Theory of Critical Elections," *Journal of Politics* 17 (1955), pp. 3-18.

[18]Walter Dean Burnham, *Critical Elections and the Mainsprings of American Politics* (New York: Norton, 1970), p. 10.

. . . Today, the interrelated Negro, suburban and Sun Belt migrations have all but destroyed the old New Deal Coalition. . . . Some Northern cities are nearly half Negro, and new suburbia is turning into a bastion of white conservatism; moreover, growing Northern-based Negro political influence has prompted not only civil rights measures obnoxious to the South but social legislation and programs anathema to the sons and daughters of Northern immigrants. As in the past, changing population patterns have set the scene for a new political alignment.[19]

According to Phillips, the future coalitional base of the Republican Party will be geographically found in the rural Midwest and West, the South (including Florida and Texas), and California, while the Democratic Party will be based in the Northeast and the Pacific Northwest. One of the by-products of this geographical realignment of the party in the electorate will be a growing ideological homogeneity, speaking for a new Republican electorate agreed on the principles that there should be "a shift away from the sociological jurisprudence, moral permissiveness, experimental residential, welfare and educational programming and massive federal spending. . . ."[20] Scammon and Wattenberg, looking at the 1968 election, see it as a useful "deviating" election which will force both political parties once again to reconsider and consolidate their party in the electorate as broad-based social and ideological coalitions. The strategy of the 1970s should not be to construct a new conservative or liberal coalition but to recognize the centrist ideological thrust of American politics and to "Hold where you are strong; beef up where you are weak."[21] They suggest that the fact that city dwellers are moving to the suburbs does not necessarily mean they are becoming Republicans at the city line. A more important criticism of the Phillips thesis is that it is unprovable until several subsequent presidential elections have occurred. You can't tell a critical election until you see whether

---

[19]Kevin Phillips, *The Emerging Republican Majority* (New York: Anchor Books, 1970), p. 39.

[20]Ibid., p. 471.

[21]Richard M. Scammon and Ben J. Wattenberg, *The Real Majority* (New York: Coward, McCann, and Geoghegan, 1970), p. 293.

the changes remain through time. A casual examination of the 1964 presidential election would lead you to think that it was a critical election since so many Republicans had voted for Johnson and there had been a shift in the proportion of the population which considered itself Republican. But the Congressional elections of 1966 and the presidential election of 1968 showed that many of the Republican defectors in 1964 returned to vote for Republican candidates after that election. The debate between Phillips and Scammon and Wattenberg is, as of this time, unresolved and unresolvable. Clues may be forthcoming from the 1972 and 1976 elections.

The party in the electorate is thus comprised of those people who consider themselves members of the party as well as those who form an electoral coalition for any particular election. Although election outcomes represent an expression of public opinion it is unclear what the party in the electorate says when it speaks. If the electoral party were composed solely of those who identify with one or the other party or who, as Phillips suggests, agree ideologically, then elections results might have some meaning for public officials. But the task of building an electoral majority requires that both parties appeal to members of the opposition party, to those of different ideological persuasions, and to those who are different in age, sex, income, education, occupation and religion. And what does that sort of coalition "say"?

Although the electorate may have mixed motives for their voting behavior, the candidates for public office see the election results as being a clear-cut expression of public opinion, with the winner seeing the results as a "mandate" from the electorate, who endorsed his campaign proposals or the party platform. The candidates feel that the electorate has been given a choice between different candidates who represent different positions on issues and the electorate has chosen the candidate with whom they most agree.[22] We have the dilemma of an elected public official imputing judgments to the electorate

---

[22]John W. Kingdon, *Candidates for Office* (New York: Random House, 1966).

which may be wrong. Thus, the candidate who is the recipient of a vote against his opponent may wrongly conclude that the electorate wholeheartedly endorses his position on issues which he felt were important.[23] The election may serve as a statement of public opinion, but the candidates and their party organizations may not be able to interpret the results correctly.

The party as electoral machine

When we think of political parties we most frequently think of them in their electoral function—running candidates for office, drafting platforms, and mobilizing the electorate. All these functions are merely necessary prerequisites for the party's primary concern—to win control of the government by nominating candidates and building electoral coalitions behind them. Does the political party, in serving as an electoral machine, act to aggregate and articulate public opinion?

Before the political party can win elections and gain control of government it must first nominate candidates. To what extent are the party nominees a faithful reflection of the opinions of their constituents? Downs argues that if a party wishes to win elections it must match the ideologies of its candidates with those of their constituents; to the extent that they deviate from the norm they are subject to defeat.[24] Evidence by Sorauf and Eldersveld indicates that such is the case.[25]

Winning candidates also have backgrounds similar to those of their constituents. As Sorauf discovered, winning candidates are the success stories of their districts.[26] If a district is heavily Irish-Catholic there is little question that the State Representative or Senator from that district will probably be Irish-Catholic—an Irish-Catholic lawyer, doctor, or busi-

---

[23]See Murray Levin, *The Alienated Voter* (New York: Holt, Rhinehart and Winston, 1960).

[24]Anthony Downs, *An Economic Theory of Democracy* (New York: Harper, 1957).

[25]Frank J. Sorauf, *Party and Representation* (New York: Atherton, 1963); and Eldersveld, *Political Parties: A Behavioral Analysis* (Chicago: Rand-McNally, 1964).

[26]Sorauf, *Party and Representation*.

nessman. Party nominees deviate from the demographic norms of their district most frequently in those districts where the party is not competitive, where there is a need for a "sacrificial" candidate. Faced with little chance of sucess the minority party has obvious difficulty encouraging candidates to run, and those whom they do encourage are unlike the constituents they seek to represent. If, by some quirk of fate, the candidate is elected, Barber finds that he is often reluctant to run for office again.[27] When Vermont Democrats elected their slate of statewide candidates in 1964 (only the third time in over a century that a Democratic candidate had won statewide office) the party organization was so surprised that they telephoned all recently elected candidates to ask if they would serve.

The fact that elected officials must share some common background with their constituents in order to be elected insures that the office holders will, perhaps unconsciously, share some political opinions in common with their constituents. At a bare minimum the official and his constituents will speak the same language and have shared somewhat common life experiences. To the extent that there will be congruence, the officeholder will rarely find himself having to resolve the dilemma of deciding whether to vote the way his constituents want or to vote his own conscience—there may be no appreciable difference.[28] In choosing candidates who reflect the characteristics of the district the political parties may pay a price. Once elected the candidate may realize that his greater obligation is to his constituents rather than to the party under whose banner he ran.

In addition to attracting candidates to run for public office, political parties also play the important role of identifying with a party label, giving the party in the electorate cues on whom to vote for. The act of nomination, an important act for party as electoral machine, serves to delimit the range of choices open to the voter on election day and to provide an effective device for

[27]James Barber, *The Lawmakers* (New Haven, Conn.: Yale University Press, 1965).
[28]Warren Miller and Donald Stokes, "Constituency Influence in Congress," *American Political Science Review* 57 (1963), pp. 45-56.

choosing between the candidates. Once the party label has been affixed, the voters can attribute to the candidate a whole series of qualities. A Democratic candidate, by definition and regardless of office, favors expansion of the government's role in the economy and supportive of labor unions and minorities. Campbell et al. suggest that,

> Merely associating the party symbol with his (the presidential candidate's) name encourages those identifying with the party to develop a more favorable image of his record and experience, his abilities, and his other personal attributes. Likewise, this association encourages supporters of the opposite party to take a less favorable view of these same personal attributes.[29]

For local nonpartisan elections we would therefore expect that the electorate would have a more difficult time differentiating between candidates and, as a result, turnout would be lower. Lee's study of local elections in California found this to be the case.[30] In addition, "surrogate" parties develop to fulfill the labelling function of political parties. These surrogates can range from the regular party organizations working under nonpartisan labels, such as the Conservative or Liberal Parties, to unofficial and ad hoc organizations which rate the candidates. Regardless of what they are called, these entities all seek to provide the electorate with cues on how to vote on election day.

Political parties also serve to mobilize the party in the electorate. They do so by attracting candidates who have appeal for the electorate and building political platforms which will have the broadest possible appeal. At the same time the party must also put its "foot soldiers" into the field to make the electorate aware of the candidate, convince them of his worth, and get them to the polls.

Writing party platforms or policy statements is not an easy task for party leaders. McClosky's study of liberalism-conservatism among party leaders and voters has shown that party

---

[29]Campbell et al., op. cit., p. 128.
[30]Eugene C. Lee, *The Politics of Nonpartisanship* (Berkeley: University of California Press, 1960).

voters are more ideologically moderate on public issues than the leaders of either party.[31] The policy differences between the two parties are most evident to those who are committed to the parties and who run for political office. Not surprisingly, there are also ideological differences within the political party hierarchies; party leaders are more ideologically committed than party workers who, in turn, are more ideologically committed than party voters.[32] The more important politics is for the individual and the more involved he is, the more likely he is to perceive differences between the policy positions of the parties.

Although there are substantial policy differences between Republican and Democratic party leaders, the need to build winning electoral coalitions makes it difficult for them to write party platforms which express those differences. We thus have the curious anomaly of party leaders writing platforms and nominating candidates more ideologically moderate than they in order to win elections. The Republican platform of 1964 and the nomination of Barry Goldwater provide a constant reminder to both parties that they can neither nominate a candidate nor write a platform which articulates the ideology of the party leaders rather than the voters. For this reason the party platforms are forced to articulate the opinions of major segments of the electorate.

When some segment of the party's ideological spectrum feels it is not being represented in the party or by the party platform, splinter groups break away from the parent party. The Progressive Party in 1912 nominated Teddy Roosevelt after dissident Republicans left the party nominating convention feeling that Roosevelt had not been given a fair chance to gain the nomination. The Dixiecrats and the Progressive Party in 1948 represented splinter groups from the Democratic party. These splinter parties rarely exist beyond a single election; their sole purpose is to make a point with party leaders. To the

---

[31]Herbert McClosky, "Consensus and Ideology in American Politics," *American Political Science Review*, LVIII (1964), pp. 361-82.
[32]Eldersveld, op. cit., pp. 183-219.

extent that they show electoral support they can obtain conces-
sions from the parent party. Strom Thurmond's candidacy in
1948 did not cost the Democrats the presidency, so they did not
feel the need to accede to the Dixiecrat demands for a weaker
civil rights plank. No political party, however, wants to have
members disgruntled and deserting the ranks. Subsequent
Democratic conventions have moved to placate southern Democrats by quashing challenges to delegate selection procedures
used by the regular party organizatons in the South.[33]

A more subtle form of the splinter party is the "counterparty", i.e., the threat of a disappointed candidate to form his
own national political party or to have his followers abstain
from voting for the party's candidate. Anti-Goldwater
Republicans in 1964 and pro-McCarthy Democrats in 1968
followed this strategy. The impact of such a move is difficult to
calculate. Would the Republicans have won the presidency in
1964 if leading Republicans had supported Goldwater? Would
Humphrey have won in 1968 with immediate and enthusiastic
support from McCarthy? The development of counterparty
groups can arise only after the national conventions and among
the losers. In the past, party nominees have attempted to forestall their development by including one or more of the losing
wings within the party campaign organization, often as vice-
presidential candidates. In bitter political contests, however, it
may be difficult to include the opposition, leaving open the possibility of the losers not supporting the party candidate and
thus handing the election to the opposition party's candidate.

The major question concerning splinter or counterparty
parties is whether they represent a sizeable segment of public
opinion within the electorate. The assumption of party regulars
is that these groups speak only in splendid isolation and it is
not until after an election like 1912 that the major party real-
izes that the splinter faction did cost them the election. The
counterparty group is even more difficult to evaluate. Did Mc-
Carthy supporters actually sit at home on election day in 1968,

---

[33]The 1972 Democratic convention was an exception due to the "take-
over" by grassroots party people.

and in sufficient numbers to deny Humphrey the election? Although a sizeable proportion of the electorate supported McCarthy prior to the Democratic convention, did they refuse to leave him after the convention?

When a sizeable segment of the electorate feels that neither party is representing its interests, we often see the development of "social protest" parties, organized groups who seek to solve specific social and economic problems by running candidates for office.[34] Many such parties maintain a curious political half-life, earning enough votes each election to reappear on the ballot in the next election but not enough to win or seriously influence the outcome of elections. As a result it is not unusual to find candidates from the Vegetarian or Temperance Parties on the ballot. In times of major discontent or social dislocation social protest parties have served to focus public discontent on policy issues which were being ignored by the two major parties and served as an electoral vehicle for the expression of that discontent. Burnham describes them in the following terms:

> They constituted attacks by groups who felt they were outsiders against an elite whom they frequently viewed in conspiratorial terms. These attacks were made in the name of democratic-humanistic universals against an established political structure which was perceived to be corrupt, undemocratic, and manipulated by insiders for their and their supporters' benefit.[35]

The social protest parties were composed of those who felt themselves on the periphery of society, whose wants, needs, and opinions were being ignored by a governmental bureaucracy and political party structure which was growing increasingly insensitive. Social protest parties have rarely succeeded in winning public office; when their electoral appeal grows so large that it cannot be ignored, the issues which they espouse are

---

[34]See Solon Buck, *The Agrarian Crusade* (New Haven: Yale University Press, 1920); William B. Hesseltine, *The Rise and Fall of Third Parties* (Washington: Public Affairs Press, 1948); and Howard P. Nash, *Third Parties in American Politics* (Washington: Public Affairs Press, 1959).

[35]Burnham, op. cit., pp. 29-30.

normally adopted by one or both of the two major parties and the electoral base of the social protest party is thereby undercut.

Social protest parties thus serve as useful indicators of public dissatisfaction with the policies and platforms of the two major political parties and the actions of the party in government. In so doing they perform an important safety-valve function for the political system, allowing voters to express their dissatisfaction within the democratic system rather than forcing them to operate outside of it. In the process of growth social protest parties continually serve to redefine the boundaries of a constantly changing American political culture, particularly defining an issue which should be legitimately considered as a policy question. Problems for the political system occur when the major parties fail to heed the warnings of the social protest parties or when the electorate no longer views them as a viable alternative to the major parties. Burnham suggests that the rise of social protest parties is the harbinger of a change in the composition of the two major parties or, as in the case of 1856, is a signal for the emergence of a new major party. There may not be unanimity, however, regarding what the rise of a protest party means. Phillips sees George Wallace as a repudiation of "liberal" political policies and the beginning of the emergence of a Republican majority; Burnham suggests that Wallace may be instrumental in restructuring the Democratic and Republican coalitions but with Wallace having no chance of electoral success; and Scammon and Wattenberg suggest that Wallace has no hope of gaining electoral success and once Wallace fades from the scene his voters will support Democratic candidates.

Political parties also seek to mobilize the electorate by face-to-face contact. The efficacy of using foot soldiers is readily accepted by professional campaign managers and party leaders.[36] Research indicates that doorbelling by party workers can act to increase the party's percentage of the two-party vote in a given

---

[36]Shadegg, op. cit.

electoral unit, particularly in campaigns for national and state-wide office.[37] When party workers canvas voters in heavily partisan districts, the dominant party's percentage of the vote has been higher than might normally have been expected, e.g., if the Republicans traditionally receive 65 percent of the vote in the precinct, doorbelling by Republican workers can raise the Republican percentage of the vote to an unexpected seventy to 75 percent. Doorbelling apparently makes politics increasingly salient for voters in the canvassed district and the minority party voters find very little support for their ideological position or party preference from among their neighbors. Two factors then become operative: increasing the salience of politics means that more people will turn out to vote but the increased salience will also make it more difficult for the minority party members to vote for their party's candidates. As a result, the majority party vote will increase or the minority party vote will fall off, resulting in the majority party receiving a greater share of the two-party vote than they might otherwise expect.

The party as an electoral machine very broadly aggregates and articulates public opinion. In mobilizing voters it serves to make politics salient for the population and to get those who are the most interested and concerned about the outcome of the election to the polls. In order to do this the party must construct an electoral majority by nominating candidates who have appeal for the electorate and constructing a party platform which articulates concerns traditionally of interest to party members and which are of current interest to the electorate in general. The presence or absence of third parties on the electoral scene gives a rough indication of the extent to which

---

[37]See Phillips Cutright and Peter Rossi, "Grass Roots Politicians and the Vote," *American Sociological Review* 23 (1958), pp. 171-79; Daniel Katz and Samuel Eldersveld, "The Impact of Local Party Activity Upon the Electorate," *Public Opinion Quarterly* 25 (Spring, 1961), pp. 1-24; Gerald H. Kramer, "The Effects of Precinct-Level Canvassing on Voter Behavior," *Public Opinion Quarterly* 34 (Winter, 1970-71), pp. 560-73; and John C. Blydenburgh, "A Controlled Experiment to Measure the Effects of Personal Contact Campaigning," *Midwest Journal of Political Science* 15 (May, 1971), pp. 365-81.

the two major parties have adequately served as channels for the electorate's policy preferences. Election results thus represent a statement of public opinion only in very broad terms; to the extent that the two major parties receive the vast bulk of the vote they know they are stressing issues which the electorate feels are important and, in that sense, the election outcome represents a partial endorsement of the party's candidate and the party platform. Regardless of whether the vote is a clearcut statement of public opinion or not, the winning candidate will perceive that it is—and will act accordingly.

The party in government

In January, 1971, 243 Democrats were sworn in as members of the U.S. House of Representatives, insuring continued Democratic control of both houses of Congress. But do these Congressmen, who call themselves Democrats, represent the Democratic Party in government? During the first few days of the session they showed almost complete unity as they made committee assignments, elected officers in both houses, met in party caucus, and began to organize Congress for another session. These manifestations of party are important but deceiving. Although the party leadership makes decisions on committee assignments it is helpless in enforcing some of its decisions. A member who does not wish to adhere to the decisions made by his party leaders runs little risk that sanctions will be applied.[38] At the same time decisions reached in caucuses rarely deal with substantive policy questions and when they do they are difficult for party leaders to enforce, particularly if the Congressman has a good reason for not following the caucus leadership. Congressional policy committees, as a result, are little more than intraparty debating societies in

---

[38]See Donald R. Matthews, *U.S. Senators and Their World* (Chapel Hill: University of North Carolina Press, 1958); Ralph K. Huitt, "The Morse Committee Assignment Controversy: A Study of Senate Norms," *American Political Science Review* 51 (1957), pp. 313-29; and Ralph K. Huitt, "The Outsider in the Senate: An Alternative Role," *American Political Science Review* 55 (1961), pp. 566-75.

which members seek to sway their colleagues' votes and make recommendations to the party members.[39]

Regardless of whether the party in government is organized or not the true test of its fulfilling its role as aggregator and articulator of public opinion is determined by the extent to which the party members vote together. Research indicates that party members vote together on some issues but not on others. Turner found in the period 1921-48 that Democrats and Republicans in Congress differed most on tariff, agricultural, and social welfare issues.[40] Examining Congressional votes for the period 1947-50 Keefe and Ogul found the two parties differed in their support of the "liberal-labor" point of view. "The Congressional parties plainly do not look at the country in the same way when it comes to legislation of this sort, although the fact is obscured partially by the behavior of a conservative band within the Democratic party and a liberal band within the Republican party."[41] Party consensus occurs on some foreign policy issues as well.[42]

Although the parties do disagree on a number of issues, the percentage of bills on which they take opposite positions is small. Turner found that only 17 percent of the Congressional roll calls were party votes,[43] while only 13 percent of the roll call votes in the Pennsylvania legislature were party votes.[44] The obvious question is: What determines the amount of partisan conflict that will occur in legislative bodies? Francis' study of legislative issues in the fifty state legislatures provides some concrete evidence.[45] He found four variables—the history

---

[39]Hugh A. Bone, *Party Committees and National Politics* (Seattle: University of Washington Press, 1958).

[40]Julius Turner, *Party and Constituency* (Baltimore: Johns Hopkins Press, 1951).

[41]William J. Keefe and Morris S. Ogul, *The American Legislative Process* (Englewood Cliffs, N.J.: Prentice-Hall, 1964), pp. 276-81.

[42]See Robert A. Dahl, *Congress and Foreign Policy* (New York: Harcourt, Brace, and World, 1950) and James A. Robinson, *Congress and Foreign-Policy-Making* (Homewood, Ill.: Dorsey, 1962).

[43]Turner, op. cit., p. 23.

[44]Sorauf, *Party and Representation*, p. 136.

[45]Wayne L. Francis, *Legislative Issues in the Fifty States* (Chicago: Rand McNally, 1967).

of election competition in the state, the pressure group content of the issues that arise, the partisan content of the issues that arise, and the percentage of seats held by the majority or minority parties in the legislature—account for seventy-four percent of the variation in partisan conflict within state legislatures. Of these four variables, two—the history of election competition and the percentage of majority and minority seats —correlate most highly with partisanship. In short, party votes are most likely to occur in highly competitive political systems which have a past history of partisanship and where political power is fairly evenly balanced. The need to hold party members in line is obviously more crucial in a situation where the party has a 51-49 margin than where the margin is 60-40.

Another factor determining party regularity is the type of constituencies of party members. MacRae has found that party regularity in the Massachusetts legislature was highest in those districts which were typical of those the party normally won. Representatives from atypical districts, recognizing that their election was something of a freak, were more prone to go against their party in order to take actions more in conformity with the wishes of their constituents.[46] Sorauf found similar evidence in the Pennsylvania legislature, as has Froman in Congress.[47]

In the face of this evidence of party cohesion in legislatures it is surprising to find that some political scientists still argue that party is not the most relevant variable in determining a legislator's vote. Sorauf, for example, concludes that the party in government "acts only infrequently out of loyalty to the national party or even in pursuit of goals and interests of the party as a party, rather than of the party as a group of individual legislators."[48] Froman, after analyzing roll call votes in the 1961 session of Congress, concluded:

---

[46] Duncan MacRae, "The Relation Between Roll Call Votes and Constituencies in the Massachusetts House of Representatives," *American Political Science Review* 46 (1952), pp. 1046-55.

[47] Sorauf, and Lewis A. Froman, Jr., *Congressmen and Their Constituents* (Chicago: Rand McNally, 1963), pp. 110-21.

[48] Sorauf, *Political Parties*, p. 128.

First, northern Democrats have more liberal voting records than do Republicans. Second, Democrats tend to come from districts with larger proportions of characteristics which are generally associated with liberalism (author's note: percent non-white, high population density, low owner-occupancy, and highly urban) than do Republicans. Third, these constituency differences are associated with liberal voting records independent of political party. Hence, Democrats have more liberal voting records partially, at least, because they tend to come from more liberal constituencies.[49]

Sorauf's study of Pennsylvania state legislators, while in basic agreement with Froman's findings, found that party regularity also was a function of the degree of party organization and the closeness of the election in each district. In districts where there was strong party organization or where the legislator had just won a difficult election battle there was more support of the party program than where the legislator came from a safe district or where there was no party organization.[50] Legislator's loyalties were to his constituencies unless there was a need for the resources which the party as electoral machine could provide. Reliance on the party as electoral machine resulted in support for the party in government.

The party in government exists, in many state legislatures and in Congress, for some members on some issues. There are a number of issues which have traditionally divided the two parties and on these issues Democrats are quite likely to vote in opposition to Republicans. On other issues, however, party members are more likely to respond to pressure from constituents than from their party, particularly if the party as an electoral machine in their district is weak and cannot provide them with assistance in gaining reelection. As a result it is difficult to argue that the party in government serves to articulate the aggregate public opinion. The votes of Democrats and Republicans in a legislative body may represent the position of a party *qua* party or they may represent the opinions of the party *qua* individual legislators concerned about representing their constituents.

---

[49]Froman, op. cit., p. 93.
[50]Sorauf, *Party and Representation*, pp. 133-46.

Interest groups

When concerned about social and political issues Americans are likely to join or form organizations to protect their interests and concerns. A five-nation study by Almond and Verba disclosed that Americans were far more likely than Britains, Germans, Italians, or Mexicans to take collective action to protest an unjust local or national law. Not only did they look to group action but they also felt their activities would have some impact.[51]

The collectivities which Americans join come in a variety of sizes and shapes. To help sort them out Kaufman has classified groups on the basis of the scope of their interests and the frequency of their intervention in governmental decision making.[52] He concludes that most group activity is organized for intervention in connection with a single issue or a narrow range of issues, i.e., the American Medical Association is concerned primarily with health- and welfare-related policy questions and disinterested in environmental questions. What differentiates between groups with a single issue focus is the frequency with which they seek to influence the policy-making process. Some groups, such as neighborhood organizations or ad hoc groups, are interested in only one specific issue while other groups, such as professional organizations or religious organizations, are interested in any issues which fall within a given policy area. The former intervene with high intensity for short periods of time, while the latter intervene with lower intensity but for substantially longer periods of time.

From this typology we can see that interest group activity in the United States is characterized by a number of stable, multi-interest groups which seek to influence governmental policy over a long period of time and a large number of single issue groups which are created and dissolved with startling rapidity. For the latter set of groups to gain permanence they

---

[51]Gabriel Almond and Sidney Verba, *The Civil Culture* (Princeton: Princeton University Press, 1963), pp. 180-213.

[52]Herbert Kaufman, *Politics and Policies in State and Local Governments* (Englewood Cliffs, N.J.: Prentice-Hall, 1963), pp. 65-87.

must broaden the range of issues in which they are concerned or they must work for an issue which stands no chance of immediate resolution.

Just because there is a large number of groups involved in the policy-making process we cannot assume that everyone who has an opinion also has an opportunity to have his opinion heard. Although Americans may be "joiners" they do not all "belong" to an organization which articulates their political interests. Not everyone who wishes can belong to or form an interest group. Some groups have membership entrance requirements—professional or occupational standing, a membership fee, or the approval of other members of the group— which preclude people from belonging. Regardless of how strongly you feel about medical care for the aged, only doctors can belong to the American Medical Association. In groups which are less restrictive in their membership, participation comes at a high cost; it takes time, interest, and skill to express an opinion and find or create organizations for it. Since time, interest, and skills are not evenly distributed in the population, those who lack them—the poor, the aged, the minorities—find their opinions underrepresented in the policy-making process. Traditional civil rights organizations, such as the National Association for the Advancement of Colored People, have frequently been the instrumentalities of middle- and upper-class blacks and white liberals. Even where the government explicitly recognizes the fact that certain segments of community opinion are not being heard and requires that they be consulted on decisions which effect them, participation has not been widespread. Participation in community action programs under the Economic Opportunities Act and community organizations under the threat of urban renewal, while initially high, has quickly declined.[53]

The assumption made by political scientists that people join interest groups in order to promote and achieve their political

[53]Stephan Thernstrom, *Poverty, Planning and Politics in the New Boston* (New York: Basic Books, 1969), Peter Rossi, *The Politics of Urban Renewal* (New York: Free Press, 1961), and Harold Kaplan, *Urban Renewal Politics* (New York: Columbia University Press, 1963).

goals has been recently criticized by the economist Mancur Olson, Jr.[54] He argues that large-scale (and long-lasting) organizations which seek to provide political rewards for their members cannot survive by providing those rewards alone. Farm organizations, for example, could not survive if all they did was to lobby Congress on agricultural policy questions; farmers would receive the rewards of that policy whether or not they belonged to the farm organization. Public policy is not confined to only those members of the political system who pressed for its adoption. As a result, Olson argues, it is foolish for a farmer to pay any fees to a farm organization in order to benefit from policies they advocate, benefits which he would also receive if he were not a member.

Why, then, do people belong to interest groups? They belong because of their interest in the "by-products" of the group effort.

> In short, by providing a helpful defense against malpractice suits, by publishing medical journals needed by its membership, and by making its conventions educational as well as political, the American Medical Association has offered its members and potential members a number of selected or noncollective benefits. It has offered its members benefits which, in contrast with the political achievements of the organization, can be withheld from nonmembers, and which accordingly provide an incentive for joining the organization.[55]

Salisbury expands Olson's theory to suggest that in large-scale interest groups the division of labor between members who are interested in the nonpolitical benefits of group membership and the leaders who provide the members with political and nonpolitical benefits allows the leadership flexibility in pursuit of the group's political policies.[56] As long as the organization provides benefits for their members the leadership can

---

[54]Mancur Olson, Jr., *The Logic of Collective Action* (Cambridge, Mass.: Harvard University Press, 1965).

[55]Ibid., p. 140.

[56]Robert H. Salisbury, "An Exchange Theory of Interest Groups," in *Interest Group Politics in America* (New York: Harper and Row, 1970), pp. 32-68.

do other things; they exchange group benefits for policy freedom.

In large organizations we find a division of labor between the membership which seeks to receive the political and nonpolitical benefits, and the organization and the leadership which is interested in perpetuating themselves in office and achieving their own political goals. Truman suggests that this division of labor must include at least a semblance of democracy; the leadership must appear to be responsive, directly or indirectly, to the needs and desires of the mass membership or the membership can remove the leadership.[57] In some organizations, such as the International Typographers Union, the members do participate in political campaigns to elect local, national, and international union leaders but do little to exercise control over the activities of their leaders between elections, preferring instead to bowl in the union leagues or read in the union libraries.[58]

The division of labor may be carried even further within the organization. The people who work to influence government policy makers may or may not be members of the organization. Milbrath found three lobbyist-organization relationships in his study of Washington lobbyists—members of the organization who served as lobbyists as part of their career pattern, hired consultants for organizations, and lobbying entrepreneurs who worked for a number of organizations on an ad hoc basis.[59] More than half the lobbyists interviewed by Zeigler and Baer in four states were officers in the organizations they represented.[60] As a result,

He may, for example, lobby for legislation which *he* thinks desirable and do so quite independent of any views his members have on the question. When he does so he cannot expect his members to agree with him, but, as long as his or-

---

[57]David Truman, *The Governmental Process* (New York: Knopf, 1951).

[58]Seymour Martin Lipset, Martin Trow, and James S. Coleman, *Union Democracy* (Glencoe, Ill.: Free Press, 1956).

[59]Lester Milbrath, *The Washington Lobbyists* (Chicago, Ill.: Rand McNally, 1963).

[60]Harmon Zeigler and Michael Baer, *Lobbying* (Belmont, Calif.: Wadsworth, 1969).

ganization survives and he with it, it does not really matter. He takes his policy positions and invests what he has in the way of profit in promoting them not because his membership demands that he do so but only because his membership makes it possible for him to pursue his private desires by asserting that they conform to those of his members.[61]

From Olson and Salisbury we find the following model of large-scale pressure groups: People join such groups not because of the political positions they take but because of the services which they provide for their members—services difficult or expensive to obtain from other sources. In return for these by-products the membership acquiesces in the political activities of the leaders of the organization. Thus, while the organization provides both political and nonpolitical benefits for the membership, the members are more interested in the nonpolitical and the leaders in the political benefits to be derived from the group.

As a result the lobbying activities of large-scale organizations do not represent an attempt to articulate the interests of the group membership. Although the lobbyist or organizational leadership may say they are representing the interests of the members, in truth they are representing their own interests, in which the membership more or less quietly acquiesces. Even if members disagreed with the political stands of the organization they would have to decide whether it was worth the effort to fight within the organization for their interests. Lacking evidence to the contrary it is difficult for a public official to believe that the AMA does not speak for all doctors or the ABA for all lawyers.

This is not to say that the organization's leaders can do what they please, so long as they provide nonpolitical benefits. The fundamental task of leadership—to maintain themselves in power—can best be attained by the artful blending of political and nonpolitical rewards, in a mix which has the greatest appeal to potential and actual members.

Olson and Salisbury argue that their model applies mainly to

[61]Salisbury, op. cit., p. 61.

large-scale groups which persist over time, implying that
short-term and/or small organizations must exist by providing
political rewards alone. Such an assumption overlooks several
important facets of group membership and activity. Membership in interest groups calls for the investment of time and
energy, at least, and the political system, slow to resist new
demands made upon it, does not respond quickly to interest
group activity. Under the circumstances it must be realized
that some groups maintain themselves, in the absence of political rewards, because the act of pursuing political rewards
becomes a reward in itself. Even those groups which appear to
be overtly political must reward their members with nonpolitical benefits—the feeling of political potency which comes from
interest group activity.

One weakness of the Olson-Salisbury argument is the assumption that the leaders and members of organized groups
have different political goals. If leaders and followers share
common political goals, one dimension of the argument
becomes trivial; if they agree, there is little need for leaders to
offer nonpolitical rewards to maintain the support of the membership for the leader's political goals. The function of nonpolitical benefits is to maintain membership in the organization,
not to insure support of the leadership.

Do group members and followers share common opinions and
goals? One of the basic tenets of pressure group theory is that
people join pressure groups in order to take concerted action
with like-minded people. To the extent that the issue is salient
for members and the organization promises to provide political
rewards there will be congruity among the members. Studies of
small groups also indicate that not only will there be
congruence of attitudes among the members but that the leaders will epitomize the attitudes and values of the group.[62] Doc
did not become the leader of the Cornerville gang by deviating
from the group's norms. Indeed, he was selected as leader
because he was the living embodiment of the values of the

---

[62]The small group research is reviewed in Clovis R. Shepherd, *Small
Groups* (San Francisco: Chandler, 1964), pp. 58-99.

group. Once chosen as head of the group Doc was not above trying to change the values of the group, actions which they tolerated because he was their leader. Like Doc, the lobbyists who are also members of the organizations they represent identify heavily with the goals of the organization. Zeigler and Baer found that officeholders were more likely than nonofficeholders to feel a personal interest in the goals of the organization.[63] As a result the organization need not fear the unrestrained activities of its lobbyists who act for the organization with which they identify.

We thus have a situation where organizational leaders do not have to adhere to the wishes of the members but, if the issue is a salient one for the organization, leaders and followers are likely to agree. Those people who join organizations to obtain political goals—and to express their opinions to governmental decision makers—are likely to find they can do so because the leaders of the organizations agree with them. In those organizations where political activity is not salient there is less need for congruence in opinions between leaders and followers.

The Olson and Salisbury model also fails to explain the small interest group which fails over time to gain its political objectives but manages to maintain its membership. The Townshend Movement in California, for example, was established as part of a nationwide campaign in the mid-1930s to pressure the federal government into supplying the elderly with a fixed amount of money per month, providing they spent that money during the month. The idea was to provide the elderly with a fixed living income and also increase the amount of money in circulation during the mid-Depression years. The Townshend Movement was undercut, however, by the passage of the Social Security Act of 1936 which accomplishd primarily what the Townshend Plan originators wanted. The Townshend Movement died soon thereafter except in California where, despite a declining membership, the Townshend Movement Clubs have weekly meetings in many locales. They had managed to survive because they had changed focus. Their weekly meetings consisted of short business meetings which were sparsely attended and which focused

---

[63]Zeigler and Baer, op. cit., p. 65.

on the political goals of the organization, after which the club opened its doors to postmeeting card parties.[64]

From the preceding discussion it is clear that most interest groups, regardless of size or duration, maintain themselves as political entities by providing their members with an artful combination of political and nonpolitical benefits. People belong to highly political groups because they are interested in the group's policies, and because they like the parties, enjoy participating in group activities of any sort, want to have access to group insurance or travel plans. As vehicles for the articulation and aggregation of public opinion, interest groups may not very well fulfill the role which we have automatically assigned to them. Instead, interest groups may be expressions of the opinions of their leaders, arguing they speak for the membership. To the extent that public officials believe them, then interest groups do aggregate and articulate opinions—of the leaders, not the members.

Given what we have said about the nature of political and nonpolitical benefits, we can draw the following conclusions. Small single issue, ad hoc groups may provide the best vehicles for the expression of public opinion on the issues of concern to them. They arise because of a concern over one issue or a narrow range of issues, they seek to mobilize public opinion quickly, and they tend to disappear as swiftly as they are formed. Because of their narrow focus, short duration, and their ability to aggregate relevant opinions they must focus on achieving political goals. The ad hoc nature of such groups also insures they will have difficulty gaining access to the policy-making process. As Truman so aptly notes, the success of interest groups is determined by their perceived legitimacy and the resources which they have at their command.[65] One of the problems with ad hoc groups is that legitimacy is garnered by continued interaction, the antithesis of the notion of a short-term organization. Thus, in order to gain access the interest group must expand its appeal and increase its membership—by

---

[64]Sheldon Messinger, "Organizational Transformation: A Case Study of a Declining Social Movement," *American Sociological Review* 20 (February, 1955), pp. 3-10.

[65]Truman, op. cit.

providing nonpolitical benefits for members and potential members—thereby expanding the group from its initial membership among the attentive public to a broader membership among the mass public. Once the organization has broadened its base, it then has the resources and legitimacy which guarantee it access to the policy-making process. But in the process of broadening its appeal the group no longer serves as the vital vehicle of public opinion on an issue—it now represents the opinions of some people who feel strongly about the issue and others who don't care.

The channels of opinion aggregation and articulation

Our definition of macro public opinion as those opinions of which the decision maker is aware forces us now to shift our focus from who communicates public opinion to the channels and the communication styles used. Choice of channel and style certainly will have an effect on whether the decision maker is aware of public opinion and whether public opinion has any impact.

Communication channels between the public and the policy makers are formal or informal. The former includes those institutionalized mechanisms within the political system whose role is the transmission of public opinion, namely the mass media and public opinion polls. Informal communication channels are those which allow one or more people to confront one another directly, i.e., by letters, telegrams, and face-to-face communications. What are the characteristics of these channels which facilitate their use as agents for the transmission of public opinion?

Formal channels: The mass media

We have seen earlier how the news-gathering process structures our perceptions of reality. Knowing what kinds of events or people the media define as newsworthy it has become possible for astute people to manipulate the media.[66] Gaining

---

[66]Dan Nimmo, *The Political Persuaders* (Englewood Cliffs, N.J.: Prentice-Hall, 1970), particularly Chapters 4 and 5.

access to the media in order to communicate with other people or governmental decision makers is less a question of what one has to say than of knowing what the media needs are and fitting what has to be said to satisfy those needs. This does not mean, however, that everyone has equal access to the media.

The "beat" system—whereby media reporters are assigned to cover on a regular basis newsworthy governmental units or people—makes it difficult for people not regularly covered to gain the attention of the media people, and gives an advantage to those people or agencies which are the focus of beat coverage.[67] When the President, the Governor, or the Mayor want to say something to the public they do not have to seek the press; the press corps assigned to them make it difficult to avoid speaking to the public—whether the public official has something to say or not. In this sense the beat reporter becomes the captive of the person or governmental unit which he is covering. The argument for beat reporters is that they develop an expertise which allows them to recognize important stories as they are developing; further, it is a far more efficient way of dealing regularly with newsworthy people. The beat reporter finds himself faced with two difficulties. First, the longer he works with a person or agency the more he knows about them and the less critical he is of his news source. It is not unusual for exposés to appear when a reporter is first assigned to a beat, but such exposés are more rare the longer the reporter covers his beat. A constant criticism of many media reporters covering governmental beats is that they become so jaded they are no longer able to report dispassionately or objectively what is happening on their beat; in covering the legislature, for example, they either become so involved with the legislature that they can't detach themselves or they become so alienated from it that they have difficulty understanding the process they are covering. Second, the beat reporter, by the very nature of his job, must rely for information on the people he is assigned to

---

[67]For a discussion of this see Douglas Cater, *The Fourth Branch of Government* (Boston: Houghton Mifflin, 1959), Dan D. Nimmo, *Newsgathering in Washington* (New York: Atherton Press, 1964), and Delmer D. Dunn, *Public Officials and the Press* (Reading, Mass.: Addison-Wesley, 1969).

cover. To the extent that access to them for vital information is a function of what he says about them, he is their servant and thus he loses some element of his independence.

The beat reporter is also faced with the difficulty of coming up with something "newsworthy" on a regular basis. The editor or the news director does not often appreciate the comment that "nothing happened today on my beat." The reason beats are established is to cover people or agencies which make news on a regular basis; for a beat reporter to say "nothing happened" is to admit there is no need for his beat. And if he likes his beat, as most do, he will rarely admit that there is little that is newsworthy. As a result beat reporters spend most of their time looking for newsworthy stories which will meet their news requirements for the day. This mitigates against the beat reporter spending a great deal of time taking an issue and following it from beginning to end.

The beat reporter may become subject to use by governmental decision makers, leading to governmental manipulation of the news and a strong role in the creation of public opinion responsive to and supportive of governmental actions. In terms of the needs of the mass media, however, they must maintain a constant coverage of "newsmakers" who are a constant source and supply of news.

As a result the mass media are most effective in transmitting the opinions of governmental officials to the public, rather than the reverse. The public can obtain access to the mass media only when they do something which is defined by the media as "newsworthy." Perhaps the most important function which the mass media performs in funneling opinions up to decision makers is that of funneling the opinions of opinion makers within the media. Front page news is not the relevant statement of public opinion for the policy maker; his public opinion arena is found on the editorial page of the newspaper or the network television "specials." These statements are important to the decision maker because they tell him what a significant segment of his public is thinking, and what they are thinking can have a role in creating public opinion, particularly among the attentive public who read the editorial page or watch television specials.

The mass public are shut off from the mass media as a means of communicating their opinions to their government. They receive no regularized coverage which would make communication possible and they must structure their actions in such a way that they become newsmakers themselves. Then their opinions can be carried by the mass media.

Public opinion polls

Public opinion polls provide one institutional channel for aggregating and articulating mass public opinion accurately. Although the early disasters of the 1936 Literary Digest Poll and the 1948 polls cast serious doubt on the ability of polls accurately to capture public opinion, the record of public opinion polls over the last decade has been quite remarkable.[68] As a result polls have become a standard part of American politics.

Candidates use the various polls to gather "horse race" information. Their primary concern is to determine how they stand vis-à-vis other candidates, how the public is responding to them as candidates, what the public thinks are the important issues of the campaign, and how the public is responding to the candidate's stand on issues. By sequential polling a candidate can tell where he stands at various times with the electorate. The candidate does not have to heed the polls, however. Mendelson and Crespi feel:

Their impact, as information to parties and candidates planning and directing their strategies, has been indirect. In this advisory capacity opinion polls, either published or confidential, act as signals for caution or concerted attack. In this indirect and limited fashion they provide a countervailing machinery to the formal institutional processes that are

[68]The *Literary Digest Magazine*, as a result of a mail poll of telephone owners, predicted that President Roosevelt would lose the 1936 Presidential election. The pollsters forgot that in the midst of the Depression not everyone could afford to maintain a telephone and subsequently their sample was biased in favor of people who could afford telephones—who were more likely to be Republicans.

The Gallup, Roper, and Crosley polls all predicted a Truman defeat in the 1948 Presidential race, based on data collected two weeks before election day. As a result they missed those people who made up their minds late in the campaign. See Norman Meier and Harold Saunders, *The Polls and Public Opinion* (New York: Henry Holt, 1949).

otherwise dominated by entrenched powers. To be effective expressions of public preference, however, they must be soundly conducted and, most importantly, listened to and correctly interpreted.[69]

After watching the 1960 gubernatorial campaign in Massachusetts Levin concluded that the candidate will heed only those polls which confirm his perceptions of the course of the campaign.[70] If the poll gives contrary evidence the candidate seems to discount the validity of the particular results or of polling in general as a method for evaluating public opinion. Barry Goldwater's evaluation of public opinion polls during the 1964 presidential campaign was that the polls did not represent the "conservative majority." The only justification for Goldwater's belief came from the "letters to the editor" column.[71] On the other hand, Kennedy's decision to confront the religion issue in the West Virginia primary in 1960 is credited to the result of a Lou Harris poll.[72]

Once elected to office, candidates continue to make extensive use of polls. The "horse race" aspect of polling carries into the official's use of polls; a study of the use of polls by U.S. senators indicated that the senators saw polls as important for determining electoral strength and areas of possible voter dissatisfaction. Most important, however, was the use of polls to determine what issues were of most concern to the electorate.

For these Senators "following the polls" does not mean accepting each poll result as a mandate as to how one should cast his vote in legislative sessions. Rather, this practice provides a signal as to whether he should take some kind of public position on the issue. The actual significance of polls in the legislative process is the fact that they can guide the development of campaign strategy and tactics, suggesting to the Senator what he should promise action on, what he should ignore, and what he should attack.[73]

---

[69]Harold Mendelsohn and Irving Crespi, *Polls, Television, and the New Politics*, (Scranton, Pa.: Chandler, 1970), pp. 55-6.

[70]Murray Levin, *The Compleat Politician* (Indianapolis: Bobbs-Merrill, 1962).

[71]Phillip E. Converse, Aage Clausen, and Warren Miller, "Electoral Myth and Reality: The 1964 Election," *American Political Science Review* 59 (June 1965): 321-36.

[72]Theodore White, *The Making of the President, 1960* (New York: Atheneum, 1961).

[73]Mendelsohn and Crespi, op. cit., p. 34.

There is little evidence that public officials act in accord with poll results when they don't agree with the official's own position. The most salient issues for the American electorate—civil rights, the war in Vietnam, and inflation—have not necessarily been the ones which decision makers have rushed to resolve. The polls then serve a supportive function for the official. They are happily received when they agree with him and they warn him when he may be going too far astray. But for many of his actions they do not provide a useful guideline for him to heed if he doesn't wish.

There are several drawbacks to using public opinion polls as channels for opinion aggregation and articulation. The cost of doing large-scale surveys is high enough to prohibit all but the wealthiest candidates from doing more than one survey during a campaign or during a term in office. Nonelectoral polls are channels from the public to decision makers, but they are channels which only carry such information as the decision maker seeks and only when he wants it. Once again the cost of polls prohibits their being done on a regular, continuing basis. The availability of public polling organizations, such as Gallup, Roper, and Harris, does not mean that officeholders receive free readings of public opinion. In order to sell their results to newspapers and the media, polling organizations must ask questions concerning "newsworthy" topics; the results most frequently reflect public opinion on current as opposed to potential issues, and current policy decisions rather than proposed policy alternatives. Correspondingly, the timing of public opinion polls may not be the best for inputting public opinion into the policy making process. As noted earlier, a government official may be interested in what issues the electorate feels are important, but he may not be able to wait until the professional organizations can get surveys into the field. By the time public opinion polls have been completed the results may no longer be relevant for the policy maker.

The kinds of questions asked and the presentation of results also seriously hamper the use of surveys for the articulation of public opinion. The easiest questions to ask are those requiring a "close-ended" response, i.e., Yes or No, Agree or Disagree, but how many important policy questions can be answered in such a facile manner? In addition, the commercial pollsters rarely present their in-depth follow-up questions to investigate the rationales behind answers to close-ended questions, although seventy percent of the population may favor a given alternative but for contradictory reasons. There is also very little in-depth analysis of the survey results. At best the pollsters break down their results by demographic categories, i.e., sex, age, residence, with little explanation as to why those categories are important.[74] There is very little attempt to present an opinion profile of the population in which opinions on one topic are related to opinions on other, corresponding topics. This type of analysis is left to academic researchers.

Informal channels

The mass media and public opinion polls are relatively inefficient and ineffective aggregators and articulators of public opinion for the reasons just discussed. Most of the opinion aggregation and articulation between the public and governmental officials is done in face-to-face or person-to-person settings where the style of the presentation is an important facet of the choice of channel. This section will focus on the informal channels which connect the public to public officials, either directly or indirectly.

Writing letters and sending telegrams

Almond and Verba have found that when people take action alone, attempting to influence governmental decision makers, they are likely to view that action in terms of written communications, particularly if the governmental decision makers are at a level psychologically and geographically distant from the citizen.[75] Over half of the U.S. citizens would try to influence their national government by directly contacting po-

---

[74]These comments refer to public pollsters who sell their results to the media and to some pollsters who do private commercial polling on a contract basis.

[75]Almond and Verba, op. cit., pp. 180-213.

litical leaders or the press, writing a letter to or visiting a local political leader, while only twenty percent suggested the same strategy for influencing their local government. Even when people take group action the group may ask them to communicate directly with their legislators. Although letter-writing and telegraph-sending are perceived by the citizenry as legitimate and readily available ways of communicating their opinions, it is informative to note that very few people have ever exercised these options. This lack of participation spares most governmental officials the task of answering multiple stacks of mail daily and makes the letter and telegraph a communication channel which is rarely overloaded. But how effective are letters and telegrams? Are they read? What kinds of letters or telegrams receive the greatest attention and have the most impact?

It is clear from research on Congress and on state legislatures that mail is read, and taken seriously.[76] Why? Dexter argues as follows:

First of all, members of Congress and their staff have no alternative but to spend an enormous amount of time reading and answering mail, and a busy man would be less than human if he were to believe he was wasting so much time. Second, congressmen often operate in a near-vacuum, uninformed about what their ultimate employers, the voters in their district or state, really want. The mail gives a sense, perhaps a spurious one, of receiving instructions on some issues. Such instructions give the man a sense of being in contact with his constituents and some notion, again perhaps spurious, as to what is likely to please his constituents and result in his re-election. Third, many junior members of the House, having no important role on major committees, appear to be frustrated at their inability to make any demonstrably effective action on major issues. Answering constituents' mail is one thing they can do which gives them the feeling of acting effectively. Fourth, writing to one's Congressman is an expression of the citizen's right of petition—treasured by most Congressmen—from perceived inequities of legislation or administrative action. Finally,

---

[76]Rowena Wyant and Herta Herzog, "Voting Via the Senate Mailbag," *Public Opinion Quarterly* 5 (Fall and Winter, 1941), pp. 359-82, 590-624.

some Congressmen, whether realistically or not, appear to regard their correspondence as rational academic discussion of issues of national importance.[77]

But not all mail is read or heeded. Organized mail campaigns, once they are recognized as such by the intended target, are normally discounted or, if pushed too hard, are liable to boomerang. One hundred post cards, bearing the same message, from the same community, are attributes of an organized campaign. Instead, policy makers are most interested in those letters which concern one topic (a bill or administrative action) and discuss that topic in the writer's own words, showing a grasp of the subject matter concerned and having an informed opinion on the matter. Legislators are most concerned with indications of informed opinion rather than a gross measure of opinion.

Analysis of mail indicates, however, that it is more concerned with requests for constituent service than with expressions of opinion on public issues.[78] The legislator seeking reelection quickly learns that this type of constituency mail is probably more important to him in the long run than the mail expressing opinions on policy questions. It is more important for the public official to know that his constituents appreciate his efforts in their behalf than for them to agree with his votes on issues about which they have no interest. In answering "service" requests from constituents the official buys support from his constituents in the policy-making realm, particularly where they are unconcerned about the policy question.

> The world's greatest publicity organ is still the mouth. . . . When you get somebody $25.00 from the Social Security Administration, he talks to his friends and neighbors about it. After a while the story grows until you've single-handedly obtained $2500 for a constituent who was on the brink of starvation.[79]

---

[77]Bauer, Pool, and Dexter, op. cit., pp. 438-39.

[78]Donald R. Matthews, *U.S. Senators and Their World* (Chapel Hill: University of North Carolina Press, 1960), p. 224, states that one third of an "average" senator's mail is "case" mail.

[79]Ibid., p. 226.

Personal contact

Studies of lobbying at the state and national level indicate that personal communication between citizen (or lobbyist) and legislator is the most effective means of communication.[80] Lobbyists feel, for example, that if they are able to talk with a legislator face-to-face, they can have some impact. Direct conversation, in the sanctity of a senator's office, is likely to be direct, honest, simple, and efficient. The lobbyist can present his case and the Senator can respond without fear of being overheard or misunderstood. The basic problem in relying on such contacts is their cost in time for the harried public official who does not have the time to spend with each of his many constituents. Subsequently, he wants to hear from those people who have something to say and whose word he can trust. When John Kennedy formed what subsequently became known as "The Executive Committee" of the National Security Council he was concerned about hearing the opinions of people whom he trusted, regardless of their official position.

Milbrath and Zeigler and Baer find that the personal contact between lobbyists and legislators seldom concerns legislation. One of the lobbyist's concerns is to maintain his credibility and his access to the governmental decision maker. As a result lobbyists are concerned about building or maintaining good will and presenting research findings, often at the behest of the legislator.[81] When the lobbyist does contact legislators he frequently must talk to them, en masse, at public hearings. Testimony at hearings is frequently downgraded as a means of presenting public opinion: "The lobbyist presents the case of his organization or clients, answers a few questions, and then retires from the witness chair to be replaced by another."[82] Milbrath lists the futility of testifying.

Hearings are often held with only one member of Congress present. Even if members are present, they may not be lis-

---

[80]Milbrath, *Washington Lobbyists;* and Ziegler and Baer, op. cit.
[81]Milbrath, and Zeigler and Baer, ibid.
[82]Matthews, p. 179.

tening. They are frequently called out of hearings to attend to something more urgent. Most members have somewhat fixed opinions about the topics on which hearings are held; thus their predispositions are likely to screen out noncongenial messages. If a member serves on a committee for several years (a common practice), he will probably have attended several hearings on the same subject. He is certain to become bored listening to the same people repeatedly saying more or less the same thing.[83]

Not all committee testimony is wasted. Testimony does become part of the public record; newsmen do cover the hearings and give broad coverage to some testimony; and failure to testify may give opponents an unfair advantage. Wildavsky argues that bureaucrats can use committee hearings to their own ends.[84] Favorable committee members can ask leading questions, and hearings allow agencies to put themselves in the best possible light before the committee. The same is true for lobbyists and others testifying.

The extent to which public opinion influences governmental policy makers is a function of the way in which it is communicated. If the message is structured in an acceptable and understandable form, sent on an appropriate channel, and sent with the appropriate loudness or frequency it can have some impact. Enough people saying they wanted an end to the war in Vietnam ultimately had an impact on U.S. foreign policy; election results have some meaning for the people they elect; and letter-writing campaigns are still an often used and referred tool for influencing elected officials.

Summary

Thus far we have focused on the institutions, channels, and styles of opinion aggregation, with the assumption that these factors all play an important role in policy making. But is this a valid assumption? Some issues, for example, may arise and become recognized as the issue becomes salient for the mass

---

[83]Milbrath, *Washington Lobbyists*, pp. 229-30.

[84]Aaron Wildavsky, *The Politics of the Budgetary Process* (Boston: Little Brown, 1964), pp. 84-90.

public; once policy makers recognize an issue exists they may be more interested in the opinions which are articulated through the activities of organized interest groups. In much the same way the channels used for expressing opinions may change with different stages of the policy-making process. The mass media may be important in making an issue salient for the mass public and for governmental officials, but the delineation of policy alternatives may be the result of face-to-face contacts with members of the public.

Another factor which must be mentioned is the openness of this system. To what extent are the institutions for opinion aggregation and articulation equally open to all people? I have earlier argued that participation in such institutions is costly, in terms of time, energy, and occasionally money. For people with few resources, working through institutions is more costly than trying to convince a policy maker in a face-to-face situation. But not all communication channels are open to all people. As we have seen, the mass media are available to those people whom the media consider to be "newsworthy" or who can afford to pay for access. Public opinion polls provide channels which the public cannot use at their own volition. Informal communication channels are less costly to use but they may not be effective.

The ability of policy makers to make decisions which have the support of the populace depends on the extent to which all public opinion has an opportunity to be heard when it is necessary. When the institutions and channels of opinion aggregation and articulation become closed to some or certain kinds of opinion, policy makers run the risk of becoming irrelevant for larger and larger segments of the public and alienating them from the policy-making process. Maintaining the system open to all types of opinions means that the policy maker is listening to opinions which may be distasteful, ill-informed, and irrelevant. But he will never be able to isolate himself from the larger public which he must serve.[85]

---

[85]George Reedy, *Twilight of the Presidency* (New York: World Publishing Company, 1970).

CHAPTER SEVEN

Public opinion and the policy-making process

Although there may be a large number of people within the political system who hold opinions on a political question, not all of them have access to the institutions which aggregate and articulate public opinion. As a result a relatively small number of people actually participate directly or indirectly in the policy-making process. The community power structure studies, while disagreeing as to whether power is concentrated or not, do agree that only a small proportion of the citizenry in a locality participate in or influence local policy-making.[1] Bauer, Pool, and Dexter found a similar lack of interest and participation in a national level policy question.[2] From these studies one would conclude that the only public opinion which is relevant in the policy-making process is the opinion of the attentive public or the opinion elite.

Such studies may be misleading, however. Careful examination of the community decision-making studies reveals that they never focus on *all* the policy decisions made within the political system; instead, they concentrate on either the most controversial decisions or those involving the greatest investment

---

[1]The literature on community power structures is too long to list or analyze here. The two seminal works are Floyd Hunter, *Community Power Structure* (Garden City: Doubleday, 1963) and Robert Dahl, *Who Governs* (New Haven, Conn.: Yale University Press, 1961).

[2]Raymond A. Bauer, Ithiel de Sola Pool, and Lewis A. Dexter, *American Business and Public Policy* (New York: Atherton, 1964).

of resources. Banfield's study of decision making in Chicago focuses on ten decisions over a four year period; Martin and Munger study cases of "all significant metropolitan action taken in Onondaga County in the last 25 years"—seven public and three quasi-public decisions; and Mowitz and Wright examine ten "crucial" policy questions which arose in Detroit during the period 1945-1960.[3] Although this research has focused on who has power and influence in local communities on "important" or "crucial" decisions, it tells us little about who is involved in influencing or settling "less-than-crucial" policy questions. This inadequacy would not be detrimental if most policy decisions in local communities were crucial, so that by studying this select group of decisions we could learn a great deal about the policy-making process in general. But the relative scarcity of cases for study in Chicago, Syracuse, and Detroit—cities where one would expect crucial decisions to occur frequently—suggests that they occur infrequently and, as a result, tell us very little about day-to-day policy-making processes in urban America. As a result, knowing that a power elite of 40 makes decisions in Atlanta doesn't really tell us who is influential in decisions to widen streets or grant dog licenses. Although Hunter might argue that street and licensing decisions aren't important in Atlanta, they probably constitute a substantially larger proportion of the policy decisions than those relating to nominations or urban redevelopment.

When we talk about the "policy-making process" we are talking about a process which results in different kinds of decisions, some of which are so routine that the policy maker doesn't stop to consider the alternatives and others so unique and awesome that officials quake in fear of the consequences of their decisions. As a result we must first distinguish between different kinds of decisions, so that we can then talk about those types of decisions where public opinion is most likely to have an impact.

---

[3]Edward C. Banfield, *Political Influence* (Glencoe, Ill.: Free Press, 1961); Roscoe C. Martin and Frank Munger, *Decisions in Syracuse* (Garden City, N.Y.: Doubleday, 1965); Robert J. Mowitz and Deil S. Wright, *Profile of a Metropolis* (Detroit: Wayne State University Press, 1962).

A typology of decisions

What makes some policy decisions crucial and others routine? Polsby argues that we use four criteria for determining whether a policy decision is important: the number of people affected by the decision, the kinds of community resources affected, how many kinds of community resources are distributed by the decision, and how the decision affects the overall distribution of resources.[4] "Important" decisions for Polsby are those which affect large numbers of people and occupy a sizeable segment of the resources of the community. Importance is thus defined by the scope of the decision, not by the controversy which it arouses. According to these criteria some decisions which affect large numbers of people and the investment of community resources, such as some highway site location decisions, which have become reasonably noncontroversial would be classified as "routine" while other kinds of decisions, such as zoning variations, while highly controversial would not be classified as "important."

Perhaps, as MacFarland suggests, these criteria are too narrow, too observer-oriented, to provide much operational utility for studying the policy-making process.[5] He contends that a more useful approach would be to classify decisions on the basis of the number of alternatives available to the decision maker. The more critical or important a decision the greater the range of alternatives and the more difficult the choice between them; routine decisions would be those where the alternatives are limited in number and specific in content. However, a typology based on the availability of alternatives alone overlooks the necessity for having criteria for choosing between them. A complex problem, with many alternatives, may not be a critical decision if the decision maker has clear-cut criteria for choosing between the alternatives. At the same time, even a decision with a limited number of alternatives is difficult if the

---

[4]Nelson Polsby, *Community Power and Political Theory* (New Haven, Conn.: Yale University Press, 1963), pp. 95-6.

[5]Andrew S. MacFarland, *Power and Leadership in Pluralist Systems* (Stanford, Calif.: Stanford University Press, 1969).

decision maker has no criteria for differentiating between them. The use of two variables—the availability of alternatives and criteria for choice—as a means for classifying types of decisions also defines the role that public opinion can play.

These two variables enable us to construct a rough continuum for classifying decisions in which the end points of the continuum are decisions that I would label as "routine" and "unique," respectively. Routine decisions are those where the range of alternatives available to the decision maker is very limited and the criteria for choosing between them are unambiguous. The clerk in city hall granting dog licenses makes a continual series of routine decisions: her alternatives are to grant or not grant the license and her criteria for making that decision are clear—does the owner have the requisite fee and has he filled out the proper form. Those are the only relevant alternatives and the operant criteria for choosing between the alternatives.

Unique decisions, on the other hand, are those where the range of alternatives is at its maximum and the criteria for choosing between them are unclear or lacking. Complex policy questions invariably produce unique decisional situations the first time they are confronted. When pollution became an important policy question in the late 1960s, decision makers were faced with the task of determining what alternatives were available to them and which available alternatives were "possible," and then developing criteria for choosing between them. Once a unique decision has been made, subsequent decisions in the same policy area become less unique and more routine; the first unique decision often becomes the benchmark for subsequent policy decisions in that policy area. Once a unique decision has been made and its effects evaluated, the policy maker is in a position to evaluate the alternatives which he considered the criteria he used, discarding in the process some of the alternatives as unfeasible and some of the criteria as irrelevant.

It must be recognized that there are very few decisions which are truly unique—where the decision maker must determine de novo his alternatives and the criteria for choice. To the extent possible the decision maker relies on roughly analogous situations where he has had to make a similar kind of decision. The decision to drop the atomic bomb on Hiroshima in 1945 was viewed by President Truman and his advisors as another example of the decision to use or not use a new military weapon. The relevant criteria for the decision centered on whether use of the atomic bomb would aid the United States militarily in its war with Japan.[6] The decision was not a new or unique one but merely a variant of an already successfully resolved policy question.

"Mixed" decisions—where the alternatives are many and the criteria clear or the alternatives few but the decisional criteria ambiguous—fall between these two poles. In the mixed cases the decision maker is confronted with the task of delineating either the alternatives or the decisional criteria. Substantial numbers of public decisions fall into this category. The question of fluoridating municipal water systems is a mixed decision, the alternatives are to fluoridate or not, but the criteria for choosing between these two are ambiguous and conflicting. The problem for the decision maker is to choose between conflicting criteria, and that decision, once made, resolves the question of which alternative to choose.

It is important to understand that a given policy decision does not necessarily remain at any one point on this continuum. Unique decisions, if made repeatedly, rapidly become routine as the alternatives become limited and the decisional criteria harden. And some decisions can become more unique. In a changing environment routine decisions may lose touch with reality if they are not constantly monitored to see whether they are accomplishing their goals. Alternatives and decision criteria which are appropriate at one point in time may not be so at another, and it is with a deep sense of shock that a decision maker finds once-routine decisions are being questioned. When the federal interstate highway program was passed in 1956 there was general agreement on the need for a network of high-speed highways to move people between and

---

[6]See Len Giovannitti and Fred Freed, *The Decision to Drop the Bomb* (New York: Coward-McCann, 1965).

FIGURE 7-1

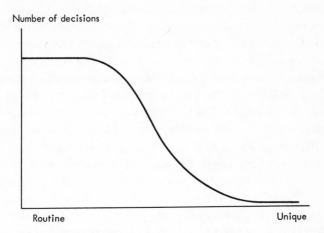

within cities. In addition, the highway program was viewed as a useful way of making the transition from a wartime economy to a peacetime economy, creating jobs in the construction industry and fostering industrial development. More recently the basic values of the program have been challenged as being irrelevant for more important environmental concerns. The values which had formed the basis for choosing a highway program have been superseded in a number of localities by other values which produce entirely different decisional outcomes, and decisions about highways which once revolved around locational disputes now focus on the utility and necessity of the interstate highway system itself.[7]

What is the distribution of decisions within a political system? There is little empirical evidence to answer the question. We know from the community power studies that the more unique decisions occur fairly infrequently at the local level. At the same time the growth of bureaucratic structure implies that the number of more routine decisions is great. Intuitively, we would expect the following distribution of decisions within a stable political system.

---

[7]Alan Lupo, Frank Colcord, and Edmund Fowler, *Rites of Way* (Boston: Little, Brown, 1971).

The fact that the political system is stable implies that most of the unique decisions have been made and that much of the policy making is done through more or less routine decisions. In fact, the very stability of the political system is based on the preponderance of routine decisions. Since the unique decisions are the most controversial and have the greatest capacity for tearing apart the fabric of the political system, the preponderance of routine decisions insures a comparatively low level of political conflict. In developing political systems, such as those in Africa and Latin America, we may find a higher incidence of more unique decisions, greater potential for disruptive conflict over unique decisions, and less stability. Once that series of initially unique decisions have been made repeatedly they become routine and the political system begins to stabilize. Apter suggests that an autocratic leader may be necessary for a developing political system in order to maintain stability in the political system while it is making important unique decisions.[8]

What use is this decision making typology for our understanding of the role of public opinion in the policy-making process? In classifying policy decisions on the basis of the number of alternatives and the criteria for choosing between alternatives, we must recognize that the major roles of public opinion are in delineating what alternatives are available (and acceptable) and in clarifying and arguing for decisional criteria. Given these roles it is clear that public opinion will have its least impact on routine decisions where the alternatives are limited and the decisional criteria are clear-cut. The clerk in the license bureau does not allow what the community thinks of the applicant or of her performance influence her decision. This information is irrelevant to her decision. The greater the uncertainty as to what decision to make, because the alternatives or criteria are unclear, the larger the role which public opinion *can* play in the policy-making process. In unique decisions public opinion can play its most important role in helping to

---

[8]David Apter, *The Politics of Modernization* (Chicago: University of Chicago Press, 1965), pp. 402-05.

define the situational context and criteria for the decision maker. We must remember, however, that while public opinion may have its greatest impact on the more unique decisions, these types of decisions constitute a relatively small proportion of the totality of policy decisions within a political system. Thus, the bulk of the day-to-day policy making which occurs within a political system is unaffected by public opinion.

In addition to determining whether public opinion can play a role in the policy-making process we must also examine the roles played by political parties and pressure groups in channeling opinion into the policy-making process.

Knowing what kinds of decisions are most likely to be affected by public opinion is useful only if we know the process by which decisions are made. Bachrach and Baratz argue, for example, that studying the decisions which are made overlooks an important field of "nondecisions," i.e., the decision not to decide.[9] To study decisions one must recognize a process in which one of the first components is the recognition that an issue exists which requires a decision. Even when a policy question is recognized there is no immediate movement toward a decision; the more unique the decision the longer it takes to clarify the policy alternatives and define the decisional criteria. Once this has been done a decision can be made or not made. That is not the end of the process, however, for the content of the policy decision is not determined so much by the decision as by its implementation. We must also recognize that not all policy questions successfully cycle through all the stages in the policy-making process. Some issues, for example, are not recognized; if recognized, they may not be regarded as important; once recognized as important, an issue may be impossible to resolve; some decisions, once made, may be impossible to implement. It is clear that policy making is a multistage process in which public opinion can play a differential role

---

[9]Peter Bachrach and Morton Baratz, "Decisions and Nondecisions: An Analytic Framework," *American Political Science Review* 57 (September, 1963), pp. 632-642; and Raymond E. Wolfinger, "Nondecisions and the Study of Local Politics," *American Political Science Review*, 65 (December, 1971), pp. 1063-1080.

depending on the stage. Recognition that the policy-making process is multistage also forces us to ask what channels are used to funnel public opinion into the process and at which stage in the process does this occur.

In the following pages we will examine a multistage model of the policy-making process, focusing on the kinds of opinion which are relevant at each stage and which institutions are operative for opinion aggregation and articulation at each stage. In order to test the utility of the model we will use it to look at President Kennedy's decision to institute a naval blockage in Cuba in 1962[10] and the U.S. Senate's decision not to confirm President Nixon's nomination of Harold Carswell to the United States Supreme Court.[11] The Cuban missile crisis case was chosen because it represents a critical foreign-policy decision which was fairly unique—the alternatives available for the removal of the missiles were many and the criteria for choosing between the alternatives were not clear. This decision also represents one of the few foreign-policy decisions which have been largely opened to public scrutiny. The Carswell nomination was chosen because it represents a normally routine domestic policy decision in which the criteria for making a decision were challenged and the decision became far from routine.

Stage I: Recognition and acceptance of the issue

There is an apochryphal study about a farmer who was seen by a neighbor beating a newly bought mule over the head with a board. When asked why he was hitting the mule the farmer replied, "I'm trying to get his attention." An analogous situation confronts the policy maker. Before he can make a decision he must recognize that a problem exists which requires a solution, and he must accept the issue, once recognized, as being one worth resolving.

Several factors are important determinants of whether a pol-

---

[10]For an excellent day-by-day account see Elie Abel, *The Missile Crisis* (New York: Lippincott, 1966). Analysis by participants can be found in Arthur M. Schlesinger, *A Thousand Days* (Boston: Houghton-Mifflin, 1965) and Theodore Sorensen, *Kennedy* (New York: Harper and Row, 1965).

[11]Richard Harris, *Decision* (New York: Dutton, 1971).

icy maker becomes aware of a problem or not. The policy maker's own values influence his ability and willingness to perceive an issue; the more salient the problem is for his own values, the more likely he is to recognize and accept it. Shortly after a son is killed in an automobile accident it would not be surprising to see his father as governor recognize the need for the development of a highway safety program within the state. Even if the policy maker's values do not lead him to recognize a problem, they do make him more or less responsive to groups seeking recognition of the problem. The fact that there are substantial numbers of veterans in Congress and of state university alumni insures that they will listen to veteran's organizations and state university presidents.

Commitments which the policy maker has made also impinge on the process of problem recognition. Political party platform planks, pledges to voters in the midst of a campaign, and acceptance of support from pressure groups insure that the policy maker will at least recognize the issues involved. Eisenhower's commitment to go to Korea if elected left him with no alternative once elected; the commitment forced him to recognize the problem and to respond to it in the way he had promised. Even if the electorate did not elect him on the basis of what he promised, elected officials tend to perceive their election as a mandate to handle the issues which they raised during the campaign.[12]

The problem may be recognized because of the nature of the problem itself, because the problem is of such a magnitude that it cannot be avoided—an earthquake which destroys half a mayor's town—or because the policy maker has never encountered the problem before—the governor of California confronted with the first oil spill to blanket large areas of the sea coast. In either case the policy-making process is responsive to, rather than anticipatory of, the problem.

One of the primary functions of public opinion at this point in the policy-making process is to raise some issues to the attention of decision makers and to establish claims of importance or urgency. The agenda-setting function is important

---

[12]John Kingdon, *Candidates for Office* (New York: Random House, 1968).

because it enables the decision maker to handle those issues which will cost him the least in political power and public opinion and will gain the most. It would pay to think of Stage I as a bottleneck which serves to choose selectively between a wide range of competing issues. Those issues which are brought to the attention of the policy maker are sufficiently different from the others that he must then decide whether they are worth consideration for solution.

The policy maker may also place an issue on the agenda even though there is little public support for it in order to see how the public responds to it as an issue. The policy maker's selection of an issue focuses public attention on it. Officials frequently choose issues on a "trial balloon" basis, hoping to generate public support so that they can recognize it as a legitimate issue. If there is no support they must be willing either to drop it or to make attempts to build public opinion on the issue. Although we tend to think of policy makers as being the targets of lobbying efforts, we must also recognize that policy makers lobby the public, other officials, pressure groups, and the mass media in order to create public acceptance of an issue.

For routine decisions the question of supportive public opinion is moot. The more unique the decision, however, the more reluctant the policy maker is to recognize and move toward acceptance of the issue without knowing the opinion environment.

Recognition that the Russians had placed offensive ballistic missiles in Cuba was difficult for Kennedy.

> In hindsight it seems obvious that the Administration should have anticipated the installation of Soviet missiles in Cuba. That it failed to do so is not the fault of any individual. The failure can be traced instead to a state of mind, an unwillingness to believe that Khrushchev would do anything so preposterous. Perhaps the crucial error on the American side was the belief at middle and senior levels of the Administration that Khrushchev, being a rational man, would not take a step that seemed to Americans as dangerously irrational.[13]

---

[13]Abel, op. cit., p. 39.

When questioned about the shipment of missiles to Cuba the Soviets replied that they were defensive missiles. The Kennedy administration was lax to question that statement. In addition Kennedy was undoubtedly sensitive about Cuba because of the Bay of Pigs invasion and any decisions on policy toward Cuba had to be based on hard data. While the Bay of Pigs invasion had taught him to rely on hard data it also taught him to be skeptical of the intelligence community as a source of information. Thus, when McGeorge Bundy, presidential assistant for national security, suggested that the Soviet missiles were offensive, his analysis was not heeded. Another factor which made it difficult was that the issue was being raised by Republican Senator Keating in an election year when the Republican Senatorial and Congressional Campaign Committees had vowed that Cuba would be the dominant campaign issue.[14]

Recognition of the Carswell nomination was no problem. The Constitutional requirement that the Senate confirm presidential nominees to the Supreme Court guaranteed that the Senate would recognize and act on the issue.

Once the decision maker is aware that an issue exists he must decide whether it is legitimate or possible to solve. Merely being placed on the public agenda does not ensure that any action will be taken on the problem. The question of legalizing abortion has long been recognized as an issue, but there has been very little movement toward a decision on the issue until recently for fear that the issue was politically explosive and morally unacceptable to substantial segments of the population. The climate of opinion regarding women's rights in general and abortion in particular became more liberal in the later 1960s as state after state began serious consideration of legalizing abortion. In order to be considered, however, policy makers had to feel that there was at least some support for legalized abortion and the development of pressure groups pushing for the measure gave them some justification for considering this an acceptable issue.

An issue may be recognized as a problem and everyone may

---

[14]Sorensen, op. cit., p. 670.

accept it as legitimate, but it may not be a solvable problem; the dimensions of the problem may be unknown or the costs of solving it too great. Poverty in the United States is a major problem whose complexity and cost make it difficult to develop an effective policy. Under these circumstances policy makers will often tackle *aspects* of the problem rather than the whole thing. By segmenting it and reducing it to manageable proportions the problem can be defined, recognized, legitimized, and action taken toward resolution. Poverty, for example, has been segmented into inadequate educational opportunities for the poor, met by the Head Start Program, or inadequate job training, met by the Manpower Training Act.[15] In the process of reacting to part of the problem, the problem itself may be redefined or the costs of handling it may be more readily assessed.

When the CIA discovered that offensive missiles were in place in Cuba, one of the first responses was to increase the number of U-2 overflights for intelligence pictures. In that way Kennedy felt he would know the magnitude of the problem and could better decide whether to mount some sort of response. The pictures offered incontrovertible evidence of the existence of offensive missiles and made some sort of response imperative, since allowing the Soviet Union to maintain offensive missiles in Cuba would upset the global political balance.[16] The critical piece of information was that the missiles were offensive rather than defensive. The Russians had earlier stipulated that they were indeed shipping missiles to Cuba but that the missiles were defensive in nature.

Recognition of the Carswell nomination as a legitimate issue is difficult under the best of circumstances since the president rarely has difficulty with his nominations gaining approval by the Senate. Prior to the Carswell nomination only two Supreme Court nominees had been defeated by the U.S. Senate and one of those defeats, that of Clement Haynsworth, had led to the

---

[15]John C. Donovan, *The Politics of Poverty* (New York: Pegasus Books, 1967).

[16]Ibid., p. 671.

nomination of Carswell. The Senate certainly was not anxious to repeat the protracted and bitter debate that had ensued over the Haynsworth nomination. As a result very few people anticipated any opposition. But, as one Republican senator who ultimately voted against Carswell observed,

> I learned that the Justice Department had rated Carswell way down below Haynsworth and a couple other candidates. . . . That made it clear that the choice of Carswell was vengeance—to make us sorry we hadn't accepted Haynsworth—and, at the same time, it was an attempt to downgrade the Supreme Court and implement the Southern strategy.[17]

Even those who thought Carswell to be a bad nominee and had led the fight against Haynsworth, particularly Senator Birch Bayh, were loath to try the patience of the Senate again. Senator Brooke, a Republican, was aware that the evidence against Carswell was strong and there was a potential base of opposition to his nomination. But to oppose Carswell would place Brooke in conflict with party leaders in the White House and Congress.

Stage II: Definition of policy alternatives and decisional criteria

If the problem is recognized as an important one requiring solution, the decision maker then begins to search for decisional alternatives. In routine decisions the alternatives are limited and clearly delineated. In unique decisions, clarifying the availability of policy alternatives may well consume a considerable amount of time. The decision maker must be concerned with discovering the range of "feasible" alternatives rather than the totality of alternatives. DeRivera accurately describes some of the constraints on the availability.

In any important decision there are constraints that restrict the formation of desirable alternatives. The President,

---

[17]Quoted in Harris, op. cit., p. 11.

in particular, may be limited by laws, by the necessity of having his alternatives accepted by important co-workers in the executive branch, accepted by the men who must carry it out, accepted by Congress, accepted by public opinion, and accepted by other nations. There are promises, traditions, and precedents that are difficult to break, and any innovation may involve the formation of a new consensus and the creation of new governmental machinery. And, of course, there is a fantastic amount of information which a President should know and that simply cannot be known by one man. The President can spend his resources to alter these constraints and allow action, but the fact that his resources are limited is yet another constraint—there is only so much money, manpower, time, credibility, patronage, etc. available.[18]

The decision maker is rarely free to do exactly what he wants, and his alternatives are limited accordingly. Lacking the power, he can wish or aspire but he cannot realistically consider some alternatives. Just as there are institutional constraints, de Rivera suggests that there are also opinion constraints.[19] The political culture of the political system helps to "define out" certain alternatives as being unacceptable, e.g., the use of nuclear weapons for offensive purposes. The range of "realistic" alternatives available to a decision maker is smaller than the totality of decisions which he could consider.

In unique decisions where time is an important factor—such as foreign policy crisis decisions—it may be impossible to explore the full range of alternatives before a decision is needed. The shortness of time thus forces the policy maker to narrow his range of alternatives to those which may not be the best but rather "the best under the circumstances." The alternatives will "satisfice," rather than satisfy,[20] and the alternatives considered will more than likely be those which are variations of already tried and tested alternatives rather than novel ones. Even when there is time to generate alternatives, the

[18]Joseph de Rivera, *The Psychological Dimension of Foreign Policy* (Columbus, Ohio: Merrill, 1968), p. 130.

[19]Ibid., pp. 70-73.

[20]Herbert Simon, *Organizations* (New York: John Wiley & Sons, Inc., 1958), pp. 140-41.

increase in the number of alternatives also increases the cost of choosing between them, since the decisional criteria have to be more fully developed and articulated.

In the Cuban missile crisis Kennedy and his advisors considered a total of six alternatives, ranging from private diplomatic negotiations to a military assault on Cuba, before narrowing the list to two serious contenders—a naval blockade or pinpoint aerial bombardment of the missile sites. This process, however, took seven days. Kennedy had learned from the Bay of Pigs invasion. Instead of relying on the CIA and the Joint Chiefs of Staff to define the alternatives, Kennedy called for a selective group of fourteen or fifteen trusted advisors (later called the Executive Committee of the National Security Council), including his brother, Attorney General Robert Kennedy. "Experience mattered little in a crisis which had no precedent. Even rank mattered little when secrecy prevented staff support. We were fifteen individuals on our own, representing the President and not different departments."[21] Although they were fifteen individuals, they had favorites among the policy proposals—the military favoring the pinpoint bombing and the Department of State people favoring a diplomatic solution. The initial problem for this group was to define the alternatives and then to choose between them.

Faced with a shortage of time in which to define alternatives the policy maker must rely on the opinions of those closest to him. To look broader for opinions would require time, a commodity in short supply.

In less unique decisions or where the press of time is less extreme, information and opinions on alternatives can be generated and transmitted to the policy maker. In fact, the more controversial the issue the greater the likelihood that the opinions of the attentive and mass publics will be solicited before a selection is made. As a result, organized public opinion has a chance to be channeled into the policy-making process; indeed, public opinion may be generated in support of an alternative. Banfield's case studies of decision making in Chicago,

---

[21]Sorensen, op. cit., p. 679.

where the mayor has sufficient political and institutional power to make decisions on his own, indicate that very frequently Mayor Daley waits for interested parties to present alternatives to him and argue in their behalf before he makes his decisions.[22] In such cases it was the opinions of interested parties which delineated the alternatives and told him the possibilities of building a consensus behind one alternative, and in that way he was able to make a decision based on knowledge of which alternative would provide him with the broadest range of public support and would be of the greatest political benefit.

Bayh's difficulty with the Carswell nomination was in getting other senators to agree that voting against confirmation was a viable alternative. He was cheered by the criticism of Carswell that was developing outside of Congress. Attacking the nomination in a speech before the local bar association in Kansas City the senator found, "The lawyers—a conservative lot, by and large, listened attentively, applauded each time he made a telling point, and gave him a standing ovation when he finished."[23] Groups of lawyers, most notably the deans of the law schools at Harvard, Yale, and Penn, also began to criticize the nomination. Another group, led by Samuel Rosenman of New York, published an open letter in the *New York Times* asking the Senate to reject the Carswell nomination. This demonstration of hostile opinion by men immediately concerned with the judicial system made it possible for the Senate to seriously consider the qualifications of the nominee rather than merely considering that he was the president's nominee.

Having delineated the alternatives the decision maker must also determine which criteria to use for choosing between them. One important criteria, of course, is cost. Economic theorists argue that a decision maker, faced with a variety of alternatives which will attain the desired end, will choose that alternative which is the least costly.[24] This assumes that one can deter-

---

[22]Banfield, *Political Influence.*
[23]Harris, op. cit., p. 71.
[24]See Anthony Downs, *An Economic Theory of Democracy* (New York: Harper and Row, 1957); Gordon Tullock, *Toward a Mathematics of Politics* (Ann Arbor: University of Michigan Press, 1967); and Kenneth Arrow, *Social Choice and Individual Values* (New York: Wiley, 1951).

mine the costs of all alternatives. Once again, in unique decisional situations where time is a factor, it may not be possible to determine the costs of all alternatives and the decision may have to be on the basis of "minimal acceptable cost." Faced with a river approaching flood stage in his community, a mayor cannot get cost estimates on all possible alternatives; any alternative which saves his community is cheap enough. And not all costs are financial. Frequently the evaluation of the desirability of policy alternatives will be in terms of their technical and political costs. It is at this point, particularly in the less unique decisions where time is not an important variable, that public opinion can play a vital role. Having advanced alternatives interested parties to the particular policy question can and will present arguments as to why their alternative is the most attractive. As we have seen earlier, lobbyists perceive their most important role in this process as that of providing technical information. In the process of providing information the groups also manifest their interest and concern with the issue and provide political information to the policy maker regarding the distribution of forces for and against various alternatives. In some cases the decision maker may find that public opinion has arrayed itself behind an alternative which is technically feasible and economically realistic. The harder decisions are those where the most feasible alternatives are the most politically costly and the most politically attractive alternatives lack technical feasibility.

In the Cuban missile crisis one of the major alternatives—precision bombing of the missile sites—was downgraded because the military could not guarantee that there would be no destruction of civilian lives and property. Without such a guarantee Robert Kennedy felt that a surprise air attack would be "a Pearl Harbor in reverse" which would not be tolerated by American public opinion.[25] A naval blockade had the advantages of being a more limited military action which avoided direct military confrontation but which could be escalated to bombings if it proved unsuccessful. Thus, the political costs

---

[25] Sorensen, op. cit., p. 684.

were manageable and the blockade was technically feasible (the U.S. Navy did have the capacity to establish and man the blockade).

The process was somewhat different with the Carswell nomination. Once senators recognized that opposition was a viable alternative, the Administration and the anti-Carswell people began to provide rationales for supporting or opposing the nomination. Attorney General Mitchell, leading the fight for confirmation, felt that Carswell would be nominated because he was strong in three areas where Clement Haynsworth had been weak: Carswell had no economic conflict of interest with cases in which he had ruled, he had shown no antilabor bias, and he was a "moderate" on civil rights. He was desirable from the Administration's view because he was a Southerner who would be a "strict constructionist" on constitutional questions. Bayh, Brooke, and their allies, on the other hand, had to construct a coalition against the nominee for entirely different reasons. Pressure was brought to bear on Senator Fong, according to Harris, by influential Hawaiians to vote against the Carswell nomination.[26] For some senators Carswell's lower court record of reversals made a convincing argument, when justified by Senator Hruska's comment,

> Even if he were mediocre, there are a lot of mediocre judges and people and lawyers. They are entitled to a little representation, aren't they, and a little chance? We can't have all Brandeises and Frankfurters and Cardozas and stuff like that there.[27]

The need for information about available alternatives and their feasibility is more urgent for critical decisions. For more routine decisions the information is readily available or, if not available, the decision maker knows what information he must have and where to get it. There are also variations within critical decisions, depending on the amount of time available to make the decision. If there is no need to make the decision immediately the search for relevant information, including public

---

[26]Harris, op. cit., pp. 141-44.
[27]Ibid., p. 110.

opinion, can be done thoroughly prior to making the decision. Given unlimited time an unlimited amount of public opinion can be fed into the policy-making process. In more unique decisions with heavy time pressure, the decision maker often must make decisions before he is aware of the full range of available alternatives or knows what criteria should be used. When the early warning system tells the president that he has 15 minutes to respond to incoming missiles he cannot consult congressional leaders or test public opinion. Knowing that he doesn't have much time and needs vital information the decision maker seeks to get all the information he can in the shortest period of time, regardless of the quality of the information. In a foreign policy crisis the president wants all the information he can get from the Department of Defense, the CIA, and people on the spot, in order to define what the situation is. He then seeks the advice of those whom he can trust, assuming that they will provide him with critical information and unswerving loyalty. The decision maker's need for information can be viewed in the following way:

FIGURE 7–2

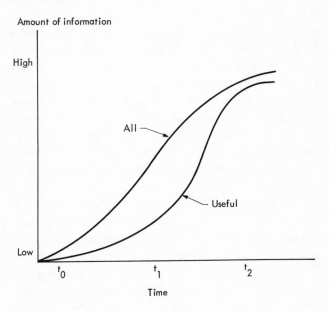

The initial flow of information is meager but then expands quickly; the amount of relevant information, relevant for the decision maker's needs, expands at a slower rate than the general flow of information. In the first few minutes or hours after the onset of a crisis there is a great deal of information incoming, much of it irrelevant. It takes time for the decision maker's intelligence network to define what information he needs and to actively seek that information. But if the decision maker must make a decision at time t_1 it is clear that although he may have information, not very much of it will be relevant to the decision he must make. Thus, it is not surprising to see a decision maker postpone a decision as long as possible in order to maximize available information. Delay, while increasing the amount of information, relevant and irrelevant, may also serve to forestall the feasibility of some alternatives or make those alternatives so costly as to be impractical. In a decisional situation with stringent time constraints the decision maker finds himself in a dilemma—to delay means to have more information on the alternatives available and allows for the development of clear criteria and, at the same time, also means that the decision maker finds himself with some options unavailable and different criteria than when the problem first arose.

The decision in the Cuban missile crisis sought to have the best of all possible worlds, an initial commitment to a naval blockade with the possibility of escalation to pinpoint bombing of missile sites if the blockade failed. The initial decision, in addition to being an important policy decision, also bought time so that its impact could be assessed along with the need for alternative future decisions. The delay in the Carswell nomination served to commit the Senate to a lengthy and fervent debate over the nomination, forestalling the possibility of a quick and near-unanimous confirmation. The delay thus guaranteed that the decision would not be a routine one.

It is clear that the more time the decision maker needs and the more information he seeks the greater the role that public opinion will play in his decision. In a time-shortened decision the initial opinions he receives will be from opinion elites who are knowledgeable about the problem and have access to him, people whose expertise he trusts. In the Cuban missile crisis, for example, the Executive Committee established by Kennedy contained his trusted advisors plus personnel from the State Department and the Joint Chiefs of Staff. Kennedy was leery, however, of the opinions of the intelligence community, particularly the CIA, which he felt had led him astray during the Bay of Pigs invasion. Reedy warns that relying on a coterie of advisors for their opinions serves to insulate the president from the consideration of some alternatives which the advisors don't think he will look favorably upon.[28] Rather than serving as the eyes and ears of the decision maker in the larger community, anticipating how that community will respond to a variety of alternatives, they may feel their primary responsibility is to preserve their own reputations and the decision maker's ego. As a result, he hears what he wants to hear, sees those alternatives he wants to see, and uses those criteria which his advisors feel will be the least uncertain.

Where time is not a consideration the policy maker can afford to wait for mass opinion to generate and become aggregated. This is not to rule out the importance of the opinions of advisors. In fact, the advisors' most important roles will be to generate opinion support for alternatives which they favor and to interpret the meaning of opinion which is articulated into the policy making process.

The discussion should not mislead us into thinking that once the decision-making process has reached the stage where alternatives are searched and evaluated then the process will grind forward to a decision. The costs of searching for alternatives may be too high. Complex problems require complex solutions and the costs of defining alternative solutions may prevent the problem from being solved unless it can be simplified. Even where the policy alternatives can be specified there may be no acceptable alternative—being "Red or dead" may not be acceptable alternatives for United States foreign policy. Where one policy alternative does not have widespread opinion support, from elites or mass, the decision maker is faced with the task of forging a coalition in support of an alternative. In the

---

[28]George Reedy, *Twilight of the Presidency* (New York: World Publishing, 1970).

process of forming that coalition he may find that the costs of compromise too greatly increase the cost of the agreed-upon alternative.[29]

Stage III: The decision

Completion of the first two stages does not guarantee that a decision will be made. The decision maker is faced with two decisions: whether to make a decision and, if he chooses to decide, which alternative to choose. In cases where there is pressure to make a decision and one alternative stands out, there is no difficulty. Where the issue is less salient and there are conflicting and costly alternative solutions, the decision to make a decision is far more difficult.

Some problems do not require a decision; the process of developing and evaluating alternatives may relieve public demand for solution of the problem, making the problem less salient and reducing public pressure for a decision. After reviewing the activities of the Kerner Commission and other riot commissions, Lipsky and Olson conclude:

> Whether or not riot commissions are created in order to buy time, it is unquestionable that they do permit public officials to avoid immediate pressures for action and to postpone decisions for many months. Not only does the creation of a commission deflect pressures from the chief executive, but it also improves his bargaining position in a conservative direction by permitting him to claim that he is constrained by other political pressures over which he has little control. In the intense crisis following the riot, people seem to appeal instinctively to the chief executive for leadership. But the opportunity for decisive leadership, for making qualitatively different decisions about national priorities, based on opportunities available only in crisis situations, may not be what the politician desires. Postponement permits the chief executive to wrap himself in the usual constraints of office where politics as usual will continue to obtain. Riot commissions also contribute to cooling of tensions by reassuring various publics in a symbolic way that their needs are being met.

---

[29]William Riker, *The Theory of Political Coalitions* (New Haven, Conn.: Yale University Press, 1962).

This may take the form of calling witnesses representative of various positions, making hortatorical appeals for justice and nonviolence, and so forth.[30]

The time lag between the creation of the commission and the completion of its duty allows the executive time to reevaluate the salience of the issue; if he feels it is still an important issue he can then accept and act upon the recommendations of the commission. Rarely is an issue so burning that it can remain salient over the lifespan of a commission. The commission members prefer to work outside the glare of publicity and so want the issue to cool. But as passions cool the commission's relevance declines, as does the pressure on the executive to act. Postponing the decision until the need for a decision has passed is still a decision—a decision not to decide.

One of the important functions for public opinion is to hold the issue salient for the decision maker and force him to reach a decision. Having forced him to recognize the problem, public opinion must then force him to act for resolution. Nonaction, however, may be fruitful for the policy maker and the groups seeking solution to the problem; in creating decisional time the decision maker has more time to sample opinions and decide whether the decision is necessary while, at the same time, allowing passions to subside.

Assuming that the decision maker is faced with making a decision he cannot or will not avoid what factors enter into his decision. To the extent that the first two stages of the decision-making process have clarified the alternatives and defined criteria for choosing between alternatives, the decision is a simple one. The easiest decisions to make are those where there is unanimity as to what should be done. In more unique decisional settings, however, the factors influencing the decision maker are incredibly complex.

The decision maker finds himself in three major crosscurrents: his personality, the goals of relevant others in the political environment, and his capacity to make and implement the

---

[30]See Michael Lipsky and David J. Olson, "Riot Commission Politics," *Trans-Action* 6 (July/August, 1969), p. 21.

decision. We have earlier discussed the role played by personality in the formulation of micro public opinion; personality plays an equally important role in decision making.[31] The "openness" of the decision maker's belief system influences his ability to understand and evaluate alternatives which are available to him. Woodrow Wilson's messianic faith in himself and his ideals resulted in his inability to compromise on policy alternatives which might have led to acceptance of the League of Nations and furthered Wilson's political career. His close-mindedness in the decision on whom to take to the Treaty Talks in Versailles prevented him from including a Republican or a congressman, which might have made congressional Republican support possible, or at least mitigated their opposition. His conviction that he was "right" led him to fight for the Versailles Treaty without modification by the Senate, thereby putting his political life and the future of the League of Nations on the block. Other policy alternatives were available but Wilson refused to recognize or consider them. In that sense the close-mindedness of his belief system made his policy decisions easy—he excluded all other criteria or alternatives other than his own.[32]

We have earlier seen how Dulles' personality influenced his perceptions of the Soviet Union. Not all decision makers, however, are as close-minded as Wilson and Dulles were. They are receptive to cues about their environment and have realistic evaluations of the environment in which they operate, for without constant reality testing they would no longer be able to function. We must not forget, nonetheless, that decision makers will seek public opinion which is favorable to their own beliefs rather than that which challenges them. In cases where the policy maker does not have strong values and beliefs, public opinion can thus have a greater impact.

When the decision maker has freedom to assess the alterna-

---

[31]See deRivera, op. cit., pp. 165-206.

[32]The best analyses of Wilson are found in Alexander and Juliette George, *Woodrow Wilson and Colonel House* (New York: Dover, 1964 ed.); Greenstein, *Personality and Politics*, pp. 69-86; and John Dos Passos, *Mr. Wilson's War* (Garden City, N.Y.: Doubleday, 1962).

tives before him he must decide how his decision will effect relevant constituencies. Neustadt argues that the president's decisions are influenced by whether they will gain or lose favor for him in the executive branch, in Congress, and outside of Washington in state houses and world capitols.[33] In a Machiavellian way the president must make those decisions which will give him the greatest reward for his investment of time and resources. At the same time he must be aware of maintaining his political capital with interested parties in his political environment, making one decision which wins favor with Congress, another which meets with the approval of the electorate, etc. The same kinds of calculations are made by all decision makers, from city councilman to president.

Neustadt's description of political leadership leaves one with the impression that the president and Lou Harris run the country, with the president responding totally to the opinions of publics which are relevant to him. Such a person would be a political version of Riesman's "other-directed" man, responding to cues from the environment without any goals or ideals of his own. Our earlier concern about the role played by the personality of the decision maker dictates that a decision is the result of the decision maker's attitudes, values, and beliefs, and the payoffs he feels he will derive from his political environment. The primary question is the relevant impact of the two variables. There are obvious difficulties with the decision maker who is guided only by public opinion; for unique decisions, made under the pressure of time, he will be unable to wait for public opinion to form and channel itself into the policy-making process. Instead he will be forced to rely on those people around him whose opinions he trusts, in the hope that mass public opinion will be supportive of the actions he takes. The other-directed man will have no time to monitor his environment when radar images are headed over the North Pole, the North Koreans invade South Korea, or the North Vietnamese cross the demilitarized zone. In more routine decisions the other-directed man may have the time to receive

---

[33] Richard Neustadt, *Presidential Power* (New York: Wiley, 1960).

some input from his environment. The close-minded decision maker, on the other hand, will not wait for public opinion to form since it is irrelevant for his decision unless it is supportive of his own values. Contrary opinions will not be perceived or heeded. The amount of time available for the decision is irrelevant for the close-minded decision maker since his belief system allows him to act regardless of the amount of information he possesses.

There is relatively little research on decision makers' abilities to perceive correctly the policy preferences of their constituents. Bauer, Pool, and Dexter found that the relevant public opinion for most congressmen on reciprocal trade were those opinions conveyed to them by lobbyists whom they trusted and with whom they agreed. There was no awareness of mass public opinion, probably because the public wasn't concerned about the issue.[34] Sigel and Friesema, studying the perceptions of thirty community leaders and over two hundred citizen advisory committee members regarding education, found the community leaders' estimates of public opinion were grossly inaccurate, with leaders misjudging both the magnitude and the direction of public opinion.[35] As one might expect, the misperceptions occurred most frequently in the areas where leaders' personal preferences varied considerably from those of their constituents. Community leaders thought there was more dissatisfaction with the educational system than there actually was and erroneously felt they shared a concern with the public over racial policy and support for innovations. In essence, the community leaders perceived that the public was as concerned as they and that the public was supportive of them, both of which were erroneous perceptions.

Two other factors are worthy of consideration when a decision maker must act: the resources which he has at his

---

[34]Bauer, Pool, and Dexter, op. cit.

[35]Roberta Sigel and H. Paul Friesema, "Urban Community Leaders' Knowledge of Public Opinion," *Western Political Quarterly* 18 (December, 1965): 881-95. See also Norman Luttbeg and Harmon Zeigler, "Attitude Consensus and Conflict in an Interest Group: An Assessment of Cohesion," *American Political Science Review* 60 (September, 1966), pp. 655-65.

disposal and his ability to implement the decision once it has been made. Neustadt argues that the decision maker has certain resources available to him as perquisites of his position—public attention, respect, constitutional and institutional bases of power. In addition he has the political capital he has accumulated with his various publics due to his previous public activities. For that reason the newly elected official is in a more tenuous position than one who has served his constituents for a period of time; he has only the institutional and constitutional bases of power and the goodwill of the electorate following his election. One could assume that a president elected by a narrow margin, such as John F. Kennedy in 1961 or Richard Nixon in 1969, would hesitate to make risky decisions lest he lose the small political capital his victory gained him with the electorate. The American people, however, are notoriously gracious to winners, regardless of the size of the margin. A president's popularity rating is often highest immediately following his election and during his first three to six months in office, which columnists have called a "honeymoon" period.[36] The public no longer responds to the candidate *qua* candidate but as president and the man they called a villain before the election becomes "President" after his victory. Thus, supportive public opinion as a resource tends to be most potent early in an official's term, declining through his term, and rallying when he takes action on an issue about which the public feels strongly.

Using the distinction made by Neustadt, between the decision maker as clerk and as leader, we find that the president who does not make the critical decisions does not risk his political capital but does not conserve it either. The president who does make decisions on important issues finds that the public approves of the fact that he has made a decision, regardless of its content. Even if Congress or some segment of the public do not like the substance of his decision—and he loses their favor—he can still recoup by his gain from the public who approve his taking a public stance. The political leader who

---

[36]See John E. Mueller, "Presidential Popularity from Truman to Johnson," *American Political Science Review* 64 (March, 1970), pp. 18-34.

sounds and acts like a leader is perceived by the public as having leadership qualities.

The political leader who seeks to act as a leader has to orchestrate the variety of publics who watch his activities. The ideal decision is that one which gains public acceptance from the mass public, the attentive public, opinion leaders, and other political leaders and competitors. There are relatively few decisions which permit this kind of opinion "gain" across the board. Instead the decision maker must be able to balance off his opinion "gains" and "losses" to see whether a decision is profitable and which alternative is the most feasible. Thus, President Nixon's 1969 decision to withdraw U.S. troops from South Vietnam while increasing the effectiveness of the South Vietnamese troops had the effect of undercutting criticism of his handling of the war and gaining some Congressional support for his policies, while losing the support of some world leaders who looked to the United States for leadership in Southeast Asia. Faced with a deteriorating military situation in early 1972 the president then moved to blockade North Vietnam and to mine the harbors to prevent the unloading of materials. The decision was not an easy one; would he be better off running the risk of suffering a military defeat in South Vietnam (and being "the first American president to lose a war") and the subsequent loss of prestige at home and abroad or would he do better by responding militarily, thus alienating those people who had approved of his Vietnamization proposals, and still running the risk of losing the war militarily?

In order effectively to make the decision the decision maker must be able to carry out his decision. First, he must be the decision maker with the proper authority to make the decision; a city official does not have the authority to declare war for the United States. Very often people who make demands on government forget that while government may be ubiquitous, there are constitutional and legal differentiations which describe what each level of government can and must do. Second, within a level of government the proper official must make the decision. It is often difficult for citizens to determine which government official has the authority to make decisions within a given policy area. The decision-making maze in the recreation field at the national level is symbolic of the confusion over who makes policy in the area. The Forest Service in the Department of Agriculture oversees recreation in the natonal forests, the National Park Service in the Department of the Interior supervises recreation in national parks and other federal facilities, and the Army Corps of Engineers are involved in building recreational facilities located adjacent to navigable waterways. As a result of these overlapping jurisdictions it is difficult for people interested in recreational policy to focus their attention and actions at the proper agents in the policy-making process. Environmental groups concerned about recreational decision making and its impact on the environment find themselves in a maze where decisions about related recreational questions are made by different policy makers, totally unaware of decisions being made elsewhere. For public opinion to have a voice in the policy-making process, the process must be decipherable for those who wish to influence it and coordinated for those who wish to understand its policy outputs. Groups which have dealt for some time with a given question have an advantage over newcomers—they at least know who is making which kinds of decisions where in the process. Third, the decision maker must have the power to make his subordinates carry out his decisions. A decision, made by a superior but not implemented by subordinates, is not a decision. Although the landmark desegregation case of *Brown* v. *The Board of Education* was decided by the Supreme Court in 1954 federal, state, and local officials are still being pushed for implementation of that decision. To be effective the decision maker must have the capacity to persuade others to carry out his wishes, which is dependent on how people perceive the mandate behind that decision. As we shall see shortly (Stage IV) the crucial test of the policy decision is the content of the policy which is administered. To the extent there is deviation between the intent of the decision and the content of the administered policy, the decision maker was not the "effective" decision maker.

Although President Kennedy used a small coterie of advisors to help clarify the alternatives and present arguments for and against them, it was he alone who had to make the decision. The decision, however, was not a single act.

> Both the case for the blockade and the case for simply living with this threat were presented. The President had already moved from the air strike to the blockade camp. He liked the idea of leaving Khrushchev a way out, of beginning at a low level that could be stepped up; and the other choices had too many insuperable difficulties. Blockade, he indicated, was his *tentative* choice. (Emphasis mine)[37]

Work was begun on a presidential address to the nation in which the blockade would be announced. To the dismay of the blockade advocates the president reopened the discussion the next day and went over the case for the naval blockade, as opposed to the air strike, with his advisors. This could have been an opportunity to reverse his position, but Sorensen feels that Kennedy wanted the opportunity to think through the blockade idea more clearly with his advisors and allow them one last chance to state their case.[38] After that discussion the president decided to pursue the naval blockade policy.

The roll call vote taken by the Senate on the Carswell nomination was the formal decision being made by the Senate. For many senators, however, the decision on how to vote had been made days earlier; all but a few senators had reached their decision and publically announced it prior to the vote. Some were undecided until the very day of the vote. At least one, Margaret Chase Smith, changed her mind during the twenty-four hours preceding the roll call vote, initially agreeing to vote for Carswell but then voting against him when she discovered that the White House had made public her vote intention.[39] The call of the roll was merely the formal recording of individual decisions which had been reached two months to two minutes before the senators' names were called.

---

[37]Sorensen, op. cit., p. 691.
[38]Ibid., p. 692 and Abel, op. cit., p. 83.
[39]Harris, op. cit., pp. 195-99.

Stage IV: Implementing the decision

Having reached a decision the decision maker must now put it into effect. Rarely does the decision maker implement the policy decision he has made; he makes decisions which others implement. The separation of the process into decisional and implementation components means that the content of a policy decision may be drastically altered in the implementation stage. It is recognized that on complex policy questions Congress will frequently pass legislation which establishes broad policy guidelines but leaves the more precise delineation of the policy to the agency which administers it. Woll suggests that this arrangement is advantageous because pressure groups often become lost in the shuffle of congressional decision making, so that the people most affected by the legislation frequently are not heard during the policy-making process. It is only when the policy must be implemented that the pressure groups and the opinions they represent can play a role in determining the content and application of the policy.[40] The policy-making process is the larger arena for the interplay of mass public opinion, while the implementation stage is the arena for the opinions of the affected publics. Some groups may have better access to the implementors of policy than to the policy makers and therefore shepherd their resources to seek to influence the implementation rather than the policy-making process itself. The broadcast industry, for example, has a close working relationship with the Federal Communications Commission, often conferring with it about implementation of legislation or regulation affecting the industry. In many cases the bureaucracy becomes a captive of the people with whom they deal. The independent regulatory commissions, designed to regulate industry and commerce in the public interest and free from political control, must have the acceptance of the people they regulate if they are to be effective. Given this need, it is not surprising that the independent regulatory commissions rarely do anything to antagonize their consumer-clients, thereby raising the question

---

[40]Peter Woll, *American Bureaucracy* (New York: Norton, 1963).

of who is regulating whom.[41] Much the same phenomenon occurs within the bureaucracy. The Department of Labor is responsive to labor union wishes just as the Department of Commerce is responsive to the business community.

The decision-maker is often helpless to correct any deviation from his policy decision. In cases where policy is made in one branch of government (the legislature) and implemented in another (the executive) there are mutual hostilities which preclude effective control by the legislature. The legislature has a potential club in its fiscal control of the bureaucracy, but budget cuts are awkward means of sanctioning action taken months earlier and are effective only in cases where there has been flagrant and consistent deviation from legislative intent.[42] Even when the decision maker and his subordinate are in the same branch of government the decision maker may find himself unable to insure compliance; the subordinate may be a member of a merit system which protects his actions except for gross cases of misfeasance or malfeasance. In addition, the subordinate may feel that his primary obligation is to his profession rather than to his superior and bases his actions on professional norms rather than the desires of the superior. There may also be institutional barriers, such as the independent commissions which are appointed by a public official but are not responsible to him, which make it difficult for a policy maker to have his decisions implemented as he would like. For these reasons it is not surprising to find that the source of "effective" policy making shifts from the official who is legally responsible for the act to the person or agency which is charged with administering it.

If it is possible to modify a policy decision in the administrative phase then public opinion can play a role. In routine policy decisions, however, the implementor has little or no discretion; it is in the more unique decisions, where the decision is imprecise or presents only broad policy guidelines, that public

---

[41]Marvin Bernstein, *Regulating Business by Dependent Commissions* (Princeton, N.J.: Princeton University Press, 1965).

[42]Aaron Wildavsky, *The Politics of the Budgetary Process* (Boston, Mass.: Little, Brown & Co., 1964).

opinion can serve to specify the content of that policy. The impact of public opinion is thus limited to those people who have a direct and vital interest in the policy area and have access to the administrators, thereby giving an advantage to those groups which are well organized, have regularized contacts with administrators, and are, in an important sense, constituents of the administrators. Groups such as the American Medical Association have more impact on the administration of policy decisions than do consumers, and a group which loses a battle to prevent a policy decision from being made can win the war by having that policy administered in ways which are less damaging to them.

In the Cuban missile crisis once Kennedy had decided on a naval blockade three tasks were involved in implementation. First, the president had to notify the parties involved—most notably the Russians and our allies—regarding the substance of the decision and to tell the American public of the danger involved in Soviet missile bases in Cuba and the decision which he had reached. It was only at this point that mass public opinion became relevant, after the decision had been reached. In order to effectively "harden" the decision and prevent implementation which deviated from his wishes the president had to create support for the decision outside the bureaucracy. Second, through his role as Commander-in-Chief, he had to implement his decision by positioning the Navy in blockade formation and monitoring their activities to make sure they were carrying out the intent of his activities. In an important sense Kennedy retained control of the implementation of his decision by requiring Navy commanders in the Caribbean to notify him of the ships which continued on toward Cuba and personally selecting the ship which was to be boarded. Third, he had to await Soviet and Cuban response to his decision in order to decide what further action would be necessary.

The Carswell decision, once the Senate had acted, needed no implementation. The public rewarded or punished some senators at the polls. President Nixon responded to the Carswell defeat by concluding, "I cannot successfully nominate to the Supreme Court any federal appellate judge from the South who believes as I do in the strict constructon of the Constitution."[43] He subsequently nominated an appellate judge from Minnesota, Warren Burger, who was approved quickly and without opposition by the Senate.

Pathways of the policy-making process

Segmenting the policy-making process into four distinct stages leaves one with the impression that issues are resolved either by having a decision made and implemented (successfully cycling through Stages I-IV) or by having the process halted at any one stage. When an issue is stopped at one stage it may cycle back to an earlier stage, seeking to build public support, define policy alternatives, or engage the attention of policy makers. (See Figure 7-3.) A tracing of the life history of most policy issues would probably show that very few of them successfully cycled through the policy-making process, from beginning to end, when they first arose to capture public attention.

FIGURE 7–3

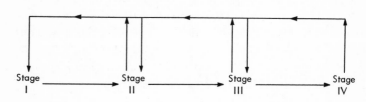

Federal aid to education is an example of the circularity of the process.[44] From 1948 to 1964 twelve federal aid to education bills were introduced in Congress and defeated. Between 1948 and 1955 the chief obstacle to passage was the House Education and Labor Committee, but by 1959 federal aid supporters had a majority on that committee. As support increased on the Edu-

---

[43]Harris, op. cit., p. 209.

[44]Eugene Eidenberg and Roy D. Morey, *An Act of Congress* (New York: Norton, 1969).

cation and Labor Committee, opposition increased in the House Rules Committee, which has the prime responsibility for scheduling legislation in the House. Even on those occasions when a bill found its way to the floor of the House it was defeated.

Why then, after sixteen years of trying, did Congress finally pass a federal aid to education bill? Eidenberg and Morey explain its passage in the following terms:

> Between 1961 and 1965 there were several major developments that paved the way for an education bill. When the 1964 Civil Rights bill was passed, the race issue in education policy was a moot point. The South had expected the filibuster to last forever; but the Senate had in 1964 cut it off—a move as significant in its own way for education legislation as the rules changes in the House in 1965.
>
> Everyone involved in the 1964 election knew the results would be read as a mandate of some kind about the education issue. Whether it was in fact such a mandate is neither debatable nor relevant. All we know was that Charlie Halleck (former House Republican Leader) had killed himself and the party on the issue with their rigid obstructionism.
>
> A protestant President could champion a bill that somehow got funds to students on nonpublic schools. The poverty problem had been drummed into peoples' minds through 1964. The Kennedy education bill gave that program the force of Presidential initiative and concern; and when the legislative vehicle for education was couched in terms of fighting poverty, it became most difficult politically to oppose.[45]

The climate of opinion, in and out of Washington, was different in 1965 than it had been earlier; the political costs of acting on an education bill had been lowered and the rewards increased. The favorable climate of opinion which existed in 1965 and allowed for the passage of the bill was transitory. The Civil Rights Act and the 1964 election were unique phenomena which combined to create a favorable public opinion toward education at that time. Perhaps, as Eidenberg and Morey argue, "If the school bill had failed in 1965, chances are it would not

---

[45]Quoted in ibid., pp. 241-42,

have been enacted subsequently, at least in the same form."[46]

The 1965 Elementary and Secondary Education Act, in turn, has made possible the passage of subsequent federal aid to education bills. Once a policy decision has been made it becomes a beachhead from which it is difficult to retreat. Difficult, but not impossible to change. Opposition to policy decisions may take one of two forms: objection to the content of the decision or objection to the way it is implemented. Seeking to reverse the content of a policy decision—the "sore-loser" syndrome—is normally a hopeless task unless it can be shown that the policy decision is not accomplishing what it was intended to accomplish. Even then the policy makers may merely acknowledge their mistake without changing the policy, as in the case of the TFX fighter-bomber,[47] because the policy decision was correct in the short-run, by taking public pressure from the policy makers and deferring criticism of the decision to the future, when the issue would be less salient. Most changes in the content of policy decisions are the result of battles over the implementation of the decision. When the Federal Communications Commission was created to regulate the burgeoning communications media, the industry moved quickly either to limit the powers of the FCC or to make the FCC dependent on the industry. It has been successful in accomplishing both its aims. In this way the loser in the policy-making battle may overtly bear the mantle of defeat while convertly savoring the wine of an operational victory.[48]

Most issues, however, cycle through Stage I or Stages I and II without being resolved. It takes a concurrence of events and forces to push an issue over the transition from Stage II to Stages III and IV. As a result of the pathway model it is possible to ask a number of interesting and exciting questions about the role of public opinion in the policy-making process.

Looking at the life histories of issues, are there any com-

---

[46]Ibid., p. 3.

[47]For background see Robert J. Ard, *The TFX Decision* (Boston: Little, Brown, and Co., 1968).

[48]The literature on independent regulatory commissions is becoming increasingly critical of their performance. See particularly Louis M. Kohlmeier, *The Regulators* (New York: Harper and Row, 1969).

*monalities in the paths they took or the length of time they took
to move from Stages I to IV?* Since are relatively few case
studies of unsuccessful issues or of classes of issues, it is
difficult to generalize about the paths of issues which have not
met success or about the pathways of classes of issues such as
highway location or water fluoridation. For routine decisions
the pathway is clearcut—a steady and rapid progression from
Stages I to IV, a process which the woman in the dog license
bureau accomplishes in slightly under four minutes. The less
routine the decision the more time the process will take and the
more circuitous the route may be; for particularly complex
issues the process may occur by fits and starts. The federal interstate highway system was first considered as an alternative
in 1939, a congressional report was submitted in 1944, but
enabling legislation was not passed by Congress until 1956.

*What kinds of public opinion are the most evident and most
influential at each stage of the policy-making process?* A variety of types of public opinion can play a role at Stage I in
bringing the issue to the attention of the policy maker. In some
cases, such as the Cuban missile crisis, it was members of the
president's immediate staff who brought the issue to his attention and convinced him of its importance and of the need for a
response. Often, however, the mass public must become involved with the issue before the decision maker will recognize
and validate it calling for the activities of pressure groups and
the statement of public opinion by public opinion polls and the
mass media. Time is an important determinant for the role of
public opinion at Stage II. Where the policy maker has time to
delineate the alternatives and explore a full range of criteria interested parties can express their opinions, seek to mobilize
others, and create coalitions in support of various alternatives
and criteria. The policy maker may find himself with the option
of either waiting for public opinion to coalesce or he may seek
to create public opinion around an option which he favors.
Where the policy maker is short of time he must rely on the
opinions of those around him whom he trusts and the amount of
opinion which he can find in the time available for him to
search.

Who are the participants in the policy-making process at each stage? In a pluralistic political system, where the policy-making process may be a long and complex one particularly for less routine decisions, we may find that certain actors intervene at one stage but not another, or they play the role of decision maker at one stage but not another. The mass media, for example, often serve as a source of problem recognition for the policy maker, bringing issues to his attention—whether he wants to consider them or not. At Stage II or III, however, the media may serve as a communication link from the policy maker downward to the public, enabling him to state which alternatives he prefers and why, or to defend his decision once it has been made. Political parties may be most relevant in the agenda-setting process where the party platform establishes priorities for the party in government. Pressure groups tend to operate throughout the process, bringing issues to the attention of public officials, rallying support, or seeking to influence the administration of a legislative enactment.

Nor does the policy-making process on an issue occur only at one governmental level. For example, a man in a small midwestern town complains to the city council that the local industry is ruining his fishing by pouring waste products into the local river. A local sportsmen's club agrees and presses a demand that the town clean up the river. Tests are taken which indicate that the pollution is at hazardous levels but the city council feels that it has neither the resources nor the statutory power to halt the industry's activities. The fisherman, with the support of others, then brings suit in state court (bringing the issue to another governmental body at another level) to halt the pollution under state law, while the city council appeals to the state legislature for funds to help construct a sewage treatment facility for the town (one group of decision makers at one governmental level seek to influence another group at a higher level). While the legal battle is being fought in the stage and, on appeal, in the federal courts, the stage decides it has neither the funds nor the statutory power to grant the town's desire for treatment facilities. In fact, the state legislature isn't sure it is much of a problem, regardless of what the fisherman or his city council think. As a result, the state's congressional delegation is consulted by a member of the city council and an interested state legislator (decision makers at the first and second level appeal to those at the third level) and legislation is introduced in Washington to establish federal aid for communities who wish to establish sewage treatment plants as an aid to combatting pollution. At the national level the battle is joined by conservationists, environmentalists, and other interested state and local officials. Once the legislation is passed and signed into law the state then establishes a pollution control agency to administer the funds received by the federal government with the advice of a citizen's advisory board (the implementation decisions are shifted from one level of government to another and interested parties have a role in determining the administration of the policy) and the local government must then apply to the state agency for funds.

Thus, the decision-making body which was initially involved in the policy-making (the city council) played a fairly minor role—it initiated the process at the state and helped at the national levels and served as client in the ultimate application of the federal statute. An apparently simple issue can become quite complex, with a variety of potential decisional points at all levels of government. Due to the complexity of the policy-making process it is difficult effectively to channel public opinion into the process at a time and in such a manner that policy makers can respond to it. One of the costs of a pluralistic system is its requirement that people who wish to influence public policy must feel strongly enough about an issue to stay with it from beginning to end, wherever the issue is shunted.

What impact does public opinion have: Does it really matter?

This book began with a discussion of what "public opinion" is and has proceeded to explore the processes by which public opinion is formed and how it is aggregated and articulated for the political system. One last question remains: what impact does public opinion have on what the political system does? Lowell argues that public opinion plays an important, if not dominant role, in the way decisions are made in a democracy.[49] Key suggests that the opinions of the political elites and the attentive public are the most relevant ones on policy questions, since these are the people who are most informed and interested[50] Bauer, Pool, and Dexter found that on an issue like reciprocal trade the mass public was unconcerned and unaware of the issue and, although pressure groups were active on the issue, members of Congress were not necessarily aware of them.[51] In more recent experience we have seen public outcry force President Nixon and the Department of Defense to reconsider their decision to ship mustard gas by rail through the Pacific Northwest. At the same time President Nixon and the Department of Defense were seemingly unimpressed by public protests in the United States and Canada against an underground atomic test at Amchitka Island in the Aleutians. What can we say to explain these diverse examples?

I have earlier suggested that public opinion serves to define how political issues are to be resolved and to define in broad terms the types of issues to be dealt with, the range of alternatives which are "acceptable," and the range of criteria to be used for choosing between the alternatives. In addition, public opinion grants legitimacy to the people who make those decisions and the rules under which they operate. With regard to any particular issue, however, we must know whose opinions the policy maker is considering when he makes his decision. Does he run to read the latest Gallup poll, does he listen to those groups and people who have an interest in the issue, or does he rely on his own judgment and that of his friends? What factors determine whose opinions he will heed?

First, the type of policy decision is important. I have argued that public opinion plays its most important role in delineating alternatives and clarifying criteria for nonroutine decisions. If

---

[49]A. Lawrence Lowell, *Public Opinion and Popular Government* (New York: Longmans, Green, and Co., 1914).

[50]V.O. Key, Jr., *Public Opinion and American Democracy* (New York: Alfred Knopf, 1961).

[51]Raymond A. Bauer, Ithiel De Sola Pool, and Lewis A. Dexter, *American Business and Public Policy* (New York: Atherton Press, 1964).

possible the policy maker also wishes to sample the widest range of possible alternatives available to him before he acts. Second, the stage of the policy-making process will also influence which opinions will be heard. As I have suggested mass opinions may be most important during the problem recognition and acceptance stage, and the attentive public may be most influential in the implementation stage. Third, the amount of time taken to make the decision influences the kind of opinion considered. As we have seen in the Cuban missile crisis, the short time span precluded extensive sampling of opinions outside the president's trusted advisors, while the Haynsworth nomination had a longer time perspective which allowed for the aggregation and articulation of the opinions of the attentive and mass publics. Fourth, access to the policy maker influences the kinds of opinions he receives. DeRivera suggests that the president tends to insulate himself from mass public opinion on foreign policy questions and relies instead on his own opinions or the opinions of his staff.[52] Reedy suggests that the isolation from public opinion is inherent in the office of the president when he surrounds himself with people who agree with him and shield him from those who disagree. "A President moves through his days surrounded by literally hundreds of people whose relationship to him is that of a doting mother to a spoiled child."[53] Fifth, the personality of the decision maker is important. For closeminded people like Woodrow Wilson or John Foster Dulles the only relevant opinions were their own, while others (Franklin Roosevelt comes to mind) seek to hear a wide range of opinions before coming to a decision. And lastly, the way the opinion is communicated will influence whether it is heeded. To the extent that the opinion is communicated clearly and loudly by someone the policy maker perceives as legitimate, he will be influenced by it. On some questions the legitimate opinion submitters may be pressure groups while on others the legitimate opinion may be that of a close friend.

With this list of variables affecting the impact of public

[52]de Rivera, op. cit.
[53]Reedy, op. cit., p. 33.

opinion it is very difficult to determine how and where public opinion influences public policy. Very few people have tried to make this connecton. Eidenberg and Morey argue that public opinion played no role in the passage of the 1964 Education Act but the bulk of their excellent case study details the activities of education lobbyists and congressmen to write an acceptable bill.[54] Mass public opinion may not have played a role but the opinions represented by the educational groups were surely important. Garceau and Silverman found that the Associated Industries of Vermont had an impact on the Vermont legislature but were not able to "control" the legislative process.[55] Much of the research on the impact of public opinion has been by means of case studies, which make generalization difficult.

Froman has attempted to study the impact of public opinion by systematically measuring the effectiveness of pressure groups in each of the states.[56] Assuming that in a highly competitive state, with strong pressure groups, each group would seek to gain advantage over others by gaining constitutional changes which benefited their interests, he hypothesized that the strength of pressure groups in the states would be reflected in the length of state constitutions, the number of amendments proposed, and the number of amendments adopted. The data confirmed his hypothesis. Unfortunately, methodological problems cast some question as to whether Froman was measuring the effectiveness of pressure group activities.[57]

The assumption that the level of party competition makes a difference in the kinds of policies which a state pursues has recently been examined by political scientists. The argument assumes that in competitive two-party states the two parties

---

[54]Eidenberg and Morey, op. cit.

[55] Oliver Garceau and Corinne Silverman, "A Pressure Group and the Pressured: A Case Report," *American Political Science Review* 48 (September, 1954), pp. 672-91.

[56]Lewis A. Froman, Jr., "Some Effects of Interest Group Strength in State Politics," *American Political Science Review* 60 (December, 1966), pp. 952-62.

[57]The difficulty stems from Froman's correlation of interest group strength, as measured in the 1960s, with constitutional length, some of which date back to 1789, when pressure group strength may have been different.

must offer discernibly different platforms and programs and, as a result, losing or gaining control of state government means a shift in the policies of the state, a shift reflective of the policy differences between the parties. Correlational research by Dye, and Dawson and Robinson[58] suggest that the strong correlation between state expenditures for various state services and party competition is eliminated when the economic development of the state is taken into account: the wealthier states are the most politically competitive and spend the most on state services, and it is the availability of money rather than party competition which determines spending.[59] It would be foolish, nonetheless, to suggest that the wealth of a state automatically determines its expenditures, so that once a state reaches a given standard of living it spends more money on state services. Wealth is a resource available to policy makers to use or not use as they see fit—it is an important parameter influencing whether a state engages in certain activities, but not the sole determinant. Subsequent research by Sharkansky suggests that policy expenditures are the result of a mixture of political and socioeconomic factors.

Highways and natural resource policies find support in the vigor of local governments, the professionalization of the public service, and the absence of industry and population concentrations. Attributes of the electoral arena, as measured by competition and turnout, as well as the levels of personal income and education, have little to do with policies in this area.

Welfare-education policies, in contrast, are related closely to levels of competition, turnout, and affluence. The most politically vigorous and well off states are the most prone to support programs for uplifting the population through

---

[58]Thomas R. Dye, *Politics, Economics and the Public* (Chicago: Rand McNally, 1966); Richard E. Dawson and James A. Robinson, "Inter-Party Competition, Economic Variables, and Welfare Policies in the American States," *Journal of Politics* 25 (May, 1963), pp. 265-89.

[59]Once again methodological problems cloud the conclusiveness of the results since the authors correlate party competition over a period of years with state expenditures in a given year, thus comparing a bag of oranges with one apple. See also Herbert Jacob and Kenneth Vines, "Epilogue," in their book *Politics in the American States* (Boston: Little, Brown, 1971), pp. 559-60.

schools and assistance to the poor. Although less important than competition-turnout and affluence, the vigor of local governments and the professionalism of the civil service supports welfare and education policies.[60]

Public policy, according to those studies, can thus be viewed as the result of a variety of factors, some institutional and some political, which determine how at least some demands by people within the political system are met.

But what happens if some members of the political system feel that their opinions have no impact on the way decisions are made, decisions which affect their lives? What happens when they lack the resources to participate in the policy-making process, lack access to governmental officials, and lack the skills adequately to represent their opinions in ways that can be understood? There is some evidence that when people become alienated from their government they react by abstaining from political action or by using the ballot box as an instrument to express their frustration.[61] Voting for the underdog, or against the front runner, or seeing the threat of Communist subversion in fluoridation proposals are often responses of those who feel they can no longer have a voice in their political system. What of those people who feel that the political system is no longer interested in their opinions and that elections are no longer legitimate vehicles for the aggregation and articulation of their opinions?

The history of recent social protest activities in the United States shows that they often began by operating within the political system to influence public opinion among the mass public and government officials but then moved outside the system. Skolnick divides the student protest movement into two phases: before 1965 and after.

---

[60] Ira Sharkansky and Richard I. Hofferbert, "Dimensions of State Policy," in *Politics in the American States*, ed. Herbert Jacob and Kenneth N. Vines (Boston: Little Brown, 1971 ed.), p. 351.

[61] Dwight Dean, "Alienation and Political Apathy," *Social Forces* 38 (March, 1960): 185-89; Murray Levin, *The Alienated Voter* (New York: Holt Rinehart and Winston, 1960); and Wayne E. Thompson and John E. Horton, "Political Alienation as a Force in Political Action," *Social Forces* 38 (March, 1960), pp. 190-95.

In phase one, the student movement embodied concern, dissent, and protest about various social issues, but it generally accepted the legitimacy of the American political community in general and especially of the university.[62]

In phase two of the student movement, a considerable number of young people, particularly the activist core, experienced a progressive deterioration of their acceptance of national and university authority.

Once they realized that political and governmental authorities were willing to allow them to demonstrate peaceably but were unwilling to listen, the political activists began to consider alternative avenues for expressing their opinions, alternatives outside the political system but which would force a response from the system. Urban blacks have experienced a similar sense of disenfranchisement from the American political system, and in which they increasingly see riots as a legitimate means of presenting their opinions to the public and public officials.[63]

Nonetheless, the urban riots of 1967 and 1968 and the riots at the 1968 Democratic convention in Chicago came as a surprise and shock to most Americans.[64] Within a climate of growing tension and following an often very minor triggering incident widespread violence occurred, lasting for days and resulting in extensive property damage. In Detroit the police raided an afterhours nightclub in the black area and arrested the patrons, which led to rock throwing the initial looting. In Chicago a police sweep of Lincoln Park at 11:00 P.M. forced hundreds of young activists onto nearby streets and into direct and violent conflict with the police, resulting several days later in the confrontation between demonstrators and the police in front of

---

[62]Jerome Skolnick, *The Politics of Protest* (New York: Simon and Schuster, 1969).

[63]William Brink and Louis Harris, *Black and White* (New York: Simon and Schuster, 1966); p. 67; and Angus Campbell and Howard Schuman, "Racial Attitudes in Fifteen American Cities," in *Supplemental Studies for the National Advisory Commission on Civil Disorders* (Washington: U.S. Government Printing Office, 1968), pp. 47-57.

[64]*The Report of the National Advisory Commission on Civil Disorders* (New York: New York Times, 1968); and Walker, *Rights in Conflict* (New York: Bantam Books, 1968).

the Conrad Hilton Hotel. In both instances the riots, more or less spontaneous, arose from a sense of frustration with the operation of the existing political system. The demonstrators in Chicago had come to express their dissatisfaction with the Johnson Administration's foreign policy in Vietnam and with what had happened at the Democratic convention.[65] A survey of blacks indicated that sixty percent of them believed that city officials pay less attention to a request from a black than a white person and "the majority of Negroes expect little from whites other than hostility, opposition, or at best indifference."[66]

These were the reasons for the disturbances. How were they viewed by the members of the political system against whom they were directed? Did the members of the Democratic convention respond by changing the platform plank on the war in Vietnam or by nominating Gene McCarthy? Did officials in Newark and Cleveland and Detroit respond to riots in their city by moving to ameliorate the problems of the ghetto?

The delegates at the Democratic convention did become aware of what was happening in downtown Chicago, five miles from the site of the convention, particularly when the police and national guard arrived to tighten security around the convention site. The activities of the demonstrators, however, had no immediate impact on the convention; after a long and sometimes bitter debate the McCarthy backers lost the fight on the Vietnam plank and for the presidential nomination.[67] As a result of the demonstration and the subsequent defeat in November, reform members of the Democratic party took the lead in suggesting changes in party organization and procedures which would ensure broader participation and input into the process of selecting presidential nominees.

The impact of the urban riots was immediate but less direct. One basic reason was that white officials and the white community had great difficulty understanding what the riots "meant."

---

[65]Ibid., pp. 13-58.

[66]Campbell and Schuman, op. cit., p. 26.

[67]For an excellent description of the convention see Lewis Chester, Godfrey Hodgson, and Bruce Page, *An American Melodrama* (New York: Dell Books, 1969), pp. 584-600.

A solid, and at points overwhelming, majority of Negroes in these 15 cities see the riots as largely spontaneous black protests against unfair treatment, economic deprivation, or a combination of the two. The main way to prevent future riots, in this view, is to remove the underlying causes. Moreover, more Negroes think the riots helped in this direction than think the riots were harmful, although the division is close.[68]

White perceptions of the riots are substantially less consistent. About one-third of the whites in the fifteen cities saw the riots in the same way blacks did, another third saw them as planned criminal acts against the political system, led by criminals and outside agitators, and the remaining third saw elements of both pictures or had no opinions. Equally important, whites are far less likely than blacks to view riots as having harmed the cause of blacks in the United States.

Although the message of urban riots is clear to blacks it is confusing to the white community. Calling in National Guard troops to suppress the "rebellion" and then calling for food and clothing for those displaced by the riots seems to suggest that big city mayors agreed with the riffraff theory that the riots were led by a small group of unemployed, unattached criminals, that only a small proportion of the urban blacks participated in the riots, and that most blacks deplored the riots. Fogelson and Hill found the riffraff theory too largely erroneous: substantial numbers of blacks participated in the riots, those who participated were employed in skilled and semiskilled jobs, they were not predominantly criminals, and the black community felt that riots may have helped their cause.[69] The response of the white community and its leadership is to what they perceive as being the causes of the riots, and their perceptions are not very accurate. Their responses, as a result, will not be relevant for urban ghetto residents.

---

[68]Campbell and Schuman, op. cit., p. 49.

[69]Robert M. Fogelson and Robert B. Hill, "Who Riots? A Study of Participation in the 1967 Riots," in *Supplemental Studies for the National Advisory Commission on Civil Disorder* (Washington: U.S. Government Printing Office, 1968), pp. 221-43.

Conclusion

V.O. Key has suggested that since most Americans aren't interested in politics, are uninformed about issues, and have relatively few opinions which they hold with any fervor, the most effective public opinion is that of the attentive publics who serve as the audience for policy makers.[70] Berelson suggests that for most people voting is a fruitful way of expressing opinions.[71] Those who wish to do more than vote can write letters to elected officials or join formal or informal organizations.

These communication channels are effective only if they are accessible to all and if the political system is responsive to the opinions which are fed into it. The riots and demonstrations of the late 1960s and 1970s suggest, however, that if people who are deeply interested and concerned about an issue are continually refused access and/or grow to feel that the political system is no longer responsive to their needs and demands, they may seek to go outside the system to make their demands heard and bring about change. The danger to a democratic political system is not that public opinion will control the policy-making process but that the people who have opinions will not have an opportunity to express them and have them heard.

We can no longer assume that people who have interests will find ways to make their interests known—that they will vote, write letters, or join organizations. For some segments of society these participatory requirements are too stringent or too alien to bring quick relief for their problems. It may no longer be possible for government to sit back and wait for the people to voice their opinions in ways which government can hear and understand. The future may well demand that government take a far more active role in asking its citizens what they want, need, and feel, and in providing channels through which opinions can more easily (for the public) be transmitted. A government which says that everything must be "all right" because no one is complaining may have lost its ability and desire to "hear."

---

[70] Key, *Public Opinion and American Democracy*, pp. 535-58.
[71] Bernard Berelson, "Democratic Theory and Public Opinion," *Public Opinion Quarterly* 16 (Fall, 1952), pp. 313-30.

Index